International Trade: a business perspective

Edited by Catrinus Jepma and André Rhoen

Longman
London and New York

Open University of the Netherlands
Heerlen

Addison Wesley Longman Limited,
Edinburgh Gate
Harlow, Essex CM20 2JE, England
and Associated Companies throughout the world.

*Published in the United States of America
by Addison Wesley Longman Publishing, New York*

First published 1996

ISBN 0 582 27760-4 PPR

British Library Cataloguing-in-Publication Data

A catalogue record for this book is
available from the British Library

Library of Congress Cataloging-in-Publication Data

International trade : a business perspective / [Catrinus] Jepma and
André Rhoen, eds.
p. cm.
Includes bibliographical references and index.
ISBN 0–582–27760–4
1. International trade. 2. International business enterprises.
3. Competition, International. 4. International economic relations.
I. Jepma, C. J. II. Rhoen, André, 1970–
HF1379.I5783 1996
382—dc20 95–50694
CIP

Set by 8 in 10/12pt Times New Roman
Produced through Longman Malaysia, TCP

Contents

Figures

Tables

Acknowledgements

The publishers would like to thank the following for permission to reproduce copyright material:

The International Civil Aviation Organisation for the tables 'Traffic of commercial air carriers – 1983, 1988 and 1992 (tonne-kilometres performed by type of service)' and 'World airline traffic, by home region of carrier, 1983 and 1992 (in % of passengers-kilometres performed by region)' from *Civil Aviation Statistics of the World – 1992*; The OECD for the tables 'Infrastructure development: number of main lines' in *Communications Outlook, 1993* and 'Notification of aid credits (mln SDR), in *Experience wth Tied and Partially Untied Aid finance under the New Rules of the Arrangement, TD/Conensus (93)*; sigma, Swiss Reinsurance Company for the tables 'Distribution of the World's total insurance premiums, 1990' and 'The main markets for reinsurance in 1990 (as % of worl demand)' in *Schweizerische Ruckversicherung-Gesellschaft, Sigma 4/1192*; The United Nations for the tables 'International incoming direct investment flows 1982–92' from the *World Investment Report 1994*; 'Sectoral development and composition of stocks of international outgoing direct investment' in *World Investment Report 1993*; 'Foreign direct investment inward flows, by region and economy 1981–91' and 'Size of intra-firm trade flows per industry, US, Japan, UK' from *UNCTC World Investment Report 1993*; 'Distribution of world tonnage by group of countries of registration on 1992' from *Review of Maritime Transport 1992*; 'Regional distribution of foreign billings of the top 20 international design firms (1986–90, US$ mln)' and 'Regional distribution of foreign construction contracts awarded to the top 250 international contractors (1986–90, US$ mln)' from *Information Technology and International Competitiveness: the case of the construction services industry*, United Nations 1993, and for the figure 'Volume of world merchandise trade and output 1980–93' from *GATT report 1625, 1994*.

Though every effort has been made to trace the owners of copyright material, in a few cases this has proved impossible and we take this opportunity to apologise to any copyright holders whose rights may have been unwittingly infringed.

Notes on contributors

Peter van Bergeijk is currently senior officer at the Ministry of Economic Affairs in The Netherlands. He studied economics at Erasmus University, Rotterdam and got his Ph.D. in 1990 at the University of Groningen (on 'Trade and Diplomacy'). From 1985 he has held appointments at the Algemene Bank Nederland, the University of Groningen and the Ministry of Economic Affairs.

He is a specialist in the field of trade policy and international relations and has published many articles and reports on these topics. His most recent books are on economic diplomacy, trade and commercial policy, and deregulation, privatisation and the macro-economy.

Elmar Bouma MA studied transportation and logistics management in Rotterdam, and economics at the University of Limburg in Maastricht, where he graduated in 1992. He is currently employed as a policy adviser on international economic relations, industrial policy and tourism policy at the Federation of Netherlands' Industry (VNO) in The Hague. His responsibilities include the Netherlands' export promotion policy, the government policy in bilateral trade and investment relations, and financial instruments for export credit insurance, mainly with respect to Asia.

H. Peter Gray, the referee of this book, is a professor of International Business at Rutgers University in Newark, New Jersey, USA. In 1952, he received his MA from Cambridge University in England, and he completed his Ph.D. at the University of California (Berkeley), in 1963. He is a past president of the International Trade and finance Association and of the Eastern (USA) Economic Association.

Philippe Gugler, Dr from the University of Fribourg, Switzerland. He studied international production and transnational corporations strategies at the Graduate School of Management, Rutgers University, USA, under the supervision of Professor John Dunning. His doctoral dissertation deals with transnational strategic alliances, and he has done research on Japanese transnational corporations for the Economic Commission for Europe/UNCTC Joint Unit on Transnational Corporations in Geneva. He also conducted some consultancy studies for the Economic Advisory Group (UK) and has worked as research fellow and is occasional lecturer at the Centre of Research in Spatial Economics of the University of Fribourg. He is employed by the Federal Office for Foreign Economic Affairs (his views expressed in Chapter 5 are those of the author and not necessarily those of the Federal Office for Foreign Economic Affairs) and was a member of the Swiss delegation to the Uruguay Round negotiations on trade in services.

Catrinus Jepma holds a Ph.D. in economics and an MA in law. He is a professor of International Economics at the Netherlands' Open University (OU), and works in the same field at Groningen University. He is a specialist in the fields of international trade and finance, North–South economic relations, and international environmental economics. He has published various books, studies, monographs and articles about these topics.

He has been a senior adviser to the OECD, convening lead author of IPCC, and served as a regular adviser to the Netherlands' Government in international economics issues. He also advises an investment fund and a mutual fund.

His most recent (1994/5) publications include books on the economics of tropical deforestation, international policy coordination and tying of aid, joint implementation, and an international economics textbook.

Eugène Kock MA studied Economics at the universities of Groningen, the Netherlands and Louvain, Belgium between 1987 and 1993. As an assistant to Prof. Jepma, he contributed to a study – commissioned by the OECD – into the effects of combining development aid with concessional export financing. In 1993, he graduated on this subject at the University of Groningen. Currently, he is employed by the Nederlandsche Credietverzekering Maatschappij (Netherlands' Credit Insurance Company) in Amsterdam as a buyerrisk underwriter.

Marcel van Marion is head of the Bureau for International Economic Relations at Philips International, charged with Philips' international trade and investment policy, as well as international economic cooperation. Earlier in his professional career, Dr van Marion was employed as an economist at the Central Board for Foreign Economic Relations, and served as a staff member of the Bureau for International Economic Relations at Philips Electronics, responsible for trade policy.

He graduated from the University of Amsterdam in 1969, and completed his doctoral thesis in Economics at the University of Groningen (1992). His publications focus on trade liberalisation and dumping (mainly with respect to Japanese manufacturers in the EU).

Dr van Marion is a member of various Dutch and European trade associations and industrial federations' committees.

Ron Meyer studied Political Science at the University of Alberta in his native Canada. After receiving his bachelor's degree he moved to the Netherlands and gained his MBA at the Erasmus University in Rotterdam. Since 1987 he has been an Assistant Professor of Strategic Management at the Rotterdam School of Management/Erasmus Graduate School of Management.

His research is mainly focused on international strategy issues. He is particularly interested in the topics of globalisation, foreign market entry strategies, geographic patterns of company development and the process of strategic management in internationally operating companies. He recently co-authored a book, together with Bob de Wit, on strategic management that is used in over 100 universities throughout Europe as a main strategy text book.

His teaching activities are focused on graduate and postgraduate programs. In the full-time MSc and MBA programs of the Rotterdam School of Management he teaches the core courses on Strategic Management and electives on International Business and International Marketing Strategy. He also teaches in numerous executive programs and in company training programs for such companies as Mercedes-Benz, Unilever, DSM, IBM, RABO Bank and the Dutch Ministry of Economic Affairs.

Dr Rajneesh Narula studied Electrical Engineering in Nigeria, and subsequently worked as an aero-electronics engineer from 1983–86. He completed an MBA from Rutgers University, Newark, USA, after which he worked in Hong Kong for IBM Asia/South Pacific as a business plans analyst. After leaving Hong Kong in 1989, he was a Research Fellow in International Business and visiting lecturer at Rutgers University, USA. He has also been a consultant for the United Nations Centre on Transnational Corporations and the European Commission. He completed his Ph.D. under the supervision of Professor John Dunning at Rutgers University. Since 1993 he has been an Assistant Professor in International Business and Research Fellow at MERIT, at the University of Limburg, Maastricht, the Netherlands. His research interests include foreign direct investment theory, competitiveness, technology accumulation, economic growth and government policy, Japan and the European Union.

André Rhoen MA studied Economics at the University of Maastricht, the Netherlands, specialising in International Management and Business Policy. In 1994, he graduated in the subject of Japanese Human Resource Management, for which he carried out a six-month field study in Japan.

Currently, he is employed as a lecturer at the Netherlands' Open University, responsible for courses on International Trade and south-east Asia.

Maarten Smeets is economic counsellor at the World Trade Organisation (Geneva). In his current function he provides technical assistance to developing countries in all matters regarding the implementation of the Uruguay Round Agreements. Previously, between 1989–95, Mr Smeets worked as an economist in the Trade Department of the Organisation for Economic Cooperation and Development (OECD) in Paris, where he held various positions. He started his professional career as an economist in the Dutch Ministry of Economic Affairs in The Hague (between 1981–87), in the department for Foreign Economic Relations, mainly dealing with multilateral trade policy. Mr Smeets graduated (masters degree) from Tilburg University (Netherlands) in 1980, where he specialised in international trade, finance and banking. He deepened his specialisation in international trade and trade policy in a post-graduate course at the Graduate Institute for International Studies in Geneva (1980–81). Between 1987 and 1989, on recommendation of the Dutch Government, Mr Smeets attended the Ecole National d'Administration in Paris.

Kathleen Steel graduated from the faculty of economics at the University of Ghent, where she specialised in development cooperation, and completed her Ph.D. She started her professional career as a research assistant and lecturer at the same institute. After being in charge of financial cooperation as a member of the General Board for Development Cooperation at the Belgian Ministry of Foreign Affairs, she became responsible for International Capital Markets at the department of Economic Studies at Belgium's Generale Bank. Currently, Dr Steel is a Senior Trade finance Manager at the Generale Bank. She is a visiting lecturer at most Belgian universities.

The International Business Programme

This volume, together with an accompanying study guide produced by the Netherlands' Open University (OU), forms an integrated 100 hour course, called 'International Trade'. The course has been developed as part of a larger (1400 hours, 42 credits) OU higher distance teaching programme on International Business, and focuses on the changing environment of – and decision-making in – internationally operating corporations.

The International Business Programme aims at junior and mid-career professionals. After completion of the programme, candidates are qualified to enter the European Master of Business Administration Programme, developed by a number of European distance teaching universities.

Although there are no formal prerequisites, students should recognise the programme's academic level when planning to enroll. All course materials have been carefully designed for distance teaching purposes, implying they can be studied without additional tools.

The main themes of the International Business Programme are:

	key couses
– International Economic Relations	Introduction in international economics, International trade
– Institutions	International economic institutions, European economic integration
– Business Administration	International financial management and accounting
– Management	International human resource management, International management 1, Strategic issues of management in an integrated European context

Students conclude the International Business Programme with an 'International Business Simulation', in which they actively deal with a 'real-world' case study in a computerised systems simulation, as members of an international team of company executives.

Although the International Business Programme has been designed as an intellectually and conceptually integrated whole, the various underlying modules of 100 hours (3 credit points) each can be studied separately. Single modules – or sets of modules – can be puchased at the Netherlans' Open University, either with or without the right to additional tutorial support or to take an official exam.

For additional information please contact:

Professor Catrinus J. Jepma or Mrs. Elise Kamphuis
co-ordinators, International Business Programme
Open University of the Netherlands, Department of Economics
P.O. box 2960
6401 DL Heerlen
The Netherlands
Tel.: +31 45 5762724
Fax: +31 45 5762123
E-mail: elise.kamphuis@ouh.nl

Introduction

The character of the volume

This volume contains the contributions of nine experts in the field of international trade and business; each has focused on one aspect of the following complex issues: how internationalisation of business has evolved, what role trade and foreign direct investment and international cooperation between corporations have played in this respect, and how businesses cope with the changing patterns of trade and international competition. Together the various chapters are intended to provide a picture of recent theory and practice of international trade and business.

The book has been designed as a graduate-level textbook for specialised courses in the fields of international business and international trade. The main part of the text presupposes a level of understanding equivalent to undergraduate in business administration or in economics.[1] In addition the book may be of interest to those active in the field of international business and trade.

International trade

World trade in goods amounted to more than 4,000 billion US dollars in 1994. In that year, total trade volume grew by 9 per cent, while total trade value increased by 12 per cent, both accounting for the highest growth figures since 1976. World trade also continues to grow faster than total world production, which increased by 3.5 per cent in 1994. As a result, trade is considered to be the motor of world economic growth.

Western Europe in particular has shown a vigorous trade revival. In 1993, Western European exports and imports shrunk by 7.5 and 10 per cent respectively. In 1994,

1. Note that this volume, together with an accompanying reader, constitutes the Open University of the Netherlands (OU) course 'International Trade', which in its turn forms part of the 1300 hour OU International Business Programme. In studying the materials of this programme the 'International Trade' course follows after, among others, the courses 'Introduction to International Economics', 'International Management', 'International Economic Institutions' and 'Strategic International Management in an European Context'. For more information about the OU International Business Programme, please contact Open University, P.O. Box 2960, 6401 DL Heerlen, The Netherlands, tel. +31-45-5762774; fax +31-45-5762123.

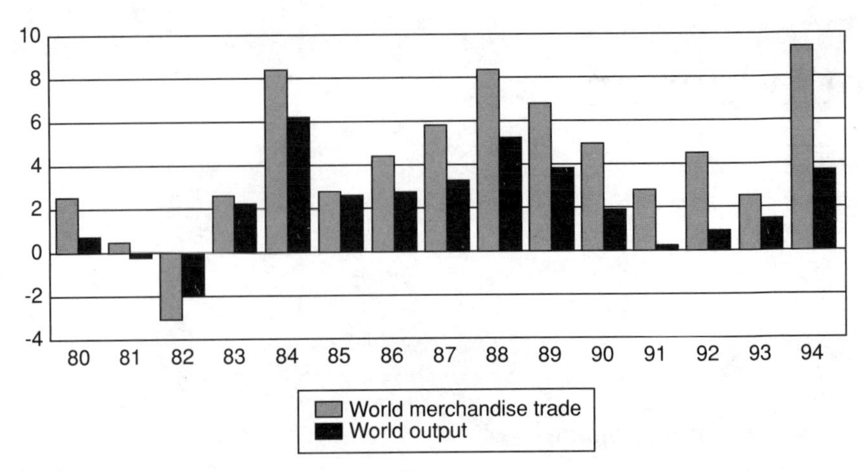

Figure 0.1 Volume of world merchandise trade and output, 1980–94

the total value of all exported and imported goods rose by 11 per cent. Due to a strong increase in imports by Western European countries, their trading partners in Eastern Europe were able to push up their exports by 20 per cent. Latin American and Asian trade figures also soared: Latin American exports rose by 15 per cent as a result of high US demand. China and Singapore experienced an export increase of 30 per cent. Africa, however, has suffered from diminishing export levels since 1990. Predictions for 1995 claimed an increase in world exports by 8 per cent, but monetary turmoil (such as the Mexico crisis) could hamper the expansion of world trade.

Clearly, apart from economic conditions, the recent developments in the liberalisation of trade can be held partly responsible for growing trade figures. However, the decision of firms to internationalise has also made an important contribution. This internationalisation and liberalisation of trade have had a profound impact on business. Few industries are left untouched by the recent moves toward trade liberalisation within, for instance, the EU and NAFTA, while the GATT negotiations of the Uruguay Round have accelerated the development toward internationalisation and even globalisation of industries.

The scope of the volume

The purpose of this volume is to provide the reader with:

- a thorough understanding of the motives for companies to internationalise their activities;
- an overview of the major internationalisation routes that firms choose and the principles their choices are based on;
- a summary of important developments and recent trends in the field of international trade such as the growing importance of foreign direct investments (FDI);

- an explanation of the motors of and barriers to international trade flows;
- an insight into the nature of international trade in goods, as distinct from trade in services.

The internationalisation and globalisation of competition (Chapter 1)

Chapter 1 provides a general background to the remaining chapters of the volume. It takes Porter's well-known five forces model as its point of departure. In every industry, national or international, the nature of competition is shaped by the objectives, strategies and abilities of all five types of industry participants. Naturally, the underlying economics are the basis for their behaviour and interaction.

The reasons why companies extend their activities beyond their national boundaries, and how they can be classified as either internal or external, proactive or reactive, are discussed subsequently. The chapter goes on to discuss the advantages and disadvantages of the major foreign market access modes.

Companies can internationalise not only by using different modes, but also by taking different paths: either evolutionary, revolutionary or a blend of these two. Firms can choose whether or not they integrate their corporate activities globally, and whether they choose a global, a multifocal, or a locally responsive business style.

Finally, the chapter discusses the impact of competitive advantages on international competition patterns, as well as the different sources of an industry's competitive advantage.

Foreign direct investments and MNCs (Chapters 2–4)

Internationalisation and globalisation are continuously growing; Chapter 1 explores the driving forces behind these trends. Generally speaking, firms internationalise by exporting products and services or by moving production factors across national borders. With the movement of production factors, foreign direct investments (FDI) have gained considerable attention over the past decade. FDI refers to transnational capital transactions between companies from different countries, such as the purchase of production resources or (parts of) companies.

Chapter 2 discusses the major trends with regard to the scale and patterns of FDI, while Chapter 3 monitors the main actors in the field of FDI, the multinational corporations (MNCs). The various forms of international cooperation between corporations are then investigated in Chapter 4.

Foreign direct investment experienced a huge growth in the 1980s, almost tripling the average level of the 1970s. The crucial factors leading to this strong increase were: the cyclical developments in the world economy; changes in the general government policy and trade policy; and the trend toward internationalisation of corporate strategies as described in Chapter 1. The links between these factors and the increase in FDI are made in Chapter 2, as well as the changes in the motives and patterns of foreign direct investments during the 1980s.

Investing abroad tends to increase the complexity of the investment decision-making process, and often enhances the risks associated with an investment. Companies planning on FDI should carefully consider such factors as the macro-economic situation and the general government policy of the host country, the economic and political risk, its economic and physical infrastructure, its regulatory and statutory investment climate, market conditions, and socio-cultural factors.

The key features of multinational corporations (MNCs), and the extent to which they internationalise their R&D activities or even globalise, are the subject of Chapter 3. A major trend in the organisation of MNCs is their increasing involvement in 'networks' through the establishment of several different modes of inter-firm cooperation.

One of the reasons for cooperating with other firms is to deal with additional risks associated with foreign direct investment. However, risk-sharing is not the only reason that companies enter into several kinds of cooperative agreements. Chapter 4 describes the reasons why firms cooperate, and the various modes they have at their disposal. Globalisation – the increasing worldwide inter-dependence of markets – encourages companies operating on a global scale to adapt their corporate strategies and organisational structures in order to sustain their competitive advantage (see also Chapter 1). Since the early 1980s, multinational corporations have increasingly focused their foreign direct investments on their core activities (see also Chapter 2). Firms are increasingly developing into 'network firms' (as described in Chapter 3). Chapter 4 discusses the linkages between MNCs, throughout different sectors and at varying stages of the value chain, established by inter-firm cooperative agreements. The chapter attempts to define inter-firm cooperative agreements, and to determine what distinguishes them from other forms of collaboration between companies. In addition, it searches for the main reasons behind the premature conclusion of many inter-firm cooperative agreements.

Trade in services (Chapter 5)

The multilateral GATT negotiations in the Uruguay Round contained several new elements, compared to the earlier Tokyo summit. An important new issue raised was the liberalisation of international trade in services, which is the topic of Chapter 5. Services cover a wide range of activities, such as banking, insurance, telecommunications, and construction. Trade in services is estimated by the World Trade Organisation (WTO) to have amounted to 1,080 billion US dollars in 1994, an increase of 6 per cent on the 1993 level.

Since total trade in services increases every year, and the share of these services in the total volume of world trade continues to grow, a thorough understanding of the underlying dynamics of trade in services becomes necessary. Trade in services is rather different from trade in goods, if only because its intangible nature often requires the physical presence of the supplier in the host country. This direct interaction between suppliers and consumers determines to a large extent the way in which different types of services are traded; it can also be held responsible for the fact that some services are more tradable than others. International trade in the construction sector is, for instance, far less developed than international banking transactions, a difference partly due to the fact that banking has benefited more from technological change.

Chapter 5 attempts to answer such questions as 'What is the distinction between goods and services with respect to their tradability?' and, as a result of this distinction, 'In what respect does trade in services differ from trade in commodities?', inevitably leading to the issue of 'Which are the most important obstacles to trade in services?'.

Financial aspects of exports (Chapters 6 and 7)

Firms use various modes to serve foreign markets, driven by a wide range of motives to internationalise their operations. However, as has been mentioned already regarding foreign direct investments, internationalisation often implies that they have to cope with an increased degree of risk. One particular risk with respect to the exports of goods to foreign countries has been mentioned earlier (in Chapter 2): the economic and political risk of non-payment faced by the exporter. Other risks involved with exporting are those occurring during transportation of the goods, exchange-rate risks, and legal and administrative risks. Chapter 6 gives an overview of the various export risks, and provides practical information about export financing (insurance).

Chapter 7 discusses the influence export promotion can have on international trade patterns, as well as on international welfare. Donor countries have used several instruments in the past to enhance exports to developing countries through concessional export financing. Concessional export financing is the combination of government aid credits or grants and official export credits, provided by national credit insurance agencies or commercial credits. Donor countries compete in offering favourable export credit conditions in order for aid to generate commercial and political benefits.

Recent inter-governmental agreements (such as the OECD Helsinki package) try to limit the use of aid budgets for export promotion by donor countries.

Political and cultural factors (Chapter 8)

As mentioned before, companies planning to internationalise their operations – however sound their motives are – have to consider a number of important risks, including the political and socio-cultural risks attached to investments in a particular country. Economic theories dealing with international trade and foreign direct investment investigate mainly the economic 'motors' and 'barriers' to trade. Comparative cost advantage is a widely quoted 'motor' of international trade. With respect to the barriers to international trade and FDI, the focus of economic theory is often on such well-known issues as import levies, import restrictions or natural barriers like physical distance and transport costs. They tend – at least partly – to overlook the influence of political and cultural factors acting as barriers to or motors of trade.

Chapter 8 deals with this gap in the theory of international trade. It provides insight into important practical aspects of international economic relations such as diplomatic barriers to trade ('inhibitors') and political factors ('motors'). In addition to these political factors, there are less tangible political preferences among consumers and policy makers, which can play a role in the deployment of trade policy instruments, such as anti-dumping measures or countervailing duties.

Finally, the impact of the cultural features of a country or a region, such as national character, language and traditions is addressed; together with political factors they have a major influence on international trade, for example, with respect to the assessment of a country's credit-worthiness (see also Chapter 6).

Note that the issues discussed in Chapter 8 could also be incorporated in, for instance, the discussion on the obstacles to trade in services, particularly since trade in services often requires the presence of the supplier in the host country, making the case of the impact of cultural factors stronger.

Anti-dumping and competitive advantage (Chapter 9)

Anti-dumping measures are briefly referred to in Chapter 8. Chapter 9 elaborates on this subject by showing how to prove a case of dumping by comparing product prices calculated by a producer in a foreign market with the prices charged in the domestic market. It then distinguishes various types of dumping, the implementation of which depends on the exporter's objective *vis-à-vis* the foreign market. Based on his own experience, the author shows that – in the case of Japanese or Korean firms – dumping can at least partly be attributed to structural differences in their national economic systems compared to EU countries' economies, making dumping difficult to prove for foreign competitors. Japanese and Korean firms in many industries are strongly vertically integrated, enabling them to enter into dumping by means of intercompany pricing.

Concluding remarks

This volume has shown that international business practices are undergoing a thorough transition due to the ever-increasing globalisation and integration of world markets. Businesses that are insufficiently aware of the most recent trends and adjustment requirements due to world market changes may well turn out to be future losers in the international competitive game; businesses that are aware of the necessary changes and turn out flexible enough to adapt to new realities posed by the international market will probably have the best chances of survival.

1 International competition

1.1 The nature of competition

1.1.1 *Definition of competition*

Economics is often referred to as the *science of scarcity*. Most of what can be witnessed in the economy is ultimately a result of the fact that our wants outstrip our means. Humans are constantly endeavouring to increase and improve their means in an attempt to satisfy their unquenchable wants. This necessarily brings people into rivalry with one another, as they want the same scarce resources: buyers compete to secure scarce goods against a low price, while suppliers compete to secure scarce customers able to pay a high price. In other words, scarcity of resources and the abundance of wants leads individuals and organisations to become rivals. In this sense economics could also be referred to as the *science of competition*.

Competition can be defined as the situation in which two or more parties come into conflict with each other because the achievement of their goals is partially or totally mutually exclusive. One form of competition is when organisations or individuals confront one another due to *similar*, but mutually exclusive, goals (e.g. both parties wish to buy or sell the same product). Organisations that strive to sell the same type of product or service are commonly referred to as 'competitors'. However, competition also takes place when organisations or individuals collide due to *dissimilar*, but mutually exclusive, goals (e.g. one party wishes to buy cheap, while the other wishes to sell dear). In this way almost everyone is in constant competition with a large number of parties in the environment.

Competition is, however, not only a nuisance. It is also the motor of economic growth, both for the economy as a whole and for the individual firm. At the micro level, competition is the force that motivates companies to search for innovative ways to achieve the same results with less inputs (*resource efficiency*) and to achieve better results with the same inputs (*resource effectiveness*). At the macro level, competition ensures that only the fittest companies survive in their continuous struggle to upgrade the use of their resources.

The conclusion for individual firms is that competition and competitiveness are essential for survival and for the achievement of company objectives. Therefore the competition phenomenon needs to be understood and the routes to competitiveness need to be explored.

1.1.2 *Determinants of competition*

According to a leading competition researcher, Michael Porter, 'the state of competition in an industry depends on five basic forces,' which are illustrated in Figure 1.1 (Porter, 1979, p. 137). In every industry, whether national or international, these forces determine the dynamics of competition and thus the potential profitability of the industry. In other words, the nature of competition within an industry depends on the objectives, strategies and abilities of all five types of industry participants (*actors*), as well as on the underlying economics (*factors*) that influence their behaviour and interaction.

This well-known five forces model is an important general framework for thinking about competition, and a good point of departure for this chapter, as it raises two important questions. First, given these general competitive forces, how do companies go about developing a competitive strategy? Secondly, what is the influence of internationalisation on competition and competitive strategy? Both questions will be discussed at length throughout the chapter.

1.1.3 *Internationalisation of competition*

It has become increasingly difficult to think of industries that have not been thoroughly influenced by internationalisation. As internal liberalisation successes have been booked, such as recently the European Union (EU), NAFTA and the Uruguay Round of the GATT, not only has international trade increased dramatically, but also the foreign direct investment of a growing number of internationalised firms. All five industry forces have witnessed increased international involvement.

This is common knowledge and clearly visible in the marketplace. It hardly requires argumentation or statistics: the internationalisation effect is known. The real issues are, what are the causes of the internationalisation of competition and what are

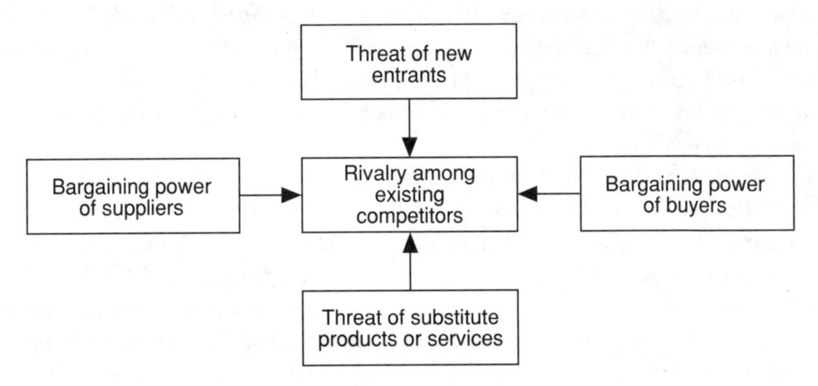

Figure 1.1 The five basic forces driving competition

Source: Porter, 1979

its consequences? Both issues will be discussed on the next pages. The general structure of this chapter will be as follows:

1.2 **From domestic competition to international competition.** The internationalisation of competitors internationalises competition. Therefore, the question must be asked: why and how do companies internationalise?
1.3 **From international competition to global competition.** The globalisation of competitors globalises international competition. Therefore, the question must be asked: why and how do companies globalise?
1.4 **From competition to competitiveness.** International competition necessitates international competitiveness. Therefore, the question must be asked: what types and sources of competitive advantage exist?

1.2 The internationalisation of competition

1.2.1 *Reasons for internationalisation*

It is often implicitly assumed that all companies internationalise for the same basic reason, namely to cash in on foreign market sales opportunities. In reality, however, there exists a wide variety of internationalisation motives among firms. To be able to understand the complexity of international competition, it is imperative also to appreciate the richness of internationalisation motives driving companies' behaviour. Figure 1.2 summarises a number of the most common reasons for companies to venture abroad.

	INTERNAL	EXTERNAL
PROACTIVE	• Managerial urge • Economies of scale • Economies of scope • Learning	• Margin opportunities • Volume opportunities • Serve internationalised customers • Locational advantages • Monitoring competitors
REACTIVE	• Bandwagon effect • Excess stock • Excess production capacity • Risk spreading	• Unsolicited orders • Unattractive home market • Retaliatory strike • Political pressure

Figure 1.2 The major reasons for internationalisation
Source: Adapted from Albaum *et al.* (1984)

MANAGERIAL URGE

Probably one of the most important reasons why companies take a leap into the big unknown is because of the personal satisfaction that this offers managers. Although most economic theories tend to minimise the influence of the individual decision-maker's personal interests, it is becoming increasingly clear that the managerial urge to expand and seek foreign adventure is a powerful driver of internationalisation. Especially in small and medium-sized companies this 'international entrepreneurial-ism' is an important motivation. Even in larger companies internationalisation efforts can result in higher status, career advancement and task enjoyment.

ECONOMIES OF SCALE

International expansion is often the quickest way to increase sales, which in turn allows for the total volume of production to be increased. In industries where significant economies of scale exist, a rise in production can have a beneficial effect on the cost per unit, thus improving a company's competitiveness,[2] both abroad and in its home market. Moreover, economies of scale of internationalisation are not only found in the area of production, but can also be realised within all other functions of a company. For instance, R&D costs can be spread over a larger sales volume and TV advertisements might be usable in more than one market. It should be noted, however, that some firms internationalise to attain the 'critical mass' dictated by economies of scale, while in reality these economies of scale do not exist. The 'big is beautiful' fallacy afflicting some industries has led to increased internationalisation, but due to the lack of scale economies, has not necessarily led to increased competitiveness.

ECONOMIES OF SCOPE

Even when economies of scale cannot be realised, because the internationalising company must adapt everything it does abroad to the local circumstances, there are still savings that can be made by manufacturing many different types of products for foreign markets. These economies of scope can be obtained if a firm uses its existing resources, skills and technologies to create new products and/or services for new foreign markets. This way, internationalisation allows a company *leverage* of its domestic assets and capabilities. For example, a firm might enter a foreign market to get more mileage out of its existing marketing know-how, its brandname, its product development ability or its service competence. Yet, here also economies of scope can often be fictitious. Companies often do lever their existing resources and skills when internationalising, but simultaneously must invest heavily in entirely new resources and skills, that are needed to operate in the new foreign environment, sometimes cancelling out the scope economies.

2. A simple firm-level definition of competitiveness is 'an adequate return on investment through time'.

LEARNING

The necessity to develop new skills to be successful in a foreign market can also be a benefit of internationalisation, if this new skill can be transferred back to the firm's domestic market. For some firms the learning opportunities presented by foreign markets are actually one of the prime motivators of internationalisation. These companies will attempt to discover 'state of the art' markets, where the pace of innovation is the highest, so that they can tap this important source of learning.

SALES MARGIN OPPORTUNITIES

The 'classical' reason for firms to internationalise is simply to sell more products at acceptable margins. So, if companies recognise foreign markets with advantageous structural characteristics that would allow for profitable extra sales – an interesting potential customer base, a tolerable level of competition and entry barriers that can be overcome – the lure to internationalise is often very strong.

SALES VOLUME OPPORTUNITIES

It is not only the margins offered by foreign markets that make internationalisation attractive, but also the sales volume that can be achieved. If the potential economies of scale and/or scope for a company are large, it is often willing to enter new foreign markets, even if the projected margins will be low. In other words, sales volume growth can be an equally strong driver of internationalisation as profit growth.

SERVE INTERNATIONALISED CUSTOMERS

As a company's customers internationalise, they often prefer to purchase the same product or service independent of the country they are in. For instance, car manufacturers setting up a factory abroad usually ask their components suppliers to service their foreign plant as well. International firms also commonly prefer to work with the same advertising agency in all their countries of operation. Companies unwilling to internationalise in step with their customers often risk losing their clients entirely to competitors that can offer a multi-country service.

LOCATIONAL ADVANTAGES

Foreign markets offer more than only sales opportunities. Other countries might present a company with the opportunity to make use of inexpensive or special local resources (e.g. people, physical infrastructure, educational and research infrastructure, government support, natural resources, geography, climate). If these foreign resources are relatively immobile, while their use would lead to a significant improvement in the cost and/or quality of a company's products, internationalisation of a number of the company's functions (mostly operations and occasionally R&D) might be considered.

MONITORING AND/OR FRUSTRATING COMPETITORS.

Of course, foreign markets offer threats, in addition to the aforementioned opportunities. Most importantly, foreign markets can be the home turf or strongholds of current competitors and the breeding ground of prospective competitors. Therefore, some companies establish a 'forward base' in their rivals' most important markets (Ayal and Zif, 1979). These advanced troops can closely monitor the competition, so that an early warning signal can be given if new initiatives seem imminent. A more aggressive task for the forward base is to engage foreign competitors in their own territory, to keep their attention away from foreign expansion and to deplete their resources (note that, for instance, a price war is almost always more expensive for the company with the highest market share). This internationalisation motive is also referred to as 'attacking the competitor's profit sanctuaries' (Prahalad and Doz, 1987). In the same vein, a company might decide to enter a 'neutral' foreign market, before a competitor from another country or a local upstart can build up a strong market presence and use the market as a profit generator. Such a strategy is referred to as a 'preemptive strike'.

BANDWAGON EFFECT

A close relative of 'managerial urge' is the 'me too' motivation to internationalise. The difference between the two is that in the case of managerial urge the motivation is proactive and largely internal, while the behaviour of the managers jumping on the bandwagon is reactive and largely externally motivated. The latter managers are engulfed by the general fashionableness of internationalisation (think of the '1992' hype that swept Europe only recently) or have witnessed the foreign ventures of a number of competitors and are gripped by the fear of being left behind. Such managers will be inclined to internationalise their firms to minimise the chance of being the odd one out in their industry.

EXCESS STOCK

A very opportunistic reason to internationalise is to get rid of excess stock. Some companies are only occasionally stuck with excess stock, but in some industries it is a structural characteristic. For instance, firms with short product life cycles are constantly trying to rid themselves of outdated products, without spoiling their own markets. So designer clothing manufacturers often export their out-of-fashion products to secondary markets, while electronics manufacturers dump their surpluses in markets with a lagging product life cycle. In other industries, quality is difficult to control throughout the production process, so that a certain level of substandard products is inevitable. These, too, are often exported to guard the image and price level in the company's primary markets.

EXCESS PRODUCTION CAPACITY

To avoid excess stock, many companies have the option of underutilizing their production capacity. However, this is never a particularly appealing solution, because it drives up the unit production costs (the same fixed costs must be covered by a lower number of products). Another alternative is to cut fixed costs, for instance by laying off employees. A less painful option is to fully use the overcapacity for production for foreign markets. This is a solution much favoured in companies where the economic and social costs of 'downsizing' are great. Also in industries with periodic or seasonal overcapacity, where companies need to maintain their total production capacity to deal with peak demand, exporting can be a way to level out capacity usage. Think, for instance, of the ski manufacturers that have been developing counter-seasonal markets in the southern hemisphere.

RISK SPREADING

Some companies prefer not to have all of their eggs in one basket. To spread risk they can either diversify their range of products or they can diversify geographically. Faced with this choice, companies that wish to remain focused on one business area will usually choose to internationalise. Moreover, if dependence on the domestic market is perceived as risky – possibly due to economic or political instability, unpredictable competition, or fickle customer demand – then the preference to diversify geographically will be more pronounced.

UNSOLICITED ORDERS

Initially, many companies do not deliberately internationalise, but have internationalisation 'thrust upon them'. It happens to them incrementally and unintentionally. They do not actively seek foreign orders, yet receive some anyway. These are filled if the margins are satisfactory and the extra bothers of dealing with foreigners can be kept at an acceptable level. These international dealings can remain infrequent indefinitely, yet many companies are gradually drawn into foreign markets by their product or service's success. This can lead to a switch in the company's mentality towards a more proactive internationalisation stance, but does not necessarily have to.

UNATTRACTIVE HOME MARKET

While foreign sales opportunities can 'pull' a company across its national borders, the lack of domestic sales opportunities can 'push' a firm to internationalise. The unattractiveness of a company's home market can be due to a variety of structural characteristics. The market might be small and present few growth opportunities, or worse, demand might even be in decline. Competition might be intense, entry barriers low, substitutes abundant, government and unions hostile, and suppliers expensive and of low quality. Any of these factors might provide a company with the motivation to seek greener pastures.

RETALIATORY STRIKE

A company confronted with an aggressive foreign competitor can react in two different ways: defensively or offensively. A defensive strategy entails 'digging in', protecting territory and limiting the entrant's 'beach head'. However, often the best defence is the offensive, which means that the company internationalises and carries the 'battle' to the aggressor's home base. Such a retaliatory strike resembles taking hostages. The retaliating company can threaten to frustrate the aggressive company in the aggressor's home market, unless the aggressive company withdraws or takes a less aggressive stance. If the aggressive foreign competitor does not cave in to this 'blackmail', then the intensity of the international competition will increase.

POLITICAL PRESSURE

In some countries, companies are influenced or forced by the government to internationalise. Such interventionist governments may have economic goals, for instance, they may wish to obtain more foreign currency or to initiate export-led economic growth. However, companies can also be pressured to internationalise for social reasons (jobs) or to fulfil political objectives (international status and power).

The conclusion that must be drawn from this discussion of Figure 1.2 is that there is a wide variety of motives for firms to internationalise. These differing motives in turn often lead to differing strategies. Hence, understanding the 'game' of international competition must start by appreciating that the participants might be playing for different reasons

1.2.2 *Forms of internationalisation*

Not only the reasons for internationalisation, but also the ways in which firms internationalise differ. Some companies internationalise only a limited part of their value-adding activities, while others internationalise every aspect of the company. Figure 1.3 and Table 1.1 depict the major forms of internationalisation that a company can choose to pursue. These forms are often referred to as *market entry modes*, although the term *market access modes* is more appropriate ('entry' is an event that happens only once, while 'access' indicates that there is a continuous channel into a foreign market). To grasp the complexity of international competition, it is important to understand this diversity of internationalisation forms that companies can adopt.

LICENSING

The main characteristic of licensing is that the item 'crossing the border' is an *intangible*, for instance, know-how or a brand name. One speaks of licensing when a company (the licensor) sells the right to use its intangible asset in a certain geographic area for a specified period of time to another company (the licensee). A company engaged in internationalisation through the sale of straightforward licences hardly needs to become internationalised at all, since none of its primary activities need to be adapted to foreign market operations. Such licensing is often largely a legal matter and therefore a staff task, although sometimes a licensing contract will require the licensor to provide certain services and support. In general, the advantages of licensing are the low need for organisational change, the low risk involved (no new

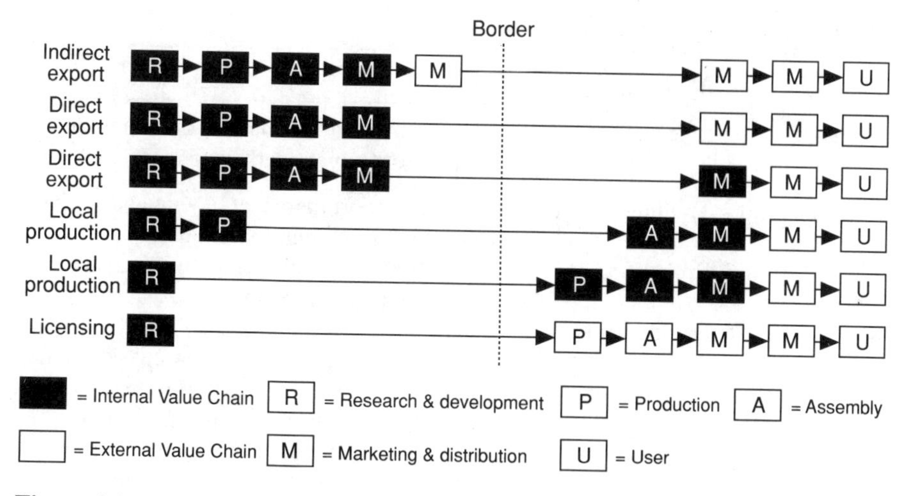

Figure 1.3 The major market access modes

investments need to be made) and the speed at which profits can be generated. Licensing can also be used when import restrictions or transport costs make exporting impossible. However, disadvantages should be noted, in that licensing negotiations can be protracted, while licensing agreements are often difficult to police. Furthermore, the licensee might damage the licensor (e.g. by leaking proprietary know-how or using a brand name unwisely) and licensees sometimes turn around to become the licensor's new competitors. Finally, licensing is hardly ever as profitable as selling the products yourself (Root, 1988).

EXPORTING

The main characteristic of exporting is that actual *physical products* cross the border. The extent to which a company must become involved in foreign markets and adapt its primary activities to the act of exporting depends largely on the type of exporting being done (see Figure 1.3 and Table 1.1). In the case of indirect exporting, most international tasks are performed by external parties (export intermediaries) and the company hardly notices that its products end up on foreign markets. In the case of direct exporting, the company's marketing and sales function deals directly with foreign parties. This requires a higher level of organisational commitment to international markets and forces companies to reflect increased internationalisation in their strategy and structure. The main attraction of exporting for a small firm – beside avoiding the pitfalls of licensing – is that it presents a relatively simple, inexpensive and gradual way to internationalise. For large firms, with extensive international experience, it allows for the concentration of production (economies of scale/scope) in the most suitable country (locational advantages). However, exporting does have its drawbacks. It is vulnerable to protectionism and other artificial trade barriers, while volatile exchange rates can also form a major impediment. Furthermore, a large physical distance between production site and market can increase transport costs and

Table 1.1 Major foreign market access modes

Category	Mode	Description
Licensing	Licensing	Company contracts out use of intangible assets for foreign markets to other company
Indirect export	Trading company	Export/import merchant buying and selling on its own account (margin basis)
	Broker	Export/import agent bringing buyers and sellers together (commission basis)
	Buying agent	Export agent representing foreign buyers in exporter's home country (commission basis)
	Resident buyer	Employee of foreign buyer stationed in exporter's home country (salary basis)
	Export agent	Domestic agent representing exporter abroad, using own name (margin or commission basis)
	Export management	Domestic agent representing exporter abroad, firm using exporter's name (margin or commission basis)
	Piggyback export	Existing channels of one exporter are used by a second (margin or commission basis)
	Export combination	Cooperative association representing several exporters abroad (commission basis)
Direct export	Import agent	Local agent representing exporter abroad, under own or exporter's name (commission basis)
	Import distributor	Local merchant fulfilling role as wholesaler (margin basis)
	Travelling salesperson	Home-based employee of exporter representing exporter abroad (salary basis)
	Sales subsidiary	Foreign-based branch of exporter representing exporter locally (salary basis)
Local production	Projects	Home-based company sends mobile units abroad to fulfil temporary contracts (sales through any of above)
	Contract production	Company contracts out production abroad to local firm (sales through any of above)
	Franchising	Company contracts out production and sales abroad to locals, but closely services and polices partners
	Greenfield	New local production subsidiary, wholly or partly owned by company
	Acquisition	Existing local production (and sales) unit is wholly or partly acquired by company

delivery time, while a large psychological distance can result in a lack of responsiveness to local market signals.

LOCAL PRODUCTION

The major characteristic of the fourth category of foreign market access modes is that *production*, rather than *products*, crosses the border. There are different ways to obtain manufacturing capacity abroad, as can be seen in Table 1.1. All methods have a high level of international involvement in common: the company must manage a broad range of value-adding activities in two or more countries. This implies that local production requires significant organisational adaptation and commitment by an internationalising firm. The main advantage of local production is that the disadvantages of exporting – transport costs and delivery time, protectionist measures and volatile exchange rates – can be avoided, and more intimate relations can be built up with local customers and/or distribution channels. It should also be noted that in the case of services – as opposed to goods – production and consumption often take place simultaneously and at one location (services usually cannot be stockpiled or transmitted over distance). This characteristic of services commonly leaves no other alternative but local production. The chief disadvantages of local production are the organisational complexities of managing across borders, the smaller economies of scale/scope that can be realised and the high risks involved in investing in foreign markets (the market might turn out to be less attractive than anticipated, while the local government might 'take the investment hostage' to extract the terms it wishes).

The conclusion that can be drawn from this discussion of internationalisation forms is that companies enter and operate in the international arena in a variety of ways. Some firms are highly committed to competing internationally, which is reflected in their choice of foreign market access modes. Other firms, with less international commitment or experience, might also be participants in the international competitive game, but they will employ foreign market access modes that allow for a lower level of international involvement. Insight into each firm's position in the international competitive game requires an understanding of the advantages and disadvantages of the internationalisation forms they have chosen.

1.2.3 *Stages of internationalisation*

The internationalisation motives and forms of companies are not static, but develop over time. Internationalisation is not a once-in-a-lifetime event for a company, but a continuous process. Every company operating in the international arena has in the past progressed through a number of phases to arrive at its current state and will probably continue to evolve in future. Early in their history, even the largest transnational companies were small domestic firms. Since then, they have gone through an extensive growth process – during which goals and access modes have constantly changed – before becoming worldwide operating companies and a major force in international competition.

Many researchers argue that most internationalising companies progress through more or less the same phases of international expansion. This would suggest that an evolutionary model of internationalisation could be put forward, with a number of fixed *stages of development*. Figure 1.4 is a simple example of such a model. The underlying idea is that companies can only gradually build up commitment, experience and the necessary resources to expand internationally over time. Therefore the initial objectives of internationalisation tend to be more short-term in orientation, while the preferred access mode is of a low risk and low investment variety. As a company's management becomes increasingly convinced of the need to internationalise and of the viability of such an endeavour, it will take a more long-term perspective on foreign expansion. Increasing international experience and growing financial resources will allow a company to adopt a higher involvement in foreign markets access mode.

Two important criticisms can be levelled at the 'stages of development' model in Figure 1.4. First, it is *determinist*, since it suggests that all firms necessarily pass through the same stages of development. In reality, however, few firms go through the phases exactly as indicated. Some skip phases, while others might even move back from local production to exporting. This criticism is widely accepted: the model should at most be seen as an indication of possible stages of development, not as a 'law' of development. The second criticism is that the model assumes that firms always behave in an *incrementalist* ('step-by-step') fashion. However, not all firms develop their international operations gradually. Some firms leap from domestic operations directly to local production. Such radical internationalisation can be due to a variety of reasons, as discussed in Section 1.2.1, for instance a company might have extremely aggressive management or international competitive pressures might neces-

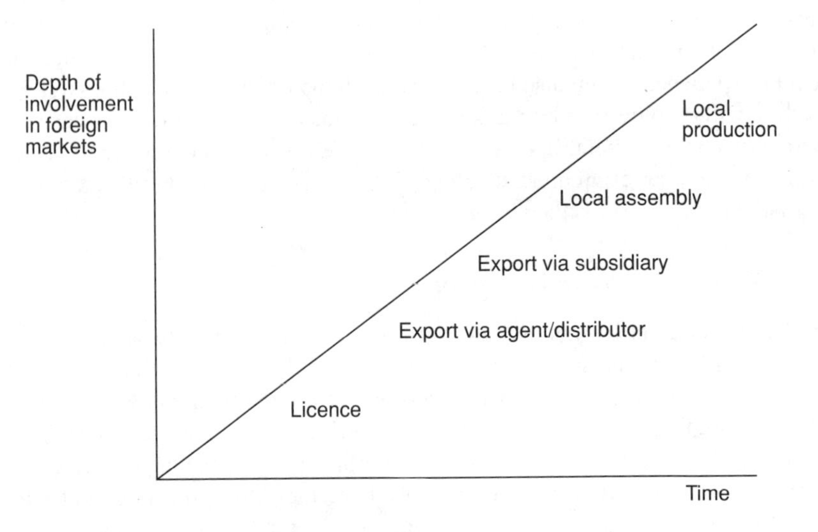

Figure 1.4 Stages of internationalisation

Source: Adapted from Rugman et al., 1986

sitate radical action. In such a case, internationalisation is not evolutionary, but revolutionary: it does not 'unfold', but is 'planned'.

Despite these criticisms, understanding that the participants in the international competitive game might be at different stages of international development is imperative for grasping the complexity of competitive interaction.

1.2.4 *Routes of internationalisation*

Complementary to the concept of 'stages of development', is the notion of 'geographic paths of development'. Companies spreading their wings internationally must choose which countries they wish to be active in. Starting from their domestic base, internationalising companies expand their foreign dealings, following a certain geographic route of advance. These geographic paths of development can vary widely. Figure 1.5 presents the three generic routes of internationalisation.

Figure 1.5 distinguishes between the internationalisation of production and sales (or more precisely, between the internationalisation of *upstream* value-adding activities, i.e. R&D and operations, and *downstream* value-adding activities, i.e. marketing, sales and service). This is an important distinction because the geographic development of a firm's *portfolio* ('set' or 'group') of production locations often differs considerably from the geographic development of its portfolio of sales markets. Each of the two requires specific further attention.

PORTFOLIO OF SALES MARKETS

When looking at the portfolio of sales markets that a company does business in, two characteristics are of strategic importance, namely its scope and composition. *Portfolio scope* refers to the *number* of sales markets that a firm is serving, while *portfolio composition* refers to the *types* of sales markets that a firm is serving (Meyer, 1991).

With regard to portfolio scope, companies can basically choose between two distinct international expansion strategies, as can be seen in Figure 1.6 (Ayal and Zif, 1978; Piercy, 1982). Given their limited managerial and financial resources, one

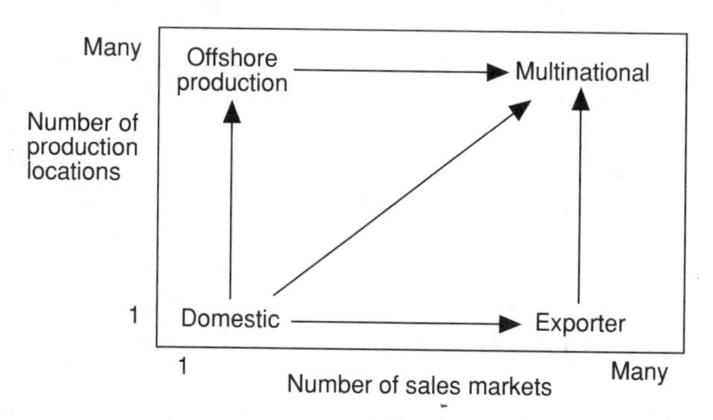

Figure 1.5 Geographic paths of internationalisation

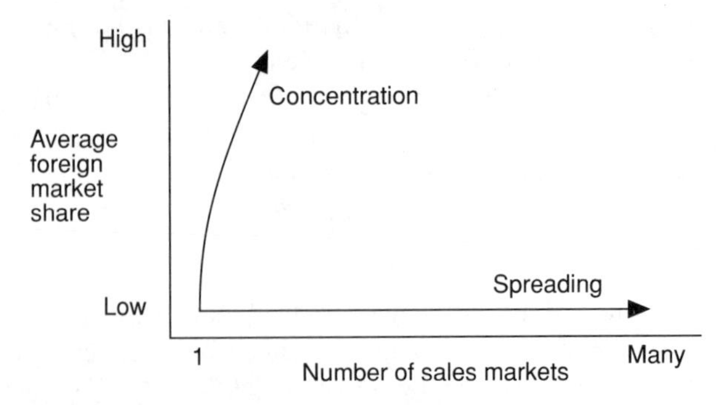

Figure 1.6 Determining sales market portfolio scope

possibility is for companies to concentrate on a small set of markets, in which they invest heavily to achieve market penetration. Alternatively, companies can spread their resources more thinly over a larger number of markets, to achieve quick access or to skim foreign markets. Of course, a wide variety of options exist between these two extremes.

Portfolio concentration and spreading have different objectives and are feasible under different circumstances, as can be seen in Table 1.2. The actual portfolio scope of a company will depend on which factors in Table 1.2 apply to the company and which are deemed most important.

Table 1.2 Factors influencing sales market portfolio scope

Objectives	Concentration	Spreading
Market entry	Overcome high entry barriers	Low entry barriers
	• High need for local adaptation	• Easily standardisable product
	• Difficult local distribution	• Accessible distribution channels
	• High customer loyalty	• Low customer loyalty
	• Name/trust/relations critical	• Product judged on merits
	• Lengthy government approval	• No regulatory barriers
	• Able to pick best markets	• Trial-and-error market selection
	• Few promising markets	• Many promising markets
Market share	Build high market share	Skim markets (low market share)
	• High economies of scale	• Low economies of scale
	• Expensive access mode	• Inexpensive access mode
	• High initial investments	• Low initial investments
	• Must build new capabilities	• Leverage existing capabilities
	• Low 'goodwill' spillover	• High 'goodwill' spillover effect
	• Sustainable advantage	• Quickly exploit temporary advantage
	• Long product life cycle	• Short product life cycle
	• Repeat sales	• Non-repeat sales
	• Complex business process	• Simple to manage across borders

Continued

Table 1.2 *Continued*

Objectives	Concentration	Spreading
Spread risk	Low risk perception • Markets less risky • Stable sales • High risk tolerance	High risk perception • Markets more risky • Volatile sales • Risk averse management
Attack competitor	Focused attack on competitor • Identifiable margin markets • Frustration value > costs • Confrontation best defence	Rapid entry into neutral territory • Poor competitive intelligence • Frustration value < costs • Encirclement best defence

With regard to portfolio composition, there is an almost endless variety of ways of putting together 'a bouquet of markets' out of the approximately 200 countries existing around the world. And indeed, when judged at face value, most companies seem to have differing portfolios of sales markets. However, if these portfolios are compared more closely, four general categories emerge: the opportunistic, evolutionary, balanced and competitive portfolios. Most sales market portfolios observed in practice fall into one of these categories, depicted in Table 1.3, or are a mixture of two or more of these 'pure' types.

The opportunistic portfolio. As the name suggests, the opportunistic portfolio is usually not intentionally put together, but emerges as the collection of sales markets that the company has jumped, stumbled, or been pushed into. The underlying logic of the portfolio is that of *chance* and *short-term gain*: the company sells in markets that accidentally cross its path (unsolicited orders and margin opportunities) or that can alleviate a short-term problem (excess stock or capacity, a poor home market and political pressure). Four types of opportunists are prevalent: the *inactive* opportunist firm, that only sells to those who knock at its door; the *reactive* opportunist firm, that only ventures abroad because outsiders (e.g. governments, banks or shareholders) force it to; the *counteractive* opportunist firm, that seeks sales possibilities abroad to alleviate the burden of overcapacity or excess stock; and the *proactive* opportunist firm, that roams foreign markets in search of easy and quick sales. This behaviour ('take the first satisfactory market you see') results in a rather unstructured zigzag route of geographic expansion. Companies with an opportunistic portfolio are inherently reactive and/or short-term in orientation and therefore prefer simple and cheap forms of internationalisation. These firms are often also characterised by a lack of commitment to internationalisation.

The evolutionary portfolio. The best way to describe an evolutionary portfolio is to emphasise that it is not 'put together', but grows. The underlying logic of the portfolio is that of *gradual development*: the company expands incrementally to bordering foreign markets, because of the relative ease of entry. There are four types of 'bordering

Table 1.3 The four general portfolio compositions

	Opportunistic	Evolutionary	Balanced	Competitive
Sub-types	Inactive Reactive Counteractive Proactive	Geographic Cultural Technical Relational	Investment risk Currency risk Product demand Resource demand	Volume Margin Warfare Learning
Main objectives	Unsolicited orders Political pressures Excess stock/ /capacity Margin opportunities Poor home market	Urge/ Bandwagon Margin opportunities Volume/ Economies Follow customers	Spread risk Margin opportunities Excess capacity	Volume/ Economies Margin opportunities Frustrate competitors Retaliation Learning effect
Preferred markets	Little adaptation Easy/quick sales Low investment	Geographically close Culturally close Technically close Existing contacts	Other risk profile Other trade block Counter-seasonal Counter-cyclical	Best volume markets Best margin markets Competitor's turf State of art markets
Market selection	Satisfying	Satisfying	Optimising	Optimising
Expansion route	Zig-zag	Centrifugal	Chequered	Campaign
Access mode	Licensing Export	All, but in stages	Export Local production	All, but context dependent
Internalisation is:	Sales opportunity	Gradual process	Resource investment	Competitive game

markets': markets can be close by *geographically* (as Germany is to Denmark), which makes physical distribution simpler, sales visits less expensive and lines of communication shorter; markets can be close by *culturally* (as Quebec is to France), which makes understanding local circumstances easier, product adaptations less necessary and local management less complex; markets can be close by *technically* (as mile/gallon/Fahrenheit countries are to one another), which makes product adaptations less necessary; and markets can be close by *relationally* (if a company follows its customer abroad), which makes understanding local markets less important and product adaptations less necessary. This movement to bordering markets results in a centrifugal geographic route of advance ('from the centre outwards'). Firms with this type of portfolio strongly follow the stages of development outlined in Figure 1.4.

The balanced portfolio. For some companies the primary concern when piecing together a portfolio of sales markets is to ensure *stability*: only markets that counter-balance existing markets will be selected. Companies can strive to achieve balance on four fronts: they can try to balance *investment risks* (e.g. low risk/low return markets can offset high risk/high return markets); they can try to balance *currency risks* (e.g. devaluations or transfer restrictions); they can try to level out (possible) fluctuations in *product demand* (e.g. seasonal or business cycles); and they can try to balance managerial and financial *resource demands*, by achieving a well-proportioned presence in embryonic, growing, mature and declining sales markets. By seeking the optimal markets to balance their portfolio, these firms produce a rather chequered pattern of geographic expansion.

The competitive portfolio. Companies engaged in fierce international competition must pick sales markets in the way that chess players select squares on a chess board: each individual position must contribute to the player's overall competitive game plan. The underlying logic of the competitive portfolio is that of *strategic advantage* The company will select those sales markets that can enhance the firm's long-term competitive position. There are four types of markets that can help firms to improve their competitive advantage: *sales volume* markets, where companies can realise economies of scale; *sales margin* markets, where companies can realise redeployable profits; *a competitor's volume or profit sanctuaries*, where a company can frustrate the competitor's efforts to build an advantage; and *state of the art* markets, where companies can detect new trends and can learn from their customers, competitors and general environment. For the competitive portfolio, market selection is focused on the best opportunities worldwide and the geographic route of advance resembles a campaign.

PORTFOLIO OF PRODUCTION LOCATIONS

Turning to the internationalisation of production, the same two important portfolio characteristics can be observed, namely scope and composition. Table 1.4 summarises the factors influencing the decision whether to concentrate production in one or just a few locations or whether to spread production over a larger number of locations. Here again, concentration and spreading are the extremes, with a number of compromise solutions in between.

With regard to portfolio composition, no general categorisation yet exists. However, Ferdows (1989) does describe the different functions that production locations can fulfil within a portfolio, as can be seen in Figure 1.7.

According to Ferdows, the three prime functions of international production locations can be to provide access to low cost inputs, to make use of local technological resources or simply to be near local customers. Depending on the function being fulfilled, six roles can be identified.

A *source* factory is a state of the art facility, often employing and improving advanced technologies, that focuses on producing for the lowest possible price. Such a factory will usually be situated in a location where low-cost inputs are available

Table 1.4 Factors influencing production location portfolio scope

Objectives	Concentration	Spreading
Lower cost	Large economies of scale	Small economies of scale
	Steep experience curve	Flat experience curve
	Low transport costs	High transport costs
	Low tariff barriers	High tariff barriers
	High inventory needed	Low inventory needed
	Location advantages important	Location advantages unimportant
	• Cheap/productive labour	• Low labour content
	• Cheap energy/raw materials	• Low energy/materials content
	• Cheap suppliers/services	• Low supplier content
	• High subsidies/low tax	• All governments offer incentives
Product quality	Technology transfer difficult	Technology transfer manageable
	Complex vertical integration	Stand alone factories possible
	Few local adaptations needed	Many local adaptations needed
	Respond to global competitors	Must respond to local competitors
	Inventory possible	Perishable product/service
	Scale advantages in learning	No scale advantages in learning
	R&D-driven innovation	Local market-driven innovation
	Concentrated location advantages	Location advantages unimportant
	• Few markets to learn from	• Many markets to learn from
	• Immobile high quality know-how	• Know-how spread/mobile
	• Quality-conscious workforce	• Quality attitude unimportant/ transferable
	• Quality suppliers/services	• Suppliers unimportant/mobile
	• Customer values country origin	• Customer is neutral/nationalistic
Customer relations	Long delivery lead times	Just-in-time delivery
	Occasional service required	Frequent service required
	Little interaction with customer	Production requires much interaction
	Low local commitment required	Must signal local commitment
	Key customers are concentrated	Customers in many markets
Spread risk	Low risk of currency appreciation	High sensitivity to currency volatility
	High risk of nationalisation	Low risk of nationalisation
	Low risk of trade barriers	High risk of trade barriers
	Technology can leak to competitors	Low risk of diffusion
	Low international experience	High international experience
	Low managerial adaptability	High managerial adaptability

Function of Production Location

Technological activities on site	Access to low cost inputs	Access to local technologies	Proximity to local customers
High	Source	Lead	Contributor
Low	Off-shore	Outpost	Server

Figure 1.7 Functions of international production locations

Source: Adapted from Ferdows, 1989

and technological development is reasonable. If the technologies used are less advanced and experience curve advantages are not expected, then the factory is a straightforward *off-shore* operation.

A *lead* factory's role is to make use of local know-how to improve product and production technologies for the firm's entire international manufacturing network. In the ideal situation a company would prefer to have its lead factory in the technologically most advanced market in the world. However, for historical, political and economic reasons companies often have their lead factory in a less than optimal location. In that case they may wish to establish an *outpost* factory in the more advanced countries to monitor developments and to report back to the lead factory.

A *server* factory's primary task is to produce for a local market. However, sometimes the technical activities carried out at these local facilities are relatively sophisticated and advancements can be realised that are of use to the firm's other factories. If such technological spin-offs are part of a local factory's role, it is referred to as a *contributor*. A company's portfolio of production locations will be a mix of these six different types of factories.

1.2.5 *Conclusion on the internationalisation of competition*

At the beginning of this chapter it was argued that it is the internationalisation of competitors that internationalises competition. Therefore, the first step towards understanding international competition has been to grasp why and how companies internationalise. The conclusion that can be drawn from the discussion in this chapter so far is that firms internationalise for many different reasons, using many different modes and following many different geographic paths.

With such varied participants it should come as no surprise that international competition varies widely among companies in the same industry. However, not only companies differ; industries do too. Some industries are global, while others are not. The extra complexity created by this fact will be further explored in the next section.

1.3 The globalisation of competition

1.3.1 *Definition of globalisation*

Few words in modern business jargon have been misused as frequently as the term *globalisation*. By some it is used as a buzzword to refer to firms and markets 'becoming very international', while others use it to indicate the 'striving towards worldwide coverage', although, ironically, the world many refer to only includes the rich, developed countries. However, nothing is particularly new about companies being very international and having worldwide coverage. Plenty of pre-Second World War companies also met these criteria. What new development then justifies the coining of the term 'globalisation'?

The new phenomenon being witnessed is that of growing *worldwide interdependence*: the events in one country are becoming increasingly linked to what happens in other countries around the world. While in the past most nations used to be relatively independent, they have grown increasingly intertwined over the last few decades. The world is no longer an *aggregation* of individual markets, but has become a *system* of interdependent markets. This can be seen, for example, by observing the speed of international dispersion of ideas and product concepts: innovative technologies introduced in one country rapidly spread to other markets, while fashions originating in one nation quickly become worldwide trends. However, the interdependence of markets goes much further than this. For instance, cost reductions achieved in one geographic region have an effect on the competitiveness of all other nations around the world. The price level in one country cannot rise too much above the prices in other countries, without triggering foreign entrants or at least arbitrage (traders buying in the low price market and selling in the high priced one). The success of a competitor in one country will have an impact on the strength of its position in other countries. In short, 'the globalisation of markets' refers to the process of worldwide market integration. A truly global market for a certain type of product is therefore one which has become fully integrated worldwide, making the entire globe basically one big market.

Such a global market for a certain type of product or service makes it necessary for companies to adapt their strategies and structures to fit into the new circumstances. Companies in global markets cannot afford to make policy decisions on a fragmented, country-by-country basis, as traditional multinational companies have done in the past. To deal with the interdependence of markets, they must develop a *global strategy*, one integrated strategy for the entire world. All company activities in the national markets must be a part of this worldwide plan. To manage this global coordination the company must also avoid having powerful national subsidiaries that are highly independence-minded, as the traditional multinational companies have. They must adopt a *global structure*, with centralised authority and responsibility for worldwide strategy formulation and implementation. In short, the global company must reflect in its policy and organisation that for a certain type of product the world is one integrated market.

This globalisation of markets and companies logically leads to the *globalisation of competition*. As markets gradually become more intertwined and companies increasingly coordinate their strategic activities across borders, the competitive games played in markets around the world also become more strongly interrelated. The consequences of competitive success or failure in one national market are no longer limited to just that one country, but have an important impact on a company's competitive position around the world. This makes the international competitive game less like blackjack – where winning or losing one hand has no consequences for the next hand – and more like chess, where the position of each piece on each field is important for a player's overall position. How this competitive game can be played will be dealt with in the following sections.

1.3.2 *Reasons for globalisation*

The roots of globalisation of a particular industry can be found in either the environment or in the strategy of one or more of the industry's participants. In some cases, globalisation is initiated by fundamental changes in market characteristics, like customer demand or production technologies. In such industries, companies largely *react* to external pressures for globalisation. In other industries, however, globalisation is triggered by a specific company, that *proactively* changes the market's underlying characteristics, so that the company can achieve a competitive advantage by pursuing a global strategy.

Independent of who causes them, there are specific market circumstances that are particularly well-suited to a global strategy. These pressures for *global integration and coordination* are summarised in Table 1.5. However, there are also many pressures on companies to be *locally responsive*. These factors, also presented in Table 1.5, are forces that inhibit the interdependence of markets: they cause the opposite of globalisation, namely international fragmentation. In markets with these characteristics a global strategy would be very difficult to implement with success.

Table 1.5 Pressures for globalisation and local responsiveness

Pressures for global integration of activities	Pressures for local responsiveness
Technology intensity	Differences in customer needs
Access to scarce resources	Differences in buying behaviour
Pressure for cost reduction	Differences in distribution channels
	Differences in media structure
Pressures for global strategic coordination	Differences in market structure
	Differences in substitutes
Importance of border-crossing customers	Differences in infrastructure
Presence of global competitors	Differences in supply structure
Investment intensity	Differences in governmental regulations
	Political impediments to trade
	Technical impediments to trade

Source: Adapted from Prahalad & Doz, 1987

PRESSURES FOR GLOBAL INTEGRATION OF ACTIVITIES

If the worldwide operational activities of a company need to be centrally managed, this is referred to as global integration. The most important reasons for such global integration are outlined below.

Technology intensity. As argued in Section 1.2.4, companies in industries using advanced technologies often prefer a concentrated portfolio of production sites, but this does require an extensive amount of operational coordination between a company's subsidiaries around the world. Having just a few lead factories allows for an easier control over quality, cost and process improvement, while the risk of secrets leaking out (technology dispersion) is also lower.

Access to scarce resources. Another reason for companies to choose a concentrated portfolio of production sites is to make use of locational advantages. These advantages normally consist of inexpensive or special local resources, such as raw materials, energy, physical infrastructure, human resources, and educational and research infrastructure. Having just a few source factories allows the firm to make use of the best or cheapest resources available worldwide, but does require operational coordination between a firm's far-flung subsidiaries.

Pressure for cost reduction. A third reason for a concentrated portfolio of production sites is to realise economies of scale. If there is a high pressure for cost reduction in an industry, a firm can coordinate all the buying it does worldwide (global sourcing) or it can build larger plants that serve multiple national markets. Both ways of reducing costs do require extensive cross-border coordination.

PRESSURES FOR GLOBAL STRATEGIC COORDINATION

Beside global integration at the operational level, firms also frequently need to coordinate at the strategic level. The coordination by headquarters of the strategies that company subsidiaries pursue in the various national markets can be necessary for the reasons outlined below.

Importance of border-crossing customers. Customers who are in a position to shop in more than one country will often try to discover where a supplier's products can be obtained at the lowest price. This is true for both individual and company buyers. Individual consumers regularly purchase products abroad, because they can be obtained there more cheaply. For years Dutch motorists bought their Mercedes cars in Germany, because the German sales division asked a lower price than the Dutch sales subsidiary. But also multinational companies that centralise their buying to negotiate lower prices will frequently play off a supplier's subsidiary in one country against the same supplier's subsidiaries in other countries to see which is most eager to drop its price and make the sale. This customer behaviour can dictate the need to coordinate pricing policy across borders. The more mobile the customer, the more subsidiaries need to coordinate, often even on a global scale.

Presence of global competitors. If an industry has one or more competitors who employ a global strategy, this in itself is an important pressure for a company to coordinate its strategy on a global scale. Such global competitors are in an ideal position to 'play global chess', attacking a company's profit sanctuaries and engaging in preemptive and retaliatory strikes. This makes it necessary for other international companies to also develop the ability to coordinate their competitive moves across borders.

Investment intensity. If an industry requires high levels of investment, the need to leverage that investment can be an important pressure for global coordination. Investments in the development of technologies, know-how, capabilities, products and brands are frequently too high to be made by each country subsidiary individually, while it is also rather inefficient for all the subsidiaries to reinvent the wheel independent from one another. Therefore, global coordination can greatly improve a company's ability to make large investments in a profitable manner.

PRESSURES FOR LOCAL RESPONSIVENESS

National markets can also have characteristics of their own that place a pressure on the international company to approach each country as a discrete entity. The main factors responsible for this fragmentation of the international market are discussed below.

Differences in customer needs. If customers in each national market have significantly different needs, companies will be forced to examine – and adapt to – markets on a country-by-country basis. The nature of these customer differences can vary from divergent cultural expectations and use characteristics, to incompatible technical systems and languages employed.

Differences in buying behaviour. Not only the customers' needs can differ across countries, but so can their buying behaviour. For example, customers can be different with regard to the way they structure buying decisions, the types of information they consider, and the relationship they wish to have with their suppliers.

Differences in distribution channels. Countries can also exhibit remarkable differences in the way their distribution channels work. For example, countries can vary with regard to the kinds of distribution channels available, the number of layers in the distribution structure, their level of sophistication, their degree of concentration and the negotiation power of each player.

Differences in media structure. National markets can also have very different media channels available for market communication purposes. In the area of television, for instance, countries vary widely with regard to the number of stations in the air (or on the cable), the types of regulation imposed, the amount of commercial time available, and its cost and effectiveness. Similarly, all other media channels may differ.

Differences in market structure. If internationally operating companies are confronted with strong local competitors, this frequently forces them to adapt to local circumstances. This need to be locally responsive is due to the fact that the strong local competitors in each country will probably implement strategies that are quite different from one another. This will require the international company to respond to a different competitive challenge in each market.

Differences in substitutes. National markets can also differ with regard to the types of indirect competition that need to be faced. In some countries, for instance, beer brewers have to deal with wine as an important rival product, while in other markets tea or soft drinks might be the most threatening substitutes.

Differences in infrastructure. Many goods and services are heavily dependent on the type of infrastructure available in a country: the more the infrastructure differs, the more locally responsive the international company must be. For example, some products rely on a digital telephone system, right-hand side driving, IBM-compatible PCs, or a national health care system. Some services require an efficient postal service, public transport, electronic banking, or cable television. Differences in any of these infrastructural elements may necessitate local adaptation.

Differences in supply structure. If a company prefers, or is pressured, to have local operations, the differences between countries with regard to their supply structures can also force the company to be more locally responsive. Not only the availability, quality and price of raw materials and components can vary widely between countries but so also can other inputs such as labour, management, capital, facilities, machinery, research, information and services.

Differences in governmental regulations. Since most government regulations are made on a country-by-country basis, they can differ significantly. Government regulations can affect almost every aspect of a company's operations, as they range from antitrust and product liability legislation, to labour laws and taxation rules. It should be noted that international efforts to coordinate governmental regulations, as attempted by, for example, the European Union and some agencies of the United Nations, are intended to reduce the international market fragmentation caused by this factor.

Political impediments to trade. Companies may also need to adapt to governmental demands that are primarily intended to inhibit trade. Sometimes home-country governments wish to impede trade in support of their political demands (e.g. boycotts), but more frequently it is the host goverment that attempts to erect import barriers. These barriers can be intended as protection for local producers or to encourage the international company to start local manufacturing. In all cases, the international company will need to be responsive to local political agendas.

Technical impediments to trade. There may also be purely technical reasons to localise operations. If transport and communication between countries is slow and/or costly, this can seriously inhibit international trade and coordination. Another important 'technical' barrier to trade is that many services, by their very nature, are rendered on the spot where they are consumed, often in cooperation with the buying party. The fact that these services cannot be stored and shipped, nor rendered at a distance, makes local operations necessary.

1.3.3 *Extent of globalisation*

As Table 1.5 indicates, there are many pressures promoting globalisation, but also many forces responsible for fragmenting international markets. There is hardly a manufacturing industry left which is undisturbed by the influence of globalisation: one would be hard-pressed to think of a market for a particular product that is still entirely internationally fragmented. Even markets for many services are globalising rapidly. Yet, on the other hand, there is also no market that is truly global; each worldwide market has some local characteristics that fragment it. Hence, it is not useful to categorise markets as global or non-global; it is the extent of globalisation and fragmentation that should be determined. The integration-responsiveness (IR) grid, developed by Prahalad and Doz (1987) and presented in Figure 1.8, is useful for this purpose.

Prahalad and Doz argue that an industry characterised by a high level of pressure for globalisation and relatively low pressures for local responsiveness normally requires a *global strategy*. Such a global strategy usually includes benefiting from a concentrated portfolio of production locations and from a relatively standardised product and marketing strategy. Implementing a global strategy demands a matching global organisational structure. The most suitable way to achieve global coordination and integration is either by means of global product divisions (one manager is responsible for the worldwide production and sale of a particular product), or through

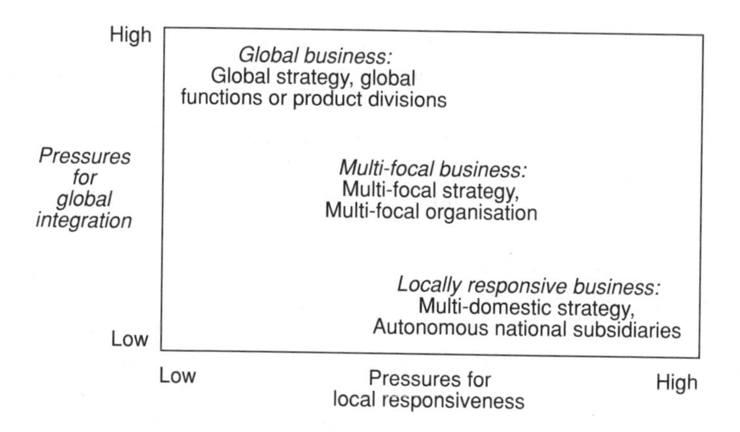

Figure 1.8 The integration-responsiveness grid

Source: Adapted from Prahalad & Doz, 1987

global functional departments (one manager is responsible for the production or marketing of all products worldwide). In both cases, the level of centralisation within the organisation is relatively high.

At the other extreme are locally responsive industries, that require a *multi-domestic strategy* (each market is treated as if it were the company's domestic market), sometimes also correctly referred to as a multinational strategy. Such a multi-domestic strategy usually includes having a widely spread portfolio of production locations and nationally tailored products and marketing strategies. The matching organisational structure is normally that of the traditional multinational, a 'federation' of relatively *autonomous national subsidiaries*.

All industries between these two extremes are more complex, because they require the delicate balancing of local demands and globalisation pressures. The industries in the upper right-hand corner of the IR grid in particular are faced with an extremely difficult balancing act: they experience high pressures for global integration *and* local responsiveness. These multi-focal businesses require a *multi-focal strategy*, sometimes also called a *transnational strategy* (in particular when referring to the upper right-hand corner of the grid). To ensure that both local responsiveness and global integration and coordination can be handled by the organisation, the preferred structure will also be multi-focal, which in practice usually means some type of *matrix* form (each employee has both a national subsidiary and global product/functional boss).

It should be noted that Figure 1.8 only gives a very generalised impression of the extent of globalisation within a particular industry. It is, however, very dangerous to generalise about an entire industry: a more detailed analysis needs to be performed. In Figure 1.9 the same IR grid is employed for a more specific evaluation of certain aspects of the publishing industry. In Figure 1.9a the publishing industry has been disaggregated into a number of *businesses* (group of strongly related product markets), that are confronted with different levels of globalisation and local responsiveness pressures.

The textbook business has been further disaggregated into a number of market segments. First, a segmentation was made between primary, secondary and university level textbook user groups, and then the university level users were further divided into English-speaking and non-English speaking groups. Finally, the English-speaking university level group was segmented on the basis of subject area, which is depicted in Figure 1.9b. It goes without saying that even further segmentation might be useful.

Figure 1.9c shows how different functional areas of a company might be faced with different pressures within the English-language university-level management textbook market. Even within functional areas, the pressures might vary considerably, as is demonstrated for the marketing function in Figure 1.9d.

The most important conclusion to be drawn from Figure 1.9 is that the general labels put on industries, such as global or multi-domestic, usually mask a more complex reality. This reality must be revealed if the industry, and the international competition within the industry, is to be understood.

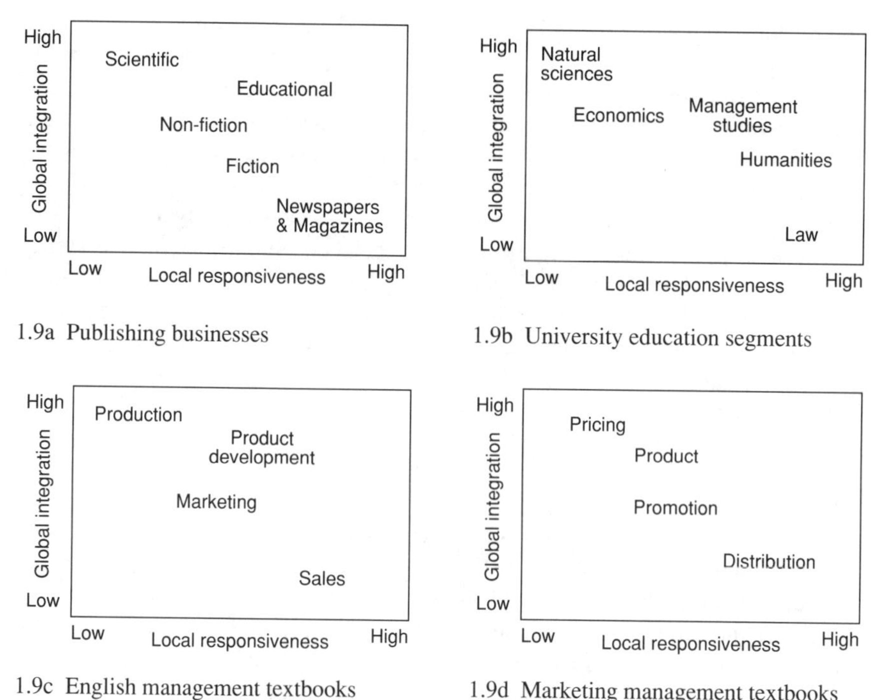

Figure 1.9 Globalisation in the publishing industry

1.3.4 *Dynamics of globalisation*

Capturing the current extent of globalisation on the IR grid is a useful exercise, but it is merely a snapshot of the existing pressures on the companies within an industry. These current demands on firms are commonly referred to as the existing *rules of the competitive game*. What such a static analysis does not reveal is how the game is played. To understand this a more dynamic analysis is necessary.

When analysing the dynamics of competition in industries that have witnessed a certain measure of globalisation, four factors seem to explain many of the patterns of competition observed. These factors are the strategic intent of the competitors, their ability to coordinate global actions, their ability to change the rules of the global game and their ability to sustain a global competitive advantage. Each factor is explored below.

THE INFLUENCE OF STRATEGIC INTENT

How a game is played is heavily dependent on what the players hope to achieve: just think how differently a football game unfolds depending on whether the teams are aiming for a victory or a draw. This is also true for the global competitive game: each company's long-term objectives will influence its current posture and therefore the nature of the competitive interaction. Prahalad and Doz (1987) refer to these long-term objectives and visions as the company's 'strategic intent'. Concrete plans and strategies are usually the result of the more fundamental strategic intent that drives a company over a longer period of time. For example, back in 1965 the small, weak, Japanese earth-moving equipment manufacturer Komatsu envisioned that it would 'encircle Caterpillar', the worldwide leader in its industry. This strategic intent acted as a guiding principle for growth and international expansion, until by the early 1980s Komatsu was strong enough to confront its rival head on. Another example is Honda, that talked about becoming a global company back in the 1950s, when it was a workshop employing 50 people. Globalising industries are often characterised by one or more of such competitors that have an aggressive and ambitious strategic intent. The higher the aspiration level of such competitors, the more intense is usually the international competitive rivalry.

THE INFLUENCE OF COORDINATED GLOBAL ACTIONS

How a game is played also depends on a team's ability to coordinate its actions on a number of fronts: just think of how differently a football match develops when a team can successfully coordinate its defenders, mid-fielders and forwards, instead of playing with 11 individualists. The same is true in globalising industries, where the patterns of competition are also more complex because a number of companies have the ability to coordinate their actions around the world. For example, a favourite competitive ploy, that is only possible if a company can coordinate across borders, is to use the profits generated in one market to attack a competitor in another market. This tactic, referred to as *cross-subsidisation*, is a powerful weapon in the global competitive game, as can be seen in the case of Komatsu and Caterpillar. In the 1970s, the giant Caterpillar had been organised on a country-by-country basis, whereby each national subsidiary had extensive autonomy, but also full responsibility for its financial results. Komatsu used Caterpillar's lack of international coordination to pick off its weaker markets one by one – financial resources generated in Komatsu's profit sanctuaries were employed to aggressively confront a Caterpillar national subsidiary that could hardly rely on other Caterpillar subsidiaries for help. Once Komatsu had bought its way into a national market and had established a strong base, it would move on to attack the next stand-alone national subsidiary of Caterpillar, thus slowly 'encircling' its competitor.

THE INFLUENCE OF CHANGING THE RULES OF THE GAME

In keeping with the football analogy, it is often the team that can force its competitors to 'play by its rules' that has the upper hand. This factor is equally important in business, where keeping the initiative and determining the basis on which competition will take place is a key element of success. In international markets, for instance, the companies that have been able to change the industry characteristics to allow for a more global strategy have often profited most from this move. In other words, firms that have innovatively been able to shift an industry on the IR grid, for example, by changing production technologies, by influencing customer needs or by overcoming barriers to trade, have commonly been best poised to benefit from these changed 'rules of the game'. Other companies are usually left disoriented by such sudden alterations of game rules and require a long period of time to recognise and develop a willingness to adapt to these exogenous changes. Philips, for example, has been struggling for two decades to align itself with the globalisation of the consumer electronics industry initiated by a number of Japanese companies, such as Sony and Matsushita, while most American consumer electronics firms have not survived the necessary transition. It should be noted, however, that shifting industries on the IR grid does not necessarily have to be in the direction of more globalisation. Companies can also attempt to change the rules by fragmenting international industries that have previously been globalised, as for instance Nokia Data has been attempting to do in the computer industry.

THE INFLUENCE OF SUSTAINING A COMPETITIVE ADVANTAGE

Finally, the way a game is played depends on who has what current competitive advantage and how each player tries to sustain or improve its competitive advantage over time. This is such a central issue to the understanding of international competition, that a separate section devoted to this topic of competitive advantage is warranted.

1.4 The roots of international competitiveness

1.4.1 *Types of competitive advantage*

A company's success in the marketplace, whether national or international, depends on whether it possesses a sustainable competitive advantage *vis-à-vis* its rivals. According to Michael Porter, there are two basic types of competitive advantage: 'lower cost than rivals, or the ability to differentiate and command a premium price that exceeds the extra cost of doing so. Any superior performing firm has achieved one type of advantage, the other, or both.' (Porter, 1991, 45). In other words, a company must be able to sustain lower costs (*cost leadership*) and/or a higher price (*differentiation*) to do better than its competitors. It should be noted that there can be only one cost leader in each market or market segment, while there might be many ways of differentiating.

Porter initially warned companies of the perils of pursuing both competitive advantages simultaneously. He referred to this situation as being *stuck in the middle* – doing both things a little, but neither properly (Porter, 1980). His reasoning was based on the premise that each dollar, yen or ecu can only be invested once, either on becoming cheaper (cost leader) or better (differentiation). By not focusing on one or the other, Porter argued, a company would be mediocre on both accounts and would be easily outclassed by the firms that did choose a clear competitive focus. However, many researchers (e.g. Gilbert and Strebel, 1989) have pointed out that some excellent firms have been able to achieve cost leadership and differentiation at the same time. These firms have invested in technologies or business systems that are simultaneously cheaper and better. For example, most firms engaged in 'total quality management' programmes and 'business system reengineering' exercises hope that these efforts will result in more streamlined production processes, that will be both less expensive and more customer friendly. Pursuing innovations that give both benefits may be more difficult than focusing on one aspect only, but can also pay off more handsomely if successful – a point Porter now seems to acknowledge.

1.4.2 *Sources of competitive advantage*

While it is important to understand competitive advantage in terms of a company's relative competitive position within an industry – the so-called external or *positioning* perspective – it is also necessary to understand the internal sources of the company's competitive advantage, also referred to as the internal or *resource-based* perspective (De Wit and Meyer, 1994). After all, both cost leadership and differentiation in the marketplace can only be attained by using the assets, competences and capabilities that a company commands. In other words, creating advantages in particular markets is only possible if a company owns, acquires or develops the resources that are necessary to perform the specific value-adding activities that lead to customer satisfaction. Therefore, if a firm aspires to sustain its competitive position in the market, it must pay explicit attention to the management and development of its internal sources of competitive advantage.

The company's resources that form the basis of competitive advantage can be divided into assets, competences and capabilities. A firm's assets consist of all the tangible and intangible resources at management's disposal that, as a rule of thumb, could be put on the firm's balance sheet. Examples of tangible assets are land, machinery, money, buildings and materials, while brand names and patents are intangible assets. Both types of assets have in common that they are easily tradable: it is relatively simple to determine their market price and sell them to other companies, because they can be easily transferred by one and absorbed by another.

A firm's *competences*, on the other hand, consist of intangible resources that are more difficult to transfer to other companies. These competences encompass all of the technical know-how and skills that a firm possesses – a firm's product and production technologies – for example, Honda is famous for its motor know-how, Sony for its miniaturisation skills and Philips for its opto-electronics ability. These competences are not easily traded for two important reasons. First, few competences hinge on one individual. On the contrary, most competences are embedded in a large number of the firm's employees and in the structure and procedures of the production system. While one individual can be traded, lured or bought, transferring an entire system is more complex. The second, related, point is that competences are usually based on extensive amounts of tacit knowledge. The more difficult it is to codify knowledge, the more difficult it is to transfer: it cannot be written down on paper and sold, but must be learnt through experience.

Much of what is true about competences is also true for the other category of intangible company resources, its *capabilities* (Stalk, Evans and Shulman, 1992). While a firm's competences are its technical skills, a firm's capabilities are based on its managerial skills. A competence refers to the mastery of a technical process, while a capability refers to the ability to manage a business process. For example, McDonald's is well known for its franchise management, Honda for its rapid product realisation and Benetton for its production and distribution network. In each example the company's competitive advantage is derived from its skill at managing an important aspect of the business system. Such management skills are usually even more difficult to transfer or imitate than technical skills, because they are wrapped up in a company's culture. Copying a management system means that a company must change its approach to doing business, which is far more complex for an organisation than imitating a technology or buying a machine.

Authors employing the resource-based perspective on competitive advantage argue that companies should strive to develop or acquire unique resources on which to base their competitive strategy. The more unique the assets, competences and capabilities of a company, the better its ability will be to differentiate itself or to become cost leader. In this view, competition in the market should be seen as companies racing to upgrade their resource base (Penrose, 1959). Sustaining a competitive edge depends on a company's ability to learn and innovate. Therefore, to understand how international competition will develop requires insight into how different companies learn and innovate differently. While much has been written on these topics, one recent theory stands out due to its explanation of observable international differences in innovativeness and competitiveness. This theory, Porter's diamond model, will be discussed in the following section.

1.4.3 *Development of competitive advantage*

In principle every company in the world would seem to have an equal opportunity to be innovative and to develop a competitive advantage. Yet each international industry has but a few successful firms, which are rarely spread at random around the globe. On the contrary, in many industries firms originating from just a few countries dominate the international market. For example, the international motion picture industry is strongly concentrated in Hollywood, the production of photography cameras is largely in the hands of a few Japanese companies and more than three-quarters of the world's cut flowers come from Holland. This suggests that some countries or regions are more suitable for the development of a competitive advantage in a particular industry than others. There seem to be strong locational sources of competitive advantage.

Traditionally, economists have almost exclusively emphasised the importance of local production factors as national sources of competitive advantage. They have focused on the availability and cost of such factors as land, capital and labour, resources referred to in Section 1.4.2. as tangible assets. However, differences in the international distribution of the factors of production explain only a very limited part of international trade and competition. Hollywood has no clear factor advantage for making movies and it would be difficult to explain Japanese success in cameras in terms of factor advantages. The Dutch flower growers actually have significant factor disadvantages: the necessary land and labour in Holland are comparatively expensive, while the weather leaves much to be desired.

According to Michael Porter (1990), the cost and availability of factors of production is just one of many locational sources of competitive advantage, and often a relatively unimportant one. In Porter's view, a firm's long-term international competitiveness usually depends much more on its capacity to continually innovate and therefore he is more interested in the national environment's influence on a firm's innovativeness. His conclusion is that the national conditions encountered by a company can actually have a rather significant impact on a firm's innovative ability and its development of competitive advantages. Four types of national conditions are of particular importance, as depicted in Figure 1.10.

FACTOR CONDITIONS

Factors need not be just homogeneous inputs for a production process, for which countries can have cost or availability advantages. Factor conditions can actually stimulate innovation. For example, outstanding educational institutions can enhance the innovative quality of labour inputs, while an advanced national infrastructure can

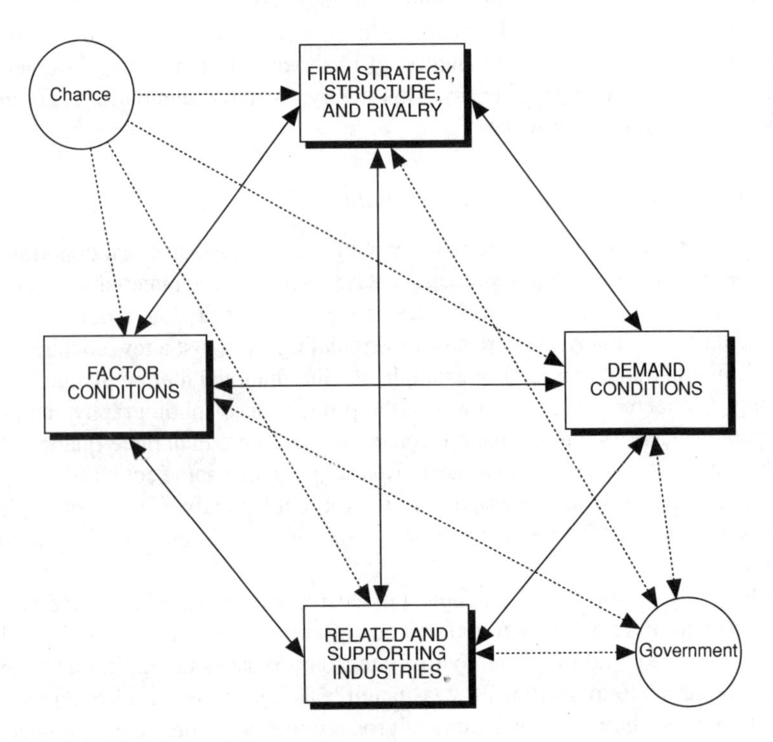

Figure 1.10 The national diamond

Source: Porter, 1990

spur the development of new business systems. In general, state of the art factors have an important positive effect on a company's potential for innovation.

DEMAND CONDITIONS

State of the art customers and distribution channels can have an equally stimulating effect. The more sophisticated and demanding the client, the harder pressed a company will be to innovate, and the more ideas the clients are bound to provide to the company willing to listen. This is especially beneficial if these advanced buyers actually foreshadow the needs that will also arise in other countries.

RELATED AND SUPPORTING INDUSTRIES

A company's innovativeness can also be encouraged by state of the art suppliers. A firm working together with world-class local suppliers can profit from exceptional cross-fertilisation opportunities. For example, the movie studios in Hollywood can produce innovative pictures due to their close cooperation with local special effects firms, stunt people and set construction companies. The Dutch flower growers are fostered by a mutually beneficial relationship with excellent local seed improvement firms, greenhouse builders and pest control companies. Beside suppliers, related industries can also prove to be an important source of innovations, as for instance the entertainment industry in California (e.g. theme parks, rock music, computer games) has cross-fertilised Hollywood.

FIRM STRATEGY, STRUCTURE AND RIVALRY

The competition that a firm encounters within its own home market is often also a force driving innovation. If a company is engaged in a prolonged struggle with a number of capable and dynamic local competitors, this situation will act as a continuous pressure on the firm to perform at its best. A company can also profit from the innovations of excellent rivals, if the company closely monitors these competitors and avoids falling into the 'not-invented-here' trap. More generally, companies can benefit from the way business is done in a specific country, if the style of management and the prevailing types of organisational structures in the nation match the industry's needs. For example, the Dutch flower growers are mostly small flexible companies that compete with one another, but simultaneously work together in a cooperative auction organisation that guards quality and the Dutch flower industry's reputation. The Dutch preference for independent units/organisations working together under the umbrella of industry-wide cooperative structures is particularly well-suited to the demands of this industry.

CHANCE AND GOVERNMENT

Historical accidents and government policy can also have an impact on a company's ability to upgrade its competitive advantage, but always through their influence on the diamond. For example, the best selling Dutch flower, the tulip, is originally

Turkish. It made its way to Holland by chance, but for the Dutch to gain a competitive advantage in producing these flowers required sophisticated consumer demand and active growers. The same is true for the role of government policy: government can 'improve or impede national advantage through its investments in factor creation, through its influence on the goals of individuals and firms, through its role as a buyer or influencer of buyer needs, through its competition policies, and through its role in related and supporting industries, among other ways.' (Porter, 1990, p. 43)

Porter argues that countries can exhibit considerable differences in all four categories of national conditions. Therefore, some national diamonds are much more suitable for the long-term development of competitive advantage than others. This, Porter believes, explains why international competition in particular industries tends to be dominated by companies from just a few countries.

Prescriptively, Porter's theory indicates that internationally operating companies would be wise to analyse the potential of their own home base for sustained development of their competitive advantage. If a company's national context offers a fertile environment for keeping up its competitiveness, the firm would do well to actively work at further improving this home base. After all, the firm has an important stake in making its national diamond a better platform for international success. If a firm is situated in a country with little potential of becoming a strong home base, it should seriously consider relocation. It should situate its activities and its headquarters at those locations in those nations where there are concentrations of sophisticated buyers, important suppliers, groups of competitors, or especially significant factor-creating mechanisms for its industry. Physical relocation can be necessary because geographic proximity makes the interchange between organisations within a cluster more intense and fluid, which improves the opportunities to build competitive advantage.

1.4.4 *Conclusions on competitive advantage*

As concluded in Section 1.2.5, to understand the nature of international competition it is necessary to study how companies continually strive to sustain a competitive advantage. In Section 1.4 it has been argued that to be competitive, firms must be cost leaders and/or be able to offer differentiated products. To sustain these competitive advantages, firms must continuously upgrade their resource base, consisting of assets, competences and capabilities. The improvement of these resources is the result of companies seizing the opportunities presented to them by their national diamond, or by other national diamonds they are able to tap. In short, companies have the freedom to develop a resource base and to conquer a competitive position within an industry, but the roots of their international competitiveness stretch back to the national environments in which they are situated.

Bibliography

Albaum, G., Strandskov, J., Duerr, E. and **Dowd, L.** (1984) *International Marketing and Export Management*, Addison-Wesley, p. 34.

Ayal, I. and **Zif, J.** (1978) Competitive market choice strategies in multinational marketing, *Columbia Journal of World Business*, Fall, pp. 72–81.

Ayal, I. and **Zif, J.** (1979) Market expansion strategies in multinational marketing, *Journal of Marketing*, vol. 43, pp. 84–94.

De Wit, B. and **Meyer, R.J.H.** (1994) *Strategy – Process, Content, Context: An International Perspective*, West.

Ferdows, K. (ed.) (1989) Managing international manufacturing, *Advanced Series in Management*, vol. 13.

Gilbert, X. and **Strebel, P.** (1989) 'From innovation to outpacing, *Business Quarterly*, Summer, pp. 19–22.

Meyer, R.J.H. (1991) International marketing strategy in threes: towards an integrative framework, in H. Vestergaard (ed.) *An Enlarged Europe in the Global Economy*, Proceedings of the 17th Annual EIBA Conference, Copenhagen Business School.

Penrose, E.T. (1959) *The Theory of the Growth of the Firm*, Basil Blackwell.

Piercy, N. (1982) Key markets vs. market spreading, *International Marketing*, Summer, pp. 56–65.

Porter, M.E. (1979) How competitive forces shape strategy, *Harvard Business Review*, no. 2, pp. 137–145.

Porter, M.E. (1980) *Competitive Strategy: Techniques for Analyzing Industries and Competitors*, Free Press.

Porter, M.E. (1990) *The Competitive Advantage of Nations,* Macmillan.

Porter, M.E. (1991) Towards a dynamic theory of strategy, *Strategic Management Journal*, Winter, pp. 95–117.

Prahalad, C.K. and **Doz, Y.** (1987) *The Multinational Mission*, The Free Press.

Root, F.R. (1988) Entering foreign markets, in I. Walter (ed.) *Handbook of International Management*, John Wiley and Sons.

Rugman, A., Lecraw, D. and **Booth, L.** (1985) *International Business: Firm and Environment*, McGraw-Hill, p. 90.

Stalk, G., Evans, P. and **Shulman, L.E.** (1992) Competing on capabilities: the new rules of corporate strategy, *Harvard Business Review*, March–April, pp. 57–69.

2 Foreign direct investments

2.1 Introduction

Before providing a description of developments in foreign direct investments, it makes sense to define the scope of the issue of 'foreign direct investments'.

The term *foreign direct investments* is used to describe transnational capital transactions made by companies from one country ('the country of origin') to another country ('the host country'). The transactions entail the purchase of production resources (such as buildings, machinery or land) or companies or stakes in them. The aim is to add value locally by means of production or services and to exercise some influence on corporate activities. Investments, that is, capital transactions with the sole aim of achieving a financial return, are therefore excluded.

It is virtually impossible to make any precise statements about the scale of foreign direct investment flows over a given period. The main reason is that many investments actually made are invisible, and it is therefore necessary to use various criteria in order to give some indication of the scale. Furthermore, there is no international standardisation in terms of recording or methods of measuring foreign direct investment.

By no means all foreign direct investments are recorded in the country of origin or the host country. In some cases only licensing applications for foreign direct investments are recorded; in many countries there is no requirement to record foreign direct investments at a central point. Capital balance sheets and the overviews of capital flows compiled by the central bank can provide some pointers, but these also include transnational investments. Furthermore, the overviews do not always include the amounts invested by the company or subsidiary established in the host country which from the perspective of the parent company are to be regarded as reinvested earnings.

With respect to the investment relationship between two countries, the picture is often affected by investments being made from a third country, for fiscal reasons, for example. The Netherlands, for instance, have had a Tax Convention with the United States, which made investment by the Netherlands in the United States fiscally very attractive. Companies from various countries have therefore made a large proportion of their investments in the United States via a holding company from the Netherlands.

In some cases it is the nationality of the parent company, in others the location of the investing subsidiary's registered office that determines the country of origin of the investment. Here too an international standard methodology is lacking.

Apart from periodical investment flows, the statistics also include data about the level (stocks) of foreign direct investments, particularly when illustrating the investment relationship between two countries. The figures on stocks are even less precise than those on investment flows, as – apart from the problems of recording and measuring described above – there are differences in the method of valuation, and in the time from which the measurement applies. In analysing investment figures, it is therefore important to check thoroughly whether one is dealing with level or stock figures or with flow figures.

In brief, data on foreign direct investments can do no more than provide a rough indication. They lack the precision they are sometimes assumed to have. A comparison of statistics between two countries on outgoing and incoming direct investments therefore often reveals disappointingly large differences.

Direct international investments are of great and ever-growing importance for the world economy. Within this framework they determine cyclical but, above all, also structural developments. Despite the measuring problems described above, the existing data can enable major developments in the geographical and sectoral patterns of foreign direct investments to be tracked and illustrated.

In the next section, the developments in the scale and patterns of foreign direct investments are dealt with, followed by a discussion on their significance for companies and governments in Sections 2.3 and 2.4.

2.2 Developments in the scale and patterns of foreign direct investments

In the light of the problems in measuring foreign direct investments described above, the most reliable data on direct international investments originate from international organisations, which standardise the figures from the various countries as far as possible, for example the OECD (Organisation for Economic Cooperation and Development) and the UN (United Nations).

2.2.1 *The importance of – and increase in – foreign direct investments*

The world economy is becoming ever more international. International trade and foreign investment are growing more rapidly than the world economy. The world economy grew by a total of 40 per cent between 1980 and 1993, but total world exports grew by 60 per cent. Between 1986 and 1993 world trade grew annually between two and four per cent more rapidly than the world economy (see Figure 2.1).

Foreign direct investment averaged more than $30 billion per annum in the 1970s, but grew in the 1980s to an average level of almost $100 billion per annum.

In the 1980s in particular, both the number and the total volume of direct international

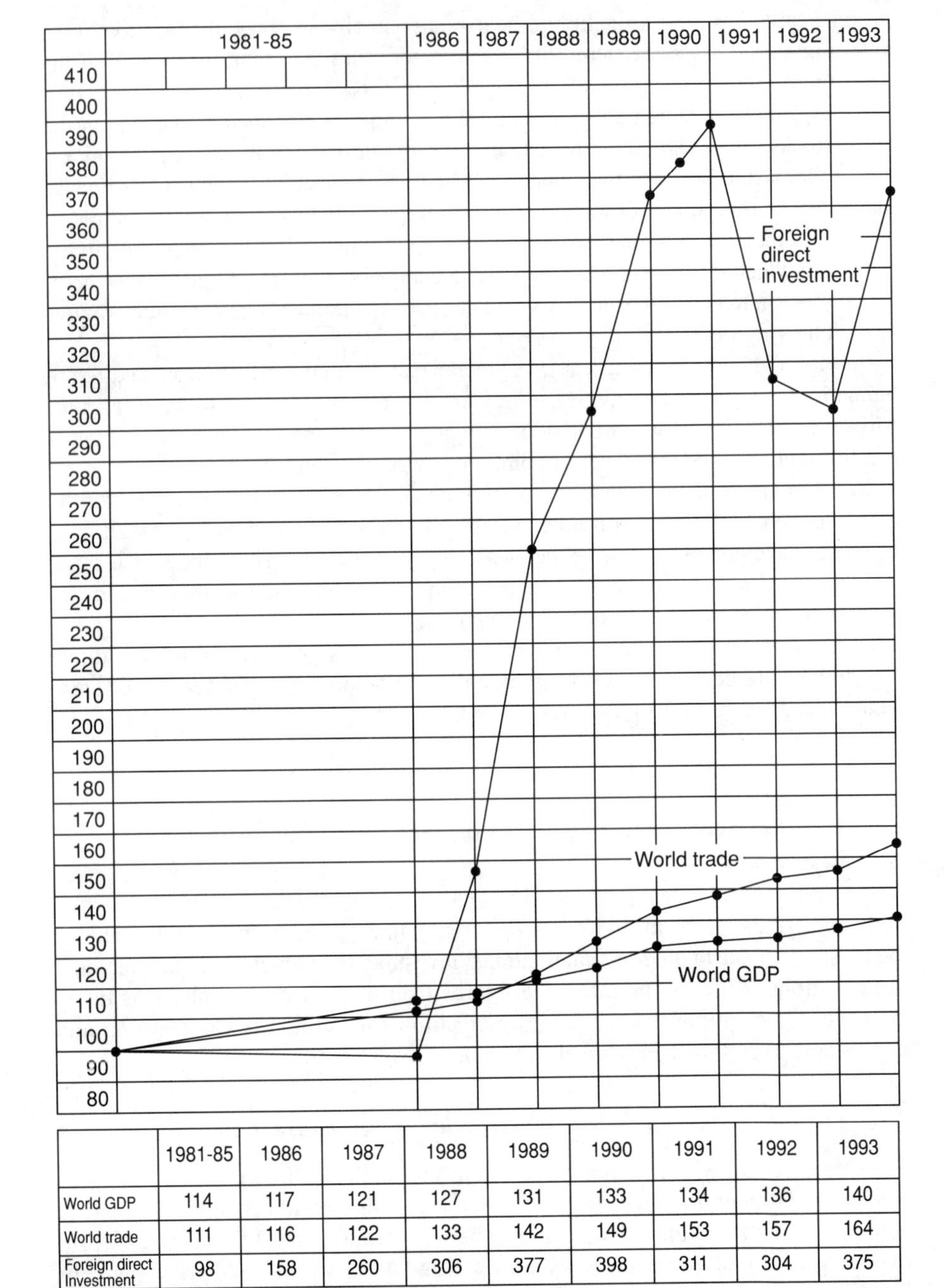

	1981-85	1986	1987	1988	1989	1990	1991	1992	1993
World GDP	114	117	121	127	131	133	134	136	140
World trade	111	116	122	133	142	149	153	157	164
Foreign direct Investment	98	158	260	306	377	398	311	304	375

Figure 2.1 Development of the volume of world-GDP, world trade and total flow of foreign direct investment (1981–1993; 1980 = 100)

Sources: GATT, 1994, UN 1994a, UN 1994b

investments in the world grew enormously, in absolute terms and also in relation to economic growth, international trade and direct domestic investment. The zenith of this wave of investment came in the second half of the 1980s when the total gross domestic product (GDP) at market prices in the world was growing annually by an average of 3.5 per cent, total exports of goods and services by an average of 6.4 per cent, and the flow of foreign direct investments by an average of 40 per cent.

In 1992 the stock of foreign direct investments in the world amounted to around $2,000 billion. The companies collectively financed by this means accounted for total sales of $5,500 billion. By way of comparison, total exports of goods and services in the world amounted to $4,000 billion in that year, one third being channelled between branches of the same company (UN 1993).

The increase in the number and volume of direct international investments, together with their characteristics, can be explained by a combination of factors which together explain the increase in direct corporate investment in general and the internationalisation patterns of those investments in particular.

These factors vary according to the extent to which they can be designated cyclical or structural and thus short-term or long-term in nature. The following classification of the factors is important, as it can help to explain and predict the level and patterns of direct international investments in different periods.

The factors will be categorised as follows:

1. Cyclical developments
2. General government policy
3. Developments in trade policy
4. Corporate strategies.

CYCLICAL DEVELOPMENTS

The favourable cyclical situation in the world economy in the second half of the 1980s gave many companies sufficient financial resources and good prospects for returns to engage in foreign direct investments and to bear the risk entailed. In the improving economic situation interest rates were falling in real terms (see Figure 2.2), while share prices were rising. Lower interest rates made it cheaper to finance direct investments. As a result, companies found themselves in a good position to engage in direct domestic but also foreign direct investment.

GENERAL GOVERNMENT POLICY

A second major factor that helps to explain the great increase in foreign direct investment is a generally more positive attitude on the part of national governments towards the private sector in general, and international trade and direct investment in particular. The more positive attitude towards the private sector in general was reflected in the privatisation of state undertakings, deregulation and the liberalisation of foreign trade and direct investment. The number of nationalisations peaked in the first half of the 1970s. Since then the number has been falling and is now negligible. The number of privatisations, by contrast, has increased dramatically since the start of the 1980s.

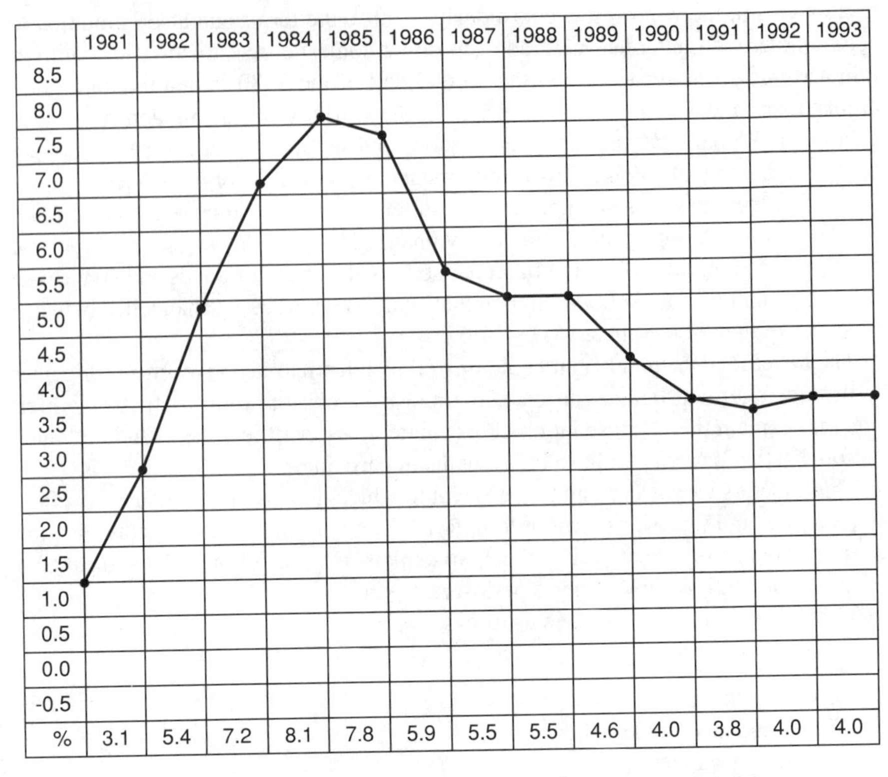

Figure 2.2 Trend in interest rates in real terms in US dollars, 1981–93

Source: OECD *Historical Statistics* 1960–89, OECD *Economic Outlook*, June 1994

The privatisation of state undertakings has admitted companies in the private sector to an increasing number of sectors. In many developing countries, but also in most countries of Southern Europe and of the former Eastern bloc, many, if not all, sectors in the economy were the exclusive domain of the government and state undertakings. In most countries the government is withdrawing from many of these sectors and is selling off state undertakings to the private sector. Even in market economies that have existed far longer, the government is withdrawing from sectors in which they have been present for a relatively long time, such as telecommunications, aviation and mineral extraction.

Deregulation is doing away with a whole range of regulations on such aspects as production, wages and prices. This created more entrepreneurial scope for the private sector, and thus in many cases a greater willingness to invest.

The more positive attitude in host countries towards foreign trade and foreign direct investment was prompted by the awareness that the assumed drawbacks, such as loss of influence on domestic production and employment, were found to be more than offset by the benefits of additional employment, capital, technological know-how and additional export revenues, and greater economic efficiency by the rise in domestic competition. There was a major shift in thinking about economic development policy. In the 1960s and 1970s this thinking was still determined by what was termed import-substitution, that is, efforts to achieve self-sufficiency in as many sectors as possible. In the 1980s the vision changed under the impact of disappointing results and, in particular, a number of developing countries began to focus successfully on developing competitive, export-oriented sectors (Todaro 1989). This was accompanied by liberalisation of international trade and foreign investment.

Initially, the more positive attitude towards foreign direct investment was still selective, expressing itself primarily in providing financial incentives, such as tax benefits and subsidies and setting up special 'export processing zones'.[3] Gradually, policies broadened to include more across-the-board deregulation and liberalisation of foreign direct investment, as reflected for example in a relaxation of the provisions pertaining to the foreign property of companies and to means of production. In the privatisation processes, foreign buyers were generally given opportunities to buy companies or parts of them.

Even in countries of origin of foreign direct investments the arguments for restrictions on the outflow of capital began to fade, when it became clear that domestic economic problems were no longer being caused by a lack of domestic capital. Instead, it came to be realised that restrictions on foreign direct investment were harmful to domestic companies wishing to strengthen their competitive position via direct investment in other countries; many privatised companies and very large companies in general also found themselves exposed to international competition and strengthened their market position by taking over companies at home and abroad.

A more or less logical consequence of the more positive attitude towards foreign direct investment was that national governments made greater efforts to improve the international legal and institutional conditions for foreign direct investment. Increasing numbers of countries signed bilateral treaties on the protection of foreign direct investment (generally including provisions on arbitration and protection against nationalisation, see Box 2.1) and aimed at avoiding double taxation. The OECD, for example, is working on standardised multilateral regulations based on the numerous and very diverse bilateral treaties that have meanwhile emerged on this point. The availability of new financing instruments has also contributed to the increase in foreign direct investment. One familiar example is debt–equity swaps, whereby developing countries in particular sell part of their foreign debt to foreign investors in exchange for local currency which can then be used to finance investment.

3. Export processing zones are special areas in which direct foreign investors are generally offered special fiscal advantages or subsidies or both, and where, generally speaking, special infrastructure or statutory provisions apply to direct foreign investments. To gain access to the facilities of an export processing zone, foreign investors usually have to export virtually their entire production. In setting up these zones, host countries were attempting to attract direct foreign investment (and thus foreign know-how), without subjecting the domestic industry unduly to major foreign competition on the home market.

Box 2.1: Investment-protection agreements

If bilateral or multilateral investment-protection agreements exist between two countries, then there is a greater guarantee for direct foreign investment against expropriation or other adverse treatment by the government of the host country. In assessing the investment climate in a country, the existence of such an agreement must therefore be included in the considerations. Most investment-protection agreements offer the following elements:

1. Non-discrimination: direct investments by domestic and foreign companies receive identical treatment.
2. Protection of the direct investment against nationalisation, or expropriation by the government. Nationalisation is generally only permitted in exceptional cases, i.e. when it is necessary for state security or other exceptional emergencies, or when it forms part of a large-scale social reform programme. In cases of nationalisations, no distinction may be made between investments by indigenous companies and foreign companies. Nationalisations must be carried out in accordance with the existing law of the country, and adequate compensation must be paid which can be freely transferred abroad in convertible currency.
3. Free transfer of profits and other proceeds – including interest and dividends, royalties, management fees and proceeds from the sale of (parts of) the direct foreign investment – in convertible currency.
4. International arbitration in the event of conflicts between the host country government and the foreign company, only if mutual negotiation fails to deliver a satisfactory result; this should be handled by the national courts or some other agreed arbitration body.
5. Clear rules and rapid procedures in granting licences for a wide range of investment and other management decisions.
6. Most-favoured clause, whereby more favourable conditions agreed by the host country with third countries are automatically applied to the present agreement.

It is generally agreed that the agreement should apply to existing as well as new investments.

DEVELOPMENTS IN TRADE POLICY

Three major developments could be discerned in the field of trade policy in the 1980s. The first has already been described in the previous section, namely, the growing liberalisation of international trade and foreign investment. The second main development was increasing regional integration, with groups of countries within regions removing barriers to mutual trade and investment. The clearest and most advanced example of this is the European Union. Other examples are:

(a) the North American Free Trade Agreement (NAFTA), of which Canada, Mexico and the United States are members;
(b) the European Free Trade Association (EFTA), of which Finland, Iceland, Liechtenstein, Norway, Austria, Sweden and Switzerland are members and have free trading relationships, and which (with the exclusion of Switzerland) together with the EU constitutes a free-trade zone (European Economic Area) and of which Sweden, Finland and Austria have acceded to the EU on 1 January 1995;
(c) the Association of Southeast Asian Nations (ASEAN), in which Brunei, the Philippines, Indonesia, Malaysia, Singapore, Vietnam and Thailand are working to reduce mutual trade barriers;
(d) some regional cooperative initiatives between developing countries in Latin America, notably Mercosur and the Andes pact, and in Africa, notably the Maghreb, Ecowas and Southern African Development Community (SADC).

Trade liberalisation and regional integration have some impact on decision-making on foreign direct investment (see Section 2.3.1); generally there is a major net positive impact on mutual direct investment of the countries involved.

A third important development lies in the increasing trade-policy tensions between the major trading blocs, with reference to the protectionist characteristics of major economies and regional cooperative ventures. Trade restrictions have been implemented on several occasions between the US, Japan and the EU, emanating as 'voluntary export restraints' and 'market-regulatory restrictions'. Not only the expansion of the number of markets that could be served from a new location via foreign direct investment in a free trade zone, but also the opportunity to circumvent the trade restrictions between the major blocs, were major incentives to investment, notably by Japan in the US and by Japan and the US in the EU.

CORPORATE STRATEGIES

The strategically determined internationalisation of corporate activities is growing. There are a number of driving forces behind this development (see also Chapter 1, and Section 2.3 of this chapter).

(a) *Structurally falling relative costs of transport and communication.* This is increasing the 'geographical market coverage' of companies. On the one hand, this development is opening up ever more distant markets for companies, while on the other hand competition in the home market comes from ever more distant origins.
(b) *Continuing acceleration of the development of technology.* This trend is shortening life cycles and thus the time window for earning a return on products. Any newly developed product must therefore be rapidly available on the largest possible market. Modifying products to cater for local preferences, and management of the sales and distribution channels, almost always require direct investment in the sales markets.
(c) *Increasing global competition.* With increasing global competition, the developments in technology, but also in marketing, demanded high levels of direct

investment in order to retain market position. This forced many companies to concentrate on one core activity or just a small number of core activities. Nevertheless, many companies now find it is almost impossible to sustain the high levels of foreign direct investment, and are seeking partners in other countries with whom to cooperate in research and development, marketing and distribution, in order to share costs and increase effectiveness. This cooperation also takes the form of strategic alliances and networks, with the companies involved investing in one another's activities or sharing capital, or both. The innovation in strategic objectives, aimed at strengthening one's position in a single core activity or a few core activities, is leading to a situation where many companies that were taken over in preceding years on the grounds of profitability have now changed owner (parent company) again (see also Section 2.3.3). Examples of industrial sectors where strategic cooperation in the field of technological development and the associated foreign direct investment have come to assume importance are computers, electronics, motor vehicles and biotechnology.

Technological, legal, and market developments, however, are in some cases causing the traditional boundaries between industries to blur, because they lead to significant benefits of synergy. For example, the services of banks and insurance companies are moving ever closer together into a total package of financial services, notably because many legal barriers have been abolished. Other examples of sectors in which this phenomenon can be found are computers and electronics, telecommunication and media (television and film). Technological developments here are frequently leading to services through which data processing, communications, the provision of news and entertainment can be integrated.

(d) *The rise of new sales markets*. In the industrialised countries of Asia in particular, and more recently in some growing economies in Latin America, the sales opportunities for companies are increasing. Foreign direct investment is often required to service these growing markets from the industrialised countries, in which most of the large companies operating internationally are present. But new markets are also emerging in industrialised countries, for example in services.

In fact, it can be said that economic and technological developments, the shifts in governmental policy and the resultant developments in corporate strategies have led to a growing international division of labour. In the process of this ever more intensive division of labour, most industrialised countries have been compelled to focus on technologically higher-value production processes with a higher added value per production factor deployed in response to the rising costs of labour, land and in some cases the price of their own currency;[4] there is a growing group of up-and-coming developing countries with low labour and land costs that is taking over more low-grade production. In addition, developing countries are making greater inroads into more high-grade production. Labour- and land-intensive production processes are therefore increasingly being transferred from Western Europe to Eastern Europe, from

4. Japanese companies in particular have transferred large sections of their most cost-sensitive production to countries with a cheaper currency as a result of the sharp rise in the yen.

North America to Latin America, and from Japan to Southeast Asia. The process is furthest advanced in the latter region, and there is now a generation of newly industrialising countries (South Korea, Taiwan, Hong Kong, Singapore), which themselves are now investing heavily in production in the low-cost countries of Southeast Asia (Thailand, Malaysia, China and the Philippines).

These factors are partly inter-related and affect one another. They provide a broad-brush explanation for the high level of foreign direct investment, particularly in the second half of the 1980s. They also explain the major developments that have occurred in the pattern of foreign direct investments.

This pattern is characterised by four aspects:

- geographical development;
- sectoral development;
- changes in the motives for foreign direct investment; and
- development in the forms of foreign direct investment.

2.2.2 *Geographical development*

The geographical pattern of foreign direct investment changed during the 1980s. This holds for both 'outgoing' and 'incoming' direct investments. One striking feature of outgoing direct investments is that EU countries have somewhat expanded their already large share. European integration has given a sharp boost to investment activity within the EU, as companies wanted to strengthen their position on the integrated market via mergers and take-overs. European companies also invested on a substantial scale in the US.

Companies from the EFTA countries and Japan also wanted to have a solid base in the EU market, and that explains the pronounced growth in direct investment from these countries. Japan was also investing on a major scale in the US, in order to avoid trade restrictions, and in Southeast Asia on account of the major cost and trade-policy advantages there (see also Box 2.2). The US was virtually absent from this investment boom and in absolute terms remained roughly at the same level. The main reasons were that high interest rates and the recession adversely affected the liquidity of many American companies.

For many US companies, borrowing from their foreign subsidiaries became attractive for fiscal reasons, and such loans serve to depress the figures for outgoing foreign direct investment by country of origin. What was striking was the rise of the newly industrialising countries in Southeast Asia, such as South Korea and Taiwan, where many companies were compelled to transfer a proportion of their activities to cheaper countries in Southeast Asia due to rising costs at home. Furthermore, companies from these countries, like their Japanese counterparts, wanted to acquire access to the US and the EU (see Table 2.1 on incoming direct investment flows).

What is striking is how the United States expanded its share in the incoming direct investment flows during the 1980s. The US especially benefited from the high levels of investment flows from Japan and Europe. The Japanese investment in the US in particular was triggered by a fear of American protectionism. The sharp fall in the

Box 2.2: The investment climate in Indonesia

Indonesia is one of the countries of Southeast Asia that has experienced pronounced economic growth in recent years. The country switched from an import-subsitution to an export-promotion strategy a few years ago. This helped it to attract a large amount of direct foreign investment in local production and sales. However, the country still suffers from the legacy of its period of import substitution. The example of the investment climate in Indonesia typifies the investment climate in many developing countries.

In 1986 a large number of sectors were opened to foreign investors. Quota and some local content rules were abolished and import duties were lowered. However, the main sectors – steel, plastics and foodstuffs – were not yet completely liberalised.

Since the time of import substitution, with limited domestic competition, many branches of industry have been dominated by a few domestic conglomerates. This is leading to relatively high prices on the domestic market for many raw materials, semi-manufactured goods, capital goods and end products. As a consequence, the indigenous group of entrepreneurs is still limited. Foreign entrepreneurs have difficulties, for example, in finding Indonesian business partners for joint ventures.

The investment climate in Indonesia has a number of drawbacks compared to Thailand and Malaysia for instance:

1. The bureaucracy in Indonesia is still large and powerful;
2. The succession of President Suharto is a very uncertain political factor;
3. The judiciary is not working very well, and the quality of the government bureaucratic system, the fiscal-legal infrastructure, entrepreneurship and the relations between employees and employers is poor;
4. Business operations in Indonesia are of low quality, particularly in the case of production;
5. There are too few accountancy firms in Indonesia, and the legal registration system does not work well.

Other factors that have hitherto hampered the establishment of substantial export-oriented direct foreign investments are:

1. A trading system which discourages export-oriented production activities;
2. High transport and handling costs, including the costs of compliance with bureaucratic regulations;
3. The slow pace of development of export processing zones (until recently);
4. The relatively low labour productivity.

Market inefficiencies, government regulations and high effective protection are also a drag on the efficiency of production and exports. Direct foreign investments are therefore focused mainly on the domestic market. The risks of high foreign debt in terms of monetary stability are reduced by the major direct foreign investments. The poor functioning of the capital market and the conservative lending policy of the Indonesian government hamper the working climate for companies. In particular, there is a shortage of trained, senior financial and economic staff. However, investment legislation has been liberalised substantially on a number of occasions in recent years.

Box 2.2: *Continued*

Indonesia pursues a tight monetary and budgetary government policy. This has brought inflation under control and ensured that the currency – the rupiah – has largely retained its value. At the same time, however, this policy restricts domestic demand. As many direct foreign investments are targeted at local sales, this leads to some slowing down in the growth of direct foreign investments.

Although direct foreign investments have played only a limited role hitherto in promoting the export of non-oil products, Indonesia offers a number of highly attractive conditions for export-oriented investments:

1. low labour costs for low-grade labour;
2. the rich basis of natural raw materials;
3. the large domestic market.

In addition to these incentives, growing protectionism in Western countries compels investors to find new Third World country bases from which to penetrate these markets.

Table 2.1 International incoming direct investment flows 1982–92 (in $ million)

Host country/economy	1982–87 (annual average)	1988	1989	1990	1991	1992
All countries	67,526	159,101	196,132	207,912	162,124	158,413
European Union (12 member-countries)	19,032	57,162	81,063	99,701	72,014	78,802
Rest Western Europe (Finland, Iceland, Norway, Austria, Sweden, Switzerland)	2,266	3,151	6,918	9,407	8,693	3,610
Northern America (US, Canada)	27,905	62,366	71,636	56,060	32,038	11,145
United States	26,927	58,571	69,010	48,422	25,446	3,388
Developing countries/ regions	14,752	27,772	27,376	31,266	39,060	51,485
East, South and South-east Asia	6,273	14,980	15,416	19,426	20,245	29,402
Latin America	6,042	9,040	6,248	6,248	15,032	17,771
Central and Eastern Europe	17	15	268	300	2,448	4,526

Source: United Nations, 1994b

value of the US dollar also made it attractive for foreign companies to invest in the US. East and Southeast Asia have also witnessed a large inflow of foreign direct investment during the 1980s, particularly from Japan. The reasons were: low local production costs, the growth of the economies, and government policy in East and Southeast Asia being friendly to foreign investment (see Box 2.3 for the role of European direct investment in East and Southeast Asia).

Latin America experienced a sharp rise in incoming direct investment flows, particularly after 1988, on account of the favourable economic developments and the liberalisations combined with the rehabilitation of government finances and of the foreign debt of many Latin-American countries. Companies were also given the opportunity via debt–equity swaps to invest at very favourable currency rates; debt–equity swaps have now become less important. For some years now the increasing number of privatisations in Latin America has attracted foreign direct investment. The foreign investment boom during the second half of the 1980s has largely bypassed Africa and the Middle East, where investments traditionally have been very

Box 2.3: Prospects for European direct investment in the ASEAN

Economic developments in Southeast Asia are attracting the attention of increasing numbers of companies in the United States, Japan and Europe. Companies are increasingly investing in Southeast Asia because of the favourable production conditions and the rapidly growing market. Companies from Europe are, however, lagging behind in this respect.

In contrast to Asian and American Companies, European firms have preferred exports and the granting of licences over direct investment. European investors, furthermore, have been frightened off more than Asian companies by the restrictive statutory provisions on ownership ratios in many Asian countries.

European companies that now wish to enter the ASEAN markets with direct investment are confronted with the dominating presence of Japanese companies. This dominance hampers access to market segments of consumer products but, as a result of Japanese companies managing to impose technical production standards on local producers, also to segments of semi-manufactured products and capital goods. The structural shifts in the ASEAN economies, however, still offer good prospects for European investors and exporters of new products.

The rationalisation of production processes in the EU following the completion of the internal market, and the reduction in government support, will encourage the transfer of activities to countries where they can be performed more efficiently. The transfer may be to countries outside the EU, by means of licensing agreements, sub-contracting or direct investment. The associated increase in intra-industrial trade will probably lead to a diminishing demand for protectionism on the part of industries in the countries involved.

much focused on mineral extraction (notably oil). The continuing political instability in many countries is probably the main cause of this. Although in Latin America and Africa the incoming direct investment flows have increased, their share in total world incoming direct investment has remained small, relatively to other regions. An additional explanation for this lies in the changing motives for carrying out foreign direct investments (see Section 2.2.4). Central and Eastern Europe have hitherto played only a marginal role in investment policy, despite the very rapidly increasing interest on the part of direct foreign investors since 1992.

2.2.3 *Sectoral development*

During the 1970s and 1980s foreign direct investments in the mining of raw materials, energy and agricultural products (the primary sector), shrank very much in relative importance to the benefit of direct investment in industry (the secondary sector) and the services sector (the tertiary sector; see Table 2.2).

One major reason for the fact that the share of direct investment in the *primary sector* has continued to drop as compared to the secondary and tertiary sector, is the ongoing fall in the prices of raw materials and crude agricultural products. The supply surplus on the world market is growing structurally, as a result of production and exports still increasing, while demand has been constant or even falling for some time now. Technological developments have enabled raw materials and energy to be used ever more efficiently, and often paved the way for cheaper substitutes (for example, sugar, rubber, copper and tin).

In order to decrease their dependence on the highly changeable prices of crude raw materials, many developing countries are pursuing a policy aimed at increasing added value at home. Foreign investors are encouraged via fiscal instruments or instruments

Table 2.2 Sectoral development and composition of stocks of international outgoing direct investment by industrialised countries*

	Average annual growth 1971–80 as %	Average annual growth 1981–90 as %	Composition		
			1970	1980	1990
Primary sector	11.7	6.1	22.7	18.5	11.2
Secondary sector	13.6	10.3	45.2	43.8	38.7
Tertiary sector	15.8	14.9	31.4	37.7	50.1
Total	13.9	11.7	100	100	100

* Australia, Canada, France, Germany, Italy, Japan, the Netherlands, Spain, United Kingdom and United States (together, these countries accounted for almost 90% of total outgoing direct foreign investment in 1990).

Source: United Nations, 1993

of trade policy or an improvement in infrastructure to invest locally in the processing of raw materials into semi-manufactured goods in the secondary sector.

Technological and capital-intensive investment has come to account for a growing share of the *secondary sector* since the start of the 1980s (from 46% in 1980 to 51% in 1990), notably in industrialised markets. This has been gained at the expense of labour-intensive investments in low-wage countries and investment in local raw-material processing (from 47% in 1980 to 38.5% in 1990; United Nations 1993).

In the secondary sector there is in general greater freedom in choice of location than in the primary sector (where the presence of raw materials is the deciding factor) or the tertiary sector (where the presence of the market decides). Many countries have become more attractive for production activities as a result of a policy aimed at strengthening the industrial structure (infrastructure, legislation) and their competitive position.

In the *tertiary sector* foreign direct investment has experienced the largest growth. As a proportion of the total, services (financial services, trade, distribution, transport and tourism) has grown from 38 per cent at the start of the 1970s to around 50 per cent at the end of the 1980s. More than 70 per cent of Japanese and around 60 per cent of US foreign direct investment now relates to the services sector.

A number of important, traditionally closed service sectors, such as financial services and transport, were exposed during the 1980s to foreign competition in increasing numbers of countries and opened up to foreign direct investment. This trend is likely to continue in the 1990s as a result of privatisation in transport, telecommunications and public utilities.

The shifts in the countries and sectors in which foreign direct investments are made are connected with the changes in the motives behind foreign direct investment.

2.2.4 *Changes in the motives for foreign direct investment*

The main motives for foreign direct investment up to the 1980s were:

1. in industrialised and developing countries (think of sales of consumer products in Brazil and India): to gain access to markets which were virtually impenetrable via exports due to severe protectionism;
2. in developing countries:
   - to mine minerals or to produce commercial agricultural products. Examples are investment in oil recovery in Nigeria, copper mining in Chile and banana production in Central America;
   - to use low wages for labour-intensive parts of the production process. (Frequently, industries that resort to this approach are designated 'footloose', allegedly willing to move quite readily to locations with lower labour costs when local labour costs rise.)

It was also part of the philosophy of forming conglomerates that prevailed in the 1970s that when a foreign company was taken over, it was mainly its profitability that was highlighted and not so much the synergy with the investor's existing activities.

Low wages for untrained labour and the availability of raw materials have become ever less important as a result of the development of technologies that increase productivity and save on raw materials. As a result of the progressive liberalisation of international trade and direct investment, gaining access to protected markets became a relatively less important motive and using the natural competitive advantages of the host country and their contribution to the strength of the investing company became more important. The higher requirements of product and service are making it increasingly important to set up operations in the outlet markets. The following motives therefore came to the fore during the 1980s:

- strengthening the company's position in one core activity or a few core activities, often with great mutual synergy;
- being part of clusters of companies and knowledge centres, in which strong technologies are developed, so as to be able to compete in the technology race;
- lowering logistical costs and gaining access to distribution channels so as to cover markets more effectively and improve service.

When a foreign company was taken over, much more attention was therefore paid to compatibility with existing corporate activities. The profitability of the company to be taken over became less important in itself, while the knowledge, market position and brand name of the company being taken over, and thus its contribution to the international competitiveness of the company taking over, gained importance. Dunning (1985) and Porter (1990) have drawn attention to the importance of the advantages of a particular location in strengthening the competitiveness of the company as a whole. Dunning asserts, for example, that because companies in various environments work with varying location-specific advantages, they can derive competitive advantages such as international transfer pricing, shifting funds between various currency areas and spreading political risk and the risk of strikes.

In short, the motives for foreign direct investment have shifted from making use of cheap local labour and local raw materials, to keeping abreast of the technology race and new trends in production and marketing (see Section 2.3.3). The availability of an adequate pool of well trained staff and an effective communication and computer infrastructure has become more important. This goes a long way towards explaining why investments are increasingly shifting towards industrialised countries, and away from developing countries.

2.2.5 *Developments in forms of foreign direct investment*

The 'traditional' form of foreign direct investment, that is, building up entirely new production and distribution facilities (generally referred to as 'greenfield investments') often demands a relatively large investment in terms of both time and money.

In highly developed markets, particularly those characterised by severe competition, building up new production capacity and distribution channels, and establishing a brand name, forces new entrants to invest heavily in plants of sufficient size, as well as in their marketing efforts. In such markets, it often proves more effective to take over an existing company which already has production capacity, distribution channels and an established brand name.

Companies lacking the resources to take over a foreign company but willing to cooperate with them – so as to benefit from their technology or market knowledge, brand name and/or distribution channels on the foreign market – are increasingly opting for strategic alliances. Strategic alliances may also be accompanied by foreign investment, for example because the companies hold minority interests in each other's equity. There are various examples in such areas as aviation, the motor vehicle sector and electronics. Under the impact of governmental regulations in countries which more recently have opened up to foreign direct investment, and in conjunction with the importance of having a good local partner in liberalising countries where government interference is still extreme, the joint venture has gained importance as a form of investment.

Apart from these investments in production resources and/or companies, companies that lack the financial resources or do not wish to accept the associated risks are increasingly opting to introduce other resources such as a product or product technology, management skills or a brand name. A payment is made in return. These *non-equity* forms of investment generally bring a lower return in the form of licence fees, royalties or management fees but also carry a lower risk.

2.3 Significance for companies

Many of the developments that have occurred in the patterns of foreign direct investment can be explained by changing management methods and new thinking about how companies can – and in many cases must – improve their competitive position.

Investment decision-making generally demands a lengthy process, with several aspects and consequences calling for close scrutiny. This is all the more true for investment in foreign countries, as many circumstances may be different from the situation at home.

Apart from the elements that have to be considered in any direct investment, it is good practice to analyse a number of specific factors with foreign direct investment, before proceeding to invest. The following sections deal with these factors.

2.3.1 *Decision-making on foreign direct investments*

The decision on a foreign direct investment is generally taken when a relationship has already lasted for a long period between the company of origin and the country where the investment is planned. In cases where the country is an outlet for the company, foreign direct investment is normally part of an entry strategy. The company has usually first been developing the market via exports. The investment is made, for example, when sales volumes and market knowledge have grown sufficiently to allow investment (via a take-over or new production resources) in a permanent production, sales and/or distribution organisation. In cases of imports from the country, the decision may actually be taken to start producing in the country, by taking over the supplier or installing one's own production capacity. In addition, the decision may of course be taken to expand existing activities – or start up new ones – in countries in which the company is already established.

In many cases the process of decision-making on a foreign direct investment therefore does not entail any selection from a number of countries. Yet, even if only one candidate is being considered, it is important to analyse thoroughly all relevant local circumstances. Furthermore, there are situations in which a company has to choose for economic reasons between a number of countries for a foreign direct investment. The fact is that many companies maintain contacts with several countries; then a number of countries may become eligible for investment for a particular period.

In addition, quite apart from the normal investment criteria, there are a number of specific circumstances to consider in deciding upon a foreign direct investment.

When selecting from countries with which a company has built up contacts, a large number of factors have usually been taken into account already. In considering an investment with a larger risk, these factors must all be thoroughly reviewed (see also the Appendix). What is more, any factors not previously considered must be reviewed to see whether they should be taken into account now. These factors may be categorised as follows:

- macro-economic and sectoral situation, and general government policy;
- economic and political risk;
- statutory, regulatory and institutional trading and investment climate;
- input and factor market conditions;
- economic infrastructure; and
- physical and socio-cultural factors.

THE MACRO-ECONOMIC AND SECTORAL SITUATION AND GENERAL GOVERNMENT POLICY

Since an investment will generally tie a company for a long period to a particular country with a particular geographical coverage, it is important to analyse and produce a long-term forecast of the trend in costs of – and the demand for – products from the planned unit. The general macro-economic situation, how it will develop and its stability are very important factors.

At a general level, the trend in costs and the scale and composition of demand are determined by the cyclical situation in the macro-economy, that is, the scale and growth in total and per capita GNP, interest rates, inflation and the trend in purchasing power. These are determined partly by the international economic situation, and partly by government policy.

Broadly speaking, there are two views of the role that the government can and should play in the economy, the economic structure and the way it develops: an intervening role or a role of restraint.

Intervening role. Some countries conduct an active economic policy, with the government attempting to offset falling demand during a recession by additional expenditure, increasing the money supply and temporary tax reductions. It is hoped that this additional expenditure will give a boost to the economy via rising demand in response to a fall in interest rates, and rising exports in response to a fall in the exchange rate. In almost all cases, these spending boosts lead to a rising government deficit, with upward pressure on inflation and downward pressure on the exchange rate. In some cases, foreign companies can benefit from the additional governmental demand and from the extra demand from consumers and companies. In times of high economic growth, the government attempts to depress demand by increasing taxes and reducing the growth in the money supply. Monetary policy (i.e. money creation) and budgetary policy (via government finances) are expansive. The consequences are usually rising interest rates, a rising exchange rate, and a curbing of demand. With respect to the structure of the economy, the government attempts to encourage the development of certain sectors and the curbing of others via special legislation, financial resources and state undertakings.

A role of restraint. Other countries pursue a policy aimed at structurally reducing the size of the civil service in relation to the economy and strengthening the working of market forces, and improving the general investment climate by curbing the government deficit, reducing regulations and investing in infrastructure and education. Governments make relatively few attempts to influence the economy. The development of sectors is left to the market, which is exposed to international competition. Monetary and budgetary policies are restrictive.

In most countries, the government leaves the cyclical and structural development of the economy increasingly to the working of market forces (Section 2.4). The government then concentrates on improving the infrastructure and education.

This process of government withdrawal started in the United States and Western Europe, to be followed by East Asia, Latin America, Eastern Europe and Africa. The process of implementing it in various countries differs in policy terms according to the country. Furthermore, if there is a change of government, there may be major shifts in government policy.

The extent to which a government intervenes in the economy generally determines the number of regulations confronting an investing company. In addition, it is important to know just how much the government wishes to stimulate a sector in which direct investment is under consideration, and whether foreign investors receive the same treatment as local companies. This also applies to concrete projects that the government is embarking upon.

At sector level, demand is determined by developments in the relevant market (notably developments in the demand and supply industries). In many cases developments in demand at a general level determine developments in demand in markets and sectors. It is therefore important to analyse and forecast the development of demand at both levels. Prior exports therefore represent a very important source of market information. The link with the market can then gradually be strengthened via various forms of investment, such as setting up a local sales office, having products manufactured under licence, taking a minority stake or entering into a joint venture or both.

Other aspects of developments in market demand that also merit attention are: the nature of the competition and strategies employed by competitors, the phase in the product life cycle at which the products find themselves on the local market, and the scope for product differentiation.

THE ECONOMIC AND POLITICAL RISK

The political risk includes a number of risks connected with the stability of the government and its policy.

The stability of the government is affected by domestic and foreign political circumstances. In assessing the investment risk it is therefore wise to look at the political situation in the country. One factor to consider is the level of support for the government in society at large. This is reflected in the strength of the opposition from other political groups in the government centre and the extent to which they are able to organise and express themselves. Other factors of importance for domestic stability are: the number of languages, races, religions, the strength of individual groups and their mutual relationships. The social situation, in terms of the distribution of wealth, is another factor that frequently has a major impact on the stability of society. Many of the rapidly growing economies of Eastern Asia owe their stability to the relatively good distribution of their prosperity. Regions with greater disparities in prosperity such as Southeast Asia and Latin America frequently have less political stability.

With regard to international political stability, the main factor to look at is relations with neighbouring countries. It is important to look at trade and political relationships between the country and neighbouring countries and how they are proceeding, particularly if the country is used as a springboard to markets in other countries.

The stability of government policy is a further risk factor to take into account. This, of course, is largely determined by the stability of the government itself, but also by its sensitivity to pressure from the opposition. Government policy may not only change in a general sense towards more or less interventionism, but also with regard to foreign economic relations.

The payment risk is a major factor. In the relationship with a foreign debtor, the risk is determined not only by the country's solvency and payment customs, but also by the general external financial situation in the country. In assessing this, one must look at the balance of payments and, above all, at the size of any deficit in relation to the overall economy. Equally important are the size and structure of the foreign debt. This size must then be related to the size of the economy and export revenues. Currency reserves must be assessed in relation to the level of imports. The point to look at is how many months of imports can be financed from the currency reserves. In brief, the general external financial situation determines the risk of government restrictions being imposed on foreign payment transactions. Payment from the country may also be very much affected by the convertibility of the currency, and by restrictions on the importing and above all the exporting of capital and currency. The rankings in the Institutional Investor, along with the countries' policy of the national credit insurance companies give a good indication of the economic and political risk of countries.

An investment agreement between the country from which the investment is being made and the country in which the investment is being made, generally offers some protection against nationalisation and expropriation of the investment (see also Box 2.1). Although the number of nationalisations has fallen dramatically since the mid-1970s, it remains conceivable that governments will seize the branches of foreign companies.

THE STATUTORY, REGULATORY AND INSTITUTIONAL TRADING AND INVESTMENT CLIMATE

The general characteristics of government policy determine to a significant degree the characteristics of the statutory, regulatory and institutional climate relating to foreign direct investment. There are diverging governmental provisions on trade and investment, such as the level of import tariffs, quantitative restrictions (quota), the need to apply for licences for imports and direct investments, and regulations governing health and safety, the environment and the origin of goods. The distribution of goods may also be highly regulated.

The institutional factors include such matters as corruption, bureaucracy, clarity and stability of regulations and the quality and reliability of the legal system and legal protection. With respect to investments in general, taxes on profits, capital and wealth are of course important, as are the charges on labour (taxes and social insurance contributions).

A large number of countries pursue a specific policy on foreign direct investment. The objectives may be to influence the type of investment and the sectors in which investments are made, and increasing the economic and technological spin-offs of foreign direct investment. As a consequence, provisions may exist regarding the required government approval of a wide range of management decisions, and the number of foreigners in management positions. Restrictions may be imposed on the number and type of activities that may be carried out. Many countries lay down performance requirements, which implies that the foreign investor is obliged to perform certain activities locally (such as research and development), to export a certain proportion of local production, or to employ a certain number of local employees.

Frequently, there are statutory restrictions on ownership ratios in a company which is the target of investment. The foreign component is usually tied to restrictions. The statutory provisions on these points, but also on such matters as location, may take the form of prohibitions, licensing requirements or even conditions governing the awarding of special incentives. These incentives may take the form of subsidies on the investment or production costs, fiscal benefits or protection against local or import competition. There may also be rules governing the purchase of products. Some countries enforce local content regulations. This implies that a product is only deemed to have been produced locally (with the associated trade preferences) if a certain minimum percentage of processed parts or other inputs have been acquired locally.

The regulations governing the repatriation of profits, interest, licence fees and capital from the country must also be reviewed, and one should also check whether there is any double taxation convention with the home country. Countries suffering from a poor balance of payments in particular, very much prefer direct foreign investors who bring their own capital. If investors were to attract capital on the local market, this would lead to an outflow of capital when profits were repatriated; this is why it is often subject to statutory provisions. However, taking their own capital carries a greater risk for investors than attracting capital on the local market. A loan by the investor's parent to the local branch leads to lower, locally taxable profits than tied-up fresh capital as a result of interest charges.

INPUT AND FACTOR MARKET CONDITIONS

If the investing company uses local production factors, availability and costs are aspects that must be studied. In the case of investments in labour-intensive processing operations in particular, there is the question of the available quantity of untrained labour; however, its relative importance is declining. Companies are also continuously transferring more high-grade and more complex activities to other countries. Many industries are proving to be less footloose than is frequently assumed. In considering the costs of relocation, companies often choose to increase the added value of local production as their answer to rising labour costs. In addition, the rapid pace of development in telecommunications is also increasing the scope for performing such activities as research and development and administration in countries with low wage costs. For example, a major European company has its software developed in India; an American company handles its administration in Mexico. This means that the availability of trained labour, qualifications and level of education becomes an important factor, along with the availability of local management, because particularly in developing countries, it is often stipulated that local management must be employed.

The importance of the level and development of labour costs in relation to productivity (or labour costs per unit product) depends upon the labour intensity of the activities. A further factor to take into account is the strength and political influence of trade unions and the risk of strikes.

Apart from labour, there are other production factors where price and availability must be considered. These may be raw materials and resources (such as energy), semi-manufactured goods, capital goods and capital. Access to technologies and the quality of the infrastructure and communications may also prove to be an important factor.

ECONOMIC INFRASTRUCTURE

In addition to the production factors listed above, the level of economic and industrial development also plays an important role. In general, the lack of an adequately developed private sector may be a problem. This general problem often brings specific problems in its wake, such as the lack of good suppliers or a good partner. The availability of a good local partner is often vital, as its knowledge of the market, ways of doing business, and contacts with the government are indispensable.

The availability of good suppliers may be important. If they are lacking, the company may be forced to import goods or services or both, which may prove substantially more expensive. The presence of good local buyers is also an important element. It is not just the customary criteria of business economics – such as solvency and payment behaviour – that are important here but also the value of the client as a source of new technological and market developments. A further factor to consider is local competition, and the formal and informal ways in which it may be receiving support from the host country's government.

PHYSICAL AND SOCIO-CULTURAL FACTORS

Important physical factors that must be taken into account in connection with the operational costs of the direct investment include geographical location and the associated domestic and international transport and communication costs. The climate may also have some bearing on operational costs, for example via the costs of air-conditioning or heating commercial premises and transport. This also applies to the costs of using land, water, energy and other natural raw materials and resources.

Finally, there remains a number of factors which are almost impossible to measure and which have a highly unpredictable but often very major influence on the success of the investment. These can be grouped under socio-cultural factors, and include labour morale, punctuality, creativity and initiative, the period for decision-making and how 'closed' employees, managers and business clients are.

The distribution of incomes, demographic characteristics and socio-cultural factors in a country have a major impact on the scale and type of consumer demand. Criminality, in all its guises, is another factor to bear in mind.

2.3.2 *Practical development of the analysis of environmental factors*

It is useful to draw up a score list in order to quantify the significance of all the environmental factors listed above. A wide range of factors may be shown on this list, with some quantitative description of their impact (weighting) on the expected risk/return ratio of the investment. This impact may range, for example, between 0 for absent to 5 for very large. The next step is to give a rating to each of these factors for a particular country. The rating may range from –2 for very poor, to +2 for very good. In this manner, a total score can be created for each country, allowing for an overall comparison between different countries. The checklist may look as shown in the Appendix to this chapter.

One must also establish how the environmental factors are taken into account in the planning for the investment.

With a direct domestic investment, the decision will be taken on the basis, for example, of the net cash value (NCV) of the cash flows (cash value of the cash flows minus the investment). If the NCV is positive, the investment is in principle acceptable.

With a foreign direct investment, there are a number of complications in this calculation. These relate primarily to the (higher) economic and political risk of the investment and the scope for transferring the return on the investment from the country to the home country, exchange rates and taxes.

A high risk can be absorbed by applying a higher discount in calculating the cash value of the investment, but generally speaking the preference is for more stringent criteria to be applied to the payback period.

The opportunities for transferring the return on the investment to the home country determine the return on the investment for the parent company. Factors to consider here are the restrictions on the export of capital and currency, and the convertibility of local currency.

These restrictions apply not only to the scope of transferring returns but also to interest on loans from the parent company to the foreign branch, along with royalties, licence fees, management fees and the proceeds from any sale of the investment (i.e. the sale of production resources or interests in a company). Sound direct or indirect local investment opportunities may be sought for the proportion of profits or interest that cannot be freely transferred abroad. This can then be used to finance expansion, for example, or income may be generated which can be transferred in periods where no profits are earned on the original investment. The parent company may also use the blocked funds to import from the country, or – against payment – to organise imports via other companies in the country.

Exchange-rate fluctuations affect the value of the return to the parent company and thus the investment risk as well. As yet, there are no reliable techniques for predicting exchange rates. Larger companies with cash flows in various currencies are often in a position to engage – to some extent – in arbitrage, in order to hedge against their exchange-rate risk. For companies not in a position to do that, covering against the exchange-rate risk on the futures market offers one means of limiting their exposure.

Taxes affect the return. It is not only local taxation that is a determining factor but also the fiscal relationship between the host country and the country to which the profit is transferred. If the country in which the parent company is established does not have an agreement with the host country on the avoidance of double taxation, a favourable option may be to make the investment from another country.

Finally, it is important to check whether the return on a particular investment should be viewed in isolation or whether the investment has some effect on the return on other activities by the same parent company in both countries or third countries. These possible effects must of course be included in the analysis of the return.

2.3.3 *Spread and concentration of corporate activities*

There are an increasing number of business activities that lend themselves to being carried out in whole or in part in another country. Each activity must be analysed on the basis of existing relationships with other countries and company strategy to see whether they are best carried out in the company's home country or in some other country (for example, the country from which goods and services are purchased, or the country in which goods or services are sold). This choice pertains to activities in the field of purchasing, research and development, production, sales, distribution and service. Each activity should be assessed to see whether it can best be concentrated in a single country, or spread over several countries. In the process, one should consider not only local circumstances for performing activities but also the need and scope for standardisation or tuning of activities to local conditions, and coordination between the various activities in the various countries.

The forces that are conducive to a concentration of activities are as follows: economies of scale, achieving major learning effects and the specific advantages of the location where the activity is carried out. Major forces behind the dispersion of activities are often government provisions (barriers to trade), or the wish to spread exchange-rate and political risks. Coordination increases the potential for benefiting from economies of scale and a more rapid response to changes in exchange rates, factor costs, customer needs and campaigns by competitors. Factors militating against coordination are, however, the high costs of international communication and the organisational requirements of good, open communication between the various organisational units. One thing to emerge from the above is that every activity can be carried out in the country with the greatest comparative benefits for that activity. Where traditional approaches to comparative advantages often confined themselves to production conditions, this approach extends the concept of comparative advantages of countries to every activity in the value chain.

In recent years, a number of forces have emerged that have led to a greater spread of activities and at the same time a stronger coordination between activities. On the one hand, new flexible production technologies are less sensitive to the economies of scale than traditional production technologies. On the other hand, the scope for international coordination is continuously improving, while the costs keep on decreasing as a result of developments in telecommunications and information technology.

With very thorough investment preparations it is also important to have, in advance, a clear-cut company policy on foreign direct investment, its setting up, its management, and on how the company will operate in the event of a joint venture or some other type of cooperative agreement. A long-term policy on – and investment in – seconded as well as local staff is very important. The reasons for the investment must be abundantly clear to all, and made explicit in strategic and operational objectives. The strategic objectives may lie in acquiring a stronger position on the market, lowering the level of costs in the company and/or gaining access to new technologies.

2.4 Significance for governments

The increasing internationalisation of trade and direct investment is creating a new economic environment in which not only companies but also countries are competing with one another. Countries are competing ever more vigorously in the area of attracting foreign direct investment, as it is clear that this is going to play an increasingly important role for employment, technology, competitive position and national income.

In an increasing number of countries government policy is becoming focused on improving the entrepreneurial climate in general, and the investment climate in particular. The scope of forcing foreign investors into local investment via trade restrictions is diminishing. First of all, there are the multilateral agreements on liberalising trade and direct investment. But furthermore, there is the general and increasing awareness that free trade ultimately creates the best conditions for healthy economic development and for the strengthening of competitiveness. In more concrete terms, this leads to an increasing focus on a number of policy elements:

1. Probably the most important are stable, reliable and clear government policies and regulations, in which companies have sufficient freedom to develop activities that can compete with those of companies from other countries;
2. Fair treatment of indigenous companies and branches of foreign companies, protection against expropriation, free repatriation of capital and the avoidance of double taxation;
3. Strengthening of infrastructure, which means investing in the infrastructure of transport and telecommunications. The increasing importance of advanced transport and communication techniques, as well as of technological and commercial cooperation in the internationalisation of corporate investment, demands substantial investments in infrastructure for transport and communication. These investments are aimed both at the direct efficiency benefits they bring to the functioning of the economy, and at remaining fully connected to international infrastructure networks;
4. A good supply of labour, in quantity as well as quality, by encouraging proper training and skills for which there is a demand among companies operating internationally;
5. A flexible labour market by reducing the taxes on labour, and streamlining regulations on such matters as working hours and dismissal;
6. A good public and private knowledge infrastructure which develops good contacts with companies in the field of research and education. Smooth cooperation makes a country very attractive for performing knowledge-intensive and high-value activities;
7. Restricting regulations and the administrative burden on companies.

National macro-economic and structure policy are becoming ever less effective. The effects of economic developments in a particular country are making their mark more and more tellingly in other countries via the strong international links between increasing numbers of companies and through the international mobility of capital. If, for example, a company achieves poor results in its home country on account of the poor economic situation, subsidiaries in other countries can often be expected to feel the impact, for example in the form of target cost reductions or a strategic realignment.

The scope for policy and regulation to influence the development of the economic structure, such as employment, social security, and the environment is on the wane because companies have increasing opportunities to perform activities in other countries with more flexible labour and environmental legislation and a lower level of taxation. Countries – isolated or otherwise – which attempt to follow their own macro-economic and economic structure policy via a protectionist trade policy are seeing investment, economic activity and thus income and prosperity increasingly disappear to other countries. More than before, macro-economic and economic structure policy can only be pursued effectively at an international level; this requires multilateral institutions and treaties at an increasingly global level (initially the EU for Western Europe, but increasingly the OECD and the WTO).

Bibliography

References

Dunning, J.H. (1985) Towards a universal theory of international production, in *Strategic Management of Multinational Corporations: The Essentials*, H. Wortzel & L. Wortzel (eds), J. Wiley.

GATT (1994) *International Trade Statistics 1993*.

Porter, M.E. (1990) *The Competitive Advantage of Nations*, Macmillan.

Todaro, M.P. (1989) *Economic Development in the Third World*, Longman.

United Nations (1993) *World Investment Report 1993*.

United Nations (1994a) *World Economic Outlook*, May.

United Nations (1994b) *World Investment Report 1994*.

Further reading

Ding, H.C. (1988) ASEAN-EC Relations: An ASEAN view, in B. Dahm and W. Harbrecht (eds) *ASEAN und Europäische Gemeinschaft, Partner, Probleme, Perspektiven*, Deutsches Uebersee Institut.

Gross, M. (1988) Entwicklung des Europäischen Engagements in ASEAN-Ländern, in B. Dahm and W. Harbrecht (eds) *ASEAN und Europäische Gemeinschaft, Partner, Probleme, Perspektiven*, Deutsches Uebersee Institut.

Appendix: Model checklist to determine the attractiveness of a country as a host country for a foreign direct investment

	weighting	**score**	**weighted score**
The macro-economic and sectoral situation and general government policy			
(a) Trend in the size and composition of domestic demand/imports			
• GNP per capita and income distribution			
• total GNP and GNP per capita growth			
• acceptance of comparable products			
• competition			
• monetary and budgetary government policy (expansive/restrictive)			

	weighting	**score**	**weighted score**

- short-, medium- and long-term plans and resultant sales prospects
- trend in purchasing power

(b) Movement in cost level
- exchange-rate policy
- inflation
- interest rates

The economic and political risks

(a) Stability of economic and social government policy
- risk of nationalisation
- movements in exchange rate

(b) Currency restrictions (freedom to transfer and convertibility) in relation to:
- balance of payments
- size and structure of foreign debt
- debt service ratio
- currency reserves

(c) Payment behaviour

(d) Social unrest and hostility arising from:
- social situation, population density, distribution of prosperity
- division of the country into political groupings, languages, races, and religions
- mentality, attitude towards foreigners, nationalism

(e) External political threat, risk of war

The statutory, regulatory and institutional trading and investment climate

(a) Provisions on trade
- import tariffs
- quantitative restrictions (quota)
- import licences
- regulations on health and safety, environment and origin of products/parts
- protection of technological know-how
- brand protection
- provisions on marketing and sales

	weighting	score	weighted score
• provisions on distribution • membership of a free-trade zone or bilateral trading agreements (for exports to third countries) • relationship in terms of trade policy between investing and host country (b) Investment climate • subsidies on investment or production costs • special fiscal advantages • protection against local or import competition • statutory provisions on number and type of activities			

Input- and factor-market conditions

(a) Labour market and labour costs
- available unskilled labour
- available skilled labour and qualifications/educational level
- management available
- labour costs and trend in wages and salaries
- labour productivity
- trade-union power and sensitivity to strikes

(b) Other production factors
- availability and price of raw materials, resources (energy) and semi-manufactured goods
- availability and price of capital goods
- access to technologies
- types of capital available
- quality of infrastructure and communications

Economic infrastructure

(a) Availability of a good local partner
(b) Availability of good suppliers of goods/services
(c) Availability of good local customers
(d) Existence of reliable judiciary
(e) Local competition, which may receive government support

	weighting	score	weighted score
Physical factors and socio-cultural factors			
(a) Geographical location			
(b) Climate			
(c) Domestic/international transport and communication costs			
(d) Cultural factors:			
• labour morale			
• time-keeping			
• creativity/initiative			
• time needed for decision-making by local partner			
• openness/reliability			
• ethnically determined industrial relations			
• historical relationships			
• population growth			
• population density			
(e) Criminality			
Weighted total score			

3 Aspects of multinational corporations (MNCs)

3.1 Introduction

Since the mid-1980s, multinational corporations have rapidly expanded business activities on a worldwide scale through foreign direct investment (FDI). This process has, on the one hand, been paralleled by structural changes in the world economy, such as trade liberalisation, the free movement of capital flows or technological developments (e.g. the availability of improved information and communication technologies that facilitate decentralised production). On the other hand, fundamental changes have taken place in the way firms organise their activities. A particular aspect of this is the strategic behaviour of firms in establishing joint ventures and alliances, and carrying out mergers and acquisitions. All these activities have experienced a major boost in recent years, making competition and cooperation two sides of the same coin.

This chapter will first briefly review the factors that drive companies to extend their activities beyond national boundaries, and then discuss the main features of MNCs and whether their activities are becoming global (Sections 3.2–3.4). Evidence is presented on trade within the multinational corporation, as well as international aspects of R&D (Sections 3.5 and 3.6). Finally the issue of multinational corporations and national authority will be addressed (Sections 3.7). It will be argued that the new structures that are currently created by the largest multinational corporations, for example, through complex networks and strategic alliances, make national boundaries largely redundant, reduce the efficacy of current policy instruments, and call for a need to revise certain concepts and/or to establish rules in some areas not (yet) well covered in an international framework relating to foreign direct investment.

3.2 Defining a multinational

There is no unique definition of an MNC. However, it is generally accepted that an MNC consists of a firm with foreign subsidiaries that extend the firm's production and marketing beyond the boundaries of a single country. International production is therefore a value-adding activity, owned or controlled, and organised by a firm (or group of firms) outside its (or their) national boundaries (Dunning, 1988). The mechanism through which the economic activities are internationalised is FDI, making it possible to acquire control over these activities. The two key concepts are thus FDI and control. What do they mean? The most common definition of FDI, applied by both OECD and IMF, is that it involves a capital investment for the purpose of acquiring a lasting interest in an enterprise, and exerting a certain degree of influence on that enterprise's operations. This essentially distinguishes FDI from portfolio investment, because the latter does not imply control. The control by an investor of 10 per cent or more of the ordinary stocks of a corporate enterprise is the normal criterion used by OECD to distinguish FDI (used also for statistics), but other factors may also be taken into account when defining FDI more precisely.[5]

Currently, there seems to be a noticeable shift in the way control is exercised by MNCs, as it increasingly involves other modalities, including contractual and co-operative agreements. This tends to blur the concept of equity (or *de jure*) to non-equity control. Different forms of international cooperation between corporations such as joint ventures, strategic alliances, mergers and acquisitions, have recently become particularly widespread. This is much related to new ways in which MNCs structure their economic activities, often referred to as 'globalisation' (see also next section). Nowadays, it is therefore sometimes argued that the interpretation of international production should be widened to include other value-adding activities in one country, if they result from activities of firms that are directly related through a contractual arrangement. This point has not yet been widely accepted, however, and the benchmark definition, that is, the 10 per cent criterion for exercising control, is still considered the only objective and recognised criterion that makes it possible to pass a judgment on the nature of the investment and to qualify it as FDI.

3.3 Multinational corporations: significance and the rationale

Since about 1980, multinational corporations have become important players in international trade. According to UNCTC (1992a), in 1990 the total number of MNCs exceeded 35,000; in total they have more than 150,000 foreign affiliates. Together they account for some 40 per cent of total exports of manufactures. There is a strong geographical concentration of MNCs, as nearly 90 per cent of them are based in developed countries; the links with developing economies are mainly through foreign

5. OECD 1992, b; see also Report of the Committee on International Investment and Multinational Enterprises, OECD Council document C(91)80, July 1991. FDI refers to investment that involves a long-term relationship reflecting a lasting interest of a resident entity in one economy (direct investor) in an entity resident in an economy other than that of the investor. The direct investor's purpose is to exert a significant degree of influence on the management of the enterprise resident in the other economy. Direct investment involves both the initial transaction between the two entities and all subsequent transactions between them and among affiliated enterprises, both incorporated and unincorporated. The concept of direct investment adopted by the group is the same as that set out by the IMF Balance of Payments Manual.

affiliates, with more than 40 per cent of the affiliates located in developing countries. Only a small number of MNCs account for the majority of outward foreign direct investment (FDI) in individual countries. Looking at the world's largest non-financial multinationals, it appears that world markets are very important for them, as foreign sales as a percentage of total sales are often quite considerable: for instance Royal Dutch/Shell (Dutch/British, 49%); Ford Motors (US, 48%); General Motors (US, 31%). In particular those multinationals that have relatively small domestic markets can have foreign sales that exceed 90 per cent (Philips, Netherlands, 93%; Nestlé, Switzerland, 98%) or which are close to that figure (Asea Brown Boveri, Switzerland/Sweden, 85%).

FDI often plays a key role in achieving effective market access, for the marketing of goods, providing after-sales service, and for establishing close customer–producer relations. In addition, FDI is often a vehicle for establishing local production facilities. This explains the surge of FDI between 1983 and 1988 by 20 per cent annually, which is almost four times higher than the increase in world trade (OECD 1992b, see also Chapter 2 on FDI). In the past decade, the stock of FDI in the OECD has almost tripled. Geographically, however, FDI flows remained mainly concentrated in the industrialised world. This can partly be explained by the existence of large consumer markets and partly by the liberalisation of capital markets, mainly within the OECD. Indeed, developed countries continued to attract more than four-fifths of worldwide FDI. Throughout the 1980s, the Triad, consisting of the EC, Japan and the United States, accounted for some 70 per cent of worldwide inflows (see Table 3.1). European and Japanese multinationals are the main direct investors in the United States, but Japan also directs important flows of FDI to Europe and South East Asia. Japan notably performs much of its production of parts and components (e.g. in consumer electronics) in neighbouring Asian countries. A particular note is the EC's attraction as a destination of FDI. The EC's share of OECD inward investment climbed to above 45 per cent in 1988–89. FDI flows from newly industrialising countries, in particular from a number of South East Asian countries, such as South Korea, towards the OECD recently have become more important as well. While the volume still remains small, the development is significant. The motivations often relate to gaining effective market access, scale economies (EC single market) or overcoming trade barriers (e.g. the application or threat – official and unofficial – of quota, anti-dumping measures, local content provisions, etc.).

There is no single general theory explaining the motivation of companies to operate on a multinational basis. Instead many theories exist, each of them providing useful insights (see Rugman 1982, Chapter 1 and UNCTC 1992b). Motives seem to vary for each company, which is understandable given the very individual character of an investment decision. In principle, a company wishing to serve a foreign market has always the choice between exports from the home country and local production in the host country. Additional key questions address topics such as what exactly triggers FDI, and what factors determine the nature, location and timing of the investment. Each decision seems to be driven by different factors and generic analysis is therefore limited. Two types of motivations are generally advanced, one related to ownership-specific advantages (e.g. product or process technology) and one related

Table 3.1 Foreign direct investment inward flows, by region and economy, 1981–91 (millions of dollars)

Host regions/countries	1981–86	1987	1989	1990	1991
Developed regions/countries	42,797	109,455	167,504	171,907	107,793
Western Europe	17,402	41,482	88,250	108,822	84,065
European Community	15,478	37,644	81,069	99,020	75,186
France	2,338	5,140	10,313	13,223	15,235
German Fed. Rep.	1,395	1,480	10,630	8,390	6,590
United Kingdom	5,041	15,696	30,553	32,669	21,537
Other Western Europe	1,924	3,838	7,181	9,802	8,879
North America	21,249	62,418	70,753	52,158	16,034
Other developed countries	3,145	5,555	8,502	10,927	7,694
Australia	2,270	3,899	7,345	6,577	4,833
Japan	317	1,170	–1,060	1,760	1,370

Source: UNCTC, 1993

to locational advantages, associated with the specific conditions of the market, including: factor costs and market proximity (which will be discussed later). While this may be so, the Mercedes Benz case illustrates that many of the elements that are decisive for the investment decision can hardly be captured in a theory or a model. Many of the decisive factors relate to the appreciation of the investors of conditions of work, discipline, infrastructure, and the way the project is handled by the local authorities. The theory can only provide some tools that help explain the driving forces behind FDI, and will briefly be reviewed below.

Much of today's theory and literature on MNCs is still based on the concept of internalisation, first developed by Coase (1937), later applied by Hymer in 1960 and published in 1976. This theory was further extended by Caves in 1971 and by other scholars, including Buckley and Casson (1976). The internalisation theory (Rugman, 1982) is largely based on market imperfections. It demonstrates that the MNC is an organisation which uses its internal market to produce and distribute products in an efficient manner in situations where a regular market fails to operate. The internal market of the MNC is a device which permits a firm to assign property rights in knowledge to itself. The firm is involved with generating knowledge via its expenditures on R&D, and in most cases it will realise an economic advantage by creating a monopolistic internal market wherein the knowledge advantage can be developed and explored in an optimal manner on a worldwide scale. According to this theory, it is more efficient for a firm to create and use an internal market than to incur the prohibitive transaction costs of an outside market. Casson based his theory of the MNC in particular on the idea of transaction costs.

Vernon's product cycle theory (1966) was among the first to provide an explanation for the process by which firms involve themselves in foreign markets; it seeks to explain the patterns of international trade and FDI in manufactured goods that occurred in the Western world. Internationalisation is considered largely to be a response to the threat of losing export markets. The international product cycle theory abandons the classical assumption that factors and products are immobile internationally, and focuses on the firm's decisions on trade and investment based on both cost and revenue conditions. Firms develop new products and processes that they introduce abroad through exports. When their export position is threatened, they establish foreign subsidiaries with lower costs or better market access in an attempt to retain their advantage. When the firm finally loses its advantage, it may move on to new products or try to create new advantages by altering the product.

Dunning's eclectic paradigm was developed in the late 1970s and refined since (Dunning, 1988). It seems to be the most comprehensive theory on MNCs in explaining the motivation of companies to move abroad. It includes the internalisation theory, and is largely based on the hypothesis that a firm will engage in foreign value-adding activities if – and when – three conditions are satisfied. These conditions relate to: ownership-specific advantages of one enterprise over another, internalisation-incentives advantages, and location-specific variables. Ownership advantages are essential in getting an intangible assets advantage over local firms. The second condition is that it must be more beneficial to the enterprise possessing these advantages to use them (or their output) itself rather than to sell or lease them to foreign firms. Even if both conditions are met it does not tell us why the MNC engages in foreign production: it must be in the global interests of the enterprise to utilise these advantages in conjunction with at least some factor inputs (including natural resources) outside the home country; otherwise foreign markets would be served entirely by exports and domestic markets by domestic production, referred to as 'locational advantages of countries'.

Porter (1990) has developed new thinking on the dynamic interplay between the competitive advantages of countries and those of companies of a particular nationality (see also Chapter 1). The notion of 'competitive advantage' means that a country has – or more specifically, local firms of a country have – the ability to use location-bound resources in a way that will enable it (or them) to be competitive in international markets. A country possesses a set of attributes which 'shape the environment in which local firms compete, that promote the creation of a competitive market' (Porter, 1990, pp. 71–72). According to Porter, the strength, composition and sustainability of a nation's competitive advantage will be revealed in the value of its national product (more particularly, the part that enters into international transactions), and/or in the rate of growth of this national product, relative to that of its leading competitors.

It seems that any analysis of multinational enterprises and FDI flows needs to make a distinction between factors that affect the decision on the micro-economic or the firm level, and those factors that are macro-economic in nature. These are complementary. The real motives, of course, can best be obtained through surveys conducted on the firm level, which would reveal a mixture of micro-economic and macro-economic factors, which cannot always be separated. At the same time, however, firms tend to give very general answers when asked about their foreign investment motives, such as the desire to enter another market with strong actual or potential demand, the overall stable economic situation of the country where it wishes to establish a subsidiary, strategic reasons, or sound business policy. Other more specific motivations include: productivity, product differentiation, input prices, transport costs, as well as exchange rate fluctuations, trade barriers, the general economic climate in the host country, and so on. But again, this does not always provide an answer to the question why a certain country or location was chosen, particularly in those cases where there are strong similarities in economic factors and conditions, as seems to be the case in a number of OECD economies.

The macro-economic conditions and environment seem to be particularly important, as economies are rapidly integrating and becoming strongly interdependent. Most OECD economies in the recent past witnessed an acceleration in deregulation and privatisation, thus creating new incentives to expand economic activities under free market conditions. In addition, the liberalisation of capital markets has probably been one of the main factors in the rapid growth of FDI. Trade and investment are increasingly intertwined, but more importantly, financial market deregulation and integration, and the growing mobility of capital as a production factor have contributed to strong financial interlinkages between economies. Many firms developed strong links with foreign markets and adopted global approaches in outlook, strategies, and operations. This was not entirely new, but the process accelerated during the 1980s as companies were forced to look beyond their national borders for new products, customers, and inputs.

According to the OECD (1992b), the surge in investment since the mid-1980s is related to strong growth in economic output in the OECD. FDI was strongly pro-cyclical during that period, affected by macro-economic swings and responding during recovery with greater vigour than either domestic investment or world trade. Locational factors played an important role in companies' decisions to invest and then sell in foreign markets, rather than limit themselves to exports. Companies want to benefit from advantages related to market access. These are to have a presence on the market for economic or purely strategic reasons, including potential economies of scale; or benefiting from comparative advantages in the host countries, for example, through the availability of highly skilled labour, technology and know-how, and infrastructure; or benefiting from government policies, geared at attracting foreign companies through fiscal incentives and local or regional subsidies, as well as (other) support measures promoting research and development.

It is often claimed that, since the late 1970s, trade policy measures – including quantitative restrictions, voluntary restraint agreements, orderly marketing arrangements, and anti-dumping rules – were important factors in explaining FDI in the 1980s. Particularly in the automobile sector, but also in consumer electronics, performance requirements, such as local content rules and rules of origin may have triggered off the decision to relocate the production facilities to the market of supply; this phenomenon proved to be highly controversial when Japanese car producers decided to manufacture their brands in the UK. Nevertheless they would generally contend that their investment decisions were largely driven by other factors, such as the strong fluctuations in exchange rates and, more important, by micro-economic factors, such as locational advantages via the introduction of new concepts in production, often referred to as Toyotism. These new patterns of production, requiring flexibility in the supply structure, include 'just-in-time' conditions for delivery of parts and components, whereby locational proximity and integration of supplier and customer plants reduce the costs of maintaining stocks of raw materials, work-in-process and even finished inventories. Based on this approach, production should occur from top to bottom in some concentrated areas, thus inducing considerable flows of outward investment from Japan to the United States and Europe. These investments initially occurred in the assembling stage of production and are now spreading to related industries, that is, parts and components industries.

The need for companies to be closer to the customer, in order to adapt the product to local taste and to the particular conditions of the local market – often referred to as 'customisation' – implies that trade and investment increasingly are two sides of the same coin. They reinforce each other, rather than being substitutes. FDI is the neglected twin of trade, since trade and not FDI has been the focus of international negotiations since the Second World War. This is perhaps because FDI flows seem so much smaller than trade flows, even after the recent surge in investments. Today, the choice is no longer trade or investment, but investment as a vehicle to enhance productivity and complement trade. Trade requires investments in order to market the good, but also to tailor it to the need of the customer. The point is that FDI itself is only the initial vehicle, through which firms establish themselves in their target market, but which at the same time triggers off new trade flows. The local purchases from suppliers and sales to customers in host markets are analogous to imports and exports. Not only are these purchases much larger than the initial FDI flow, but they generally go on for many years after the investment takes place. This has been particularly noticeable in the automobile industry, where both intra- and inter-regional trade in parts and components have largely outpaced trade in assembled cars. In addition, it can be observed that investments increasingly spread out to related activities, including R&D and design, but also investments in sales distribution systems and after-sales service, as well as related activities. This also explains the rapid growth of investments in services, often related to the sales of goods. In fact, the financial sector itself became the object of extensive investment activity. This gave a new dimension to FDI. The United States, in the early 1970s, noted a strong influx of foreign banks and securities firms, which were attracted to the United States by their multinational clients who had already settled there. The growth of Japanese banks has been particularly important, keeping pace with the spread of Japanese business and foreign investments.

An illustration of the complex relationship between FDI and trade, and the difficulties encountered in explaining the rationale of multinational enterprises to move abroad, is provided by so-called 'transplants'. While there is no definition of a transplant, it is often associated with Japanese investments in automobile production facilities. The main concern with transplants was the low value-added they were feared to generate in the host country; hence, the term 'screwdriver' applied to assembly plants which leave the higher value-added parts in the production process to the home country (Smeets, 1990). Related to this is the general concern that transplants hardly have any substantial links to the domestic economy, and that they do not provide opportunities for employment to nationals of the host country. Transplants are perceived as an investment to undermine or circumvent the trade balance of the host country by promoting imports of parts and components. From the MNC point of view, the relocation of parts of the production process is driven by efficiency reasons and changing conditions in production and the market of supply.

Transplants have largely been perceived as the 'Trojan horse' in Europe and the United States. This particularly explains the initial reticence in welcoming Japanese investment. Transplants were thus often perceived as a form of FDI hardly desirable from a host country's perspective, because the benefits are considered to accrue primarily to the home country. Attitudes have evolved over time, as it became clear with the establishment of local R&D facilities that the roots of these production facilities are growing much deeper, becoming integral parts of the economy of the countries where they are created.

A discussion on the rationale of multinational enterprises cannot be conclusive, as there are many factors at play, both on the macro and micro level, such as the nature of the product, the demand perspectives, size of the market and the country's infrastructure, as well as subsidies provided by governments to attract foreign capital. But non-economic reasons such as political stability and cultural aspects, as well as the language spoken in the host country, are other factors that can be decisive. In addition to this, the attitude of the host country to the foreign investor is critical, as is well illustrated by Japanese investments in the automobile sector. In Europe, the British government took a very open attitude, welcoming the inflow of FDI, whereas France took a very defensive stance, in view of economic interests in the French automobile industry. However, France's position has gradually changed, as it became clear that it would miss out on investment flows and, related to this, new employment opportunities, while not being able to stop UK-built Japanese cars in the context of the EU single market. It is often easier to explain an FDI decision *ex post*, once the firm has established its subsidiary, than *ex ante*.

3.4 Features of multinational corporations

The explosive growth of FDI since the mid-1980s has led to changes in the structure of multinational enterprises, and the organisation and dispersal of economic activities and siting of firm operations. Many companies now have become global operators (Porter, 1986). Nevertheless, strategies of firms vary greatly in the way they internationalise production and the extent to which they create backward and forward linkages in the value-added chain (UNCTC, 1993). There is not one single mode of operation: some MNCs take the world market as their field of action; others continue focusing on individual markets, or, alternatively, concentrate their activities regionally. This depends largely on the nature of the product, but also on the barriers companies may face in obtaining market access. Some products, such as consumer electronics, can easily be marketed worldwide, with minor adaptations to adjust the product to local standards or consumer preferences. Also, certain foodstuffs can be found worldwide, with adaptation occurring mainly on the level of packaging and sometimes taste, to adapt it to local customs and preferences. Other products, which can be considered global in their very nature, for example, pharmaceutical products (drugs having a very specific curing effect), require adaptation to local market conditions, given the high degree of government regulation in this industry.

A product requiring more of a regional approach seems to be the automobile: the largest manufacturers now separately concentrate on Europe, North America and Asia, with top to bottom production facilities in each of the regions. This is much related to changes in production techniques for manufacturing automobiles and market conditions. Whereas at the beginning of the 20th century and until recently, markets could be supplied either through exports or local production, or a combination of both, as mass production resulting in standard products was characteristic for the industry, current conditions necessitate a complete production line in the market of supply in order to meet local standards and tastes. Differentiation and customisation have forced MNCs to switch their approach to 'lean' production, showing more similarities with the skill that characterised production of cars in the early days of the industry (Womack, Jones and Roos, 1990).

Porter's studies on competition in global industries suggest that the pattern of international competition differs markedly from industry to industry, as they vary along a spectrum from 'multi-domestic' to global in their competitive scope. In multi-domestic industries, competition essentially depends on competition in other countries. A multi-domestic industry is one that is present in many countries, but one in which competition occurs on a country-by-country basis. The competitive advantages of the firm are largely specific to the country in which it operates. According to Porter's theory, a 'global' industry is an industry in which a firm's competitive position in one country is significantly affected by its position in other countries or vice versa. Therefore, the international industry is not merely a collection of domestic industries, but a series of linked domestic industries in which the rivals compete against each other on a worldwide basis. This distinction has direct implications for the international strategy of firms. In a multi-domestic industry, Porter argues, a firm can and should manage its international activities like a portfolio. Subsidiaries should have a large degree of autonomy. This is different in a global industry, where a firm must in some way integrate its activities on a worldwide basis to capture the linkages among countries. This integration will require more than transferring intangible assets among countries, though it will include such a transfer (on competitiveness, see also Chapter 1).

A global strategy thus means integrating activities within a global framework, implying increased interdependence between the geographically separate activities of subsidiaries and the parent company. At the same time it includes optimising the local advantages of each subsidiary and satisfying local demand conditions. As T. Levitt of Harvard Business School has said 'companies should think global, but act local'. A global strategy combines integration, co-ordination, segmentation and differentiation, with a view to promoting flexible adaptation to changes in technology and demand. Or, to put it differently, a global strategy aims at harnessing the gains deriving from the synergy between subsidiaries located in a number of countries (Michalet, 1991). The trend is towards specialisation by subsidiaries in types of production which make use of the comparative advantage of the host country. Labour-intensive manufacturing is located in cheap labour areas; R&D laboratories are built close to major universities in countries with the strongest science and technology potential. In a way, the globalisation process could be compared with international trade specialisation, but on the micro level, that is within the MNC. It is a new way of looking at the internalisation process discussed in the previous chapters.

Policy-makers, both in governments and in international organisations, monitor multinational activity, and in particular the globalisation of firms, and analyse consequences for policy (see Section 3.7). While there is no agreed definition of globalisation, in line with the above, the view is held that globalisation consists of a new organisational structure of companies and business behaviour (OECD, 1992c). Globalisation refers to the stage now reached – and the forms taken today – in what is known as 'international production', namely the value-adding activities owned or controlled and organised by a firm (or group of firms) outside its (or their) national boundaries. It pertains to a set of conditions in which an increasing fraction of value and wealth is produced and distributed worldwide through a system of interlinking private networks. Large multinational firms (MNCs) operating within concentrated world supply structures, and capable of taking full advantage of financial globalisation, are at the centre of this process (OECD, 1992a). The result is that borderlines between previously fairly distinct channels and processes of international relationships have become increasingly blurred. Collaboration among firms combines technology, inputs and production across countries. Investment in foreign countries and companies spreads the location, assets and ownership of firms among nations.

Globalisation gained importance during the 1980s, the aim of the multinational firms being to find a balance between reaping some of the scale advantages of global markets yet exploiting the often geographically determined diversity of consumers and production factors. The large multinational firm's organisational as well as production and information technology gives it the necessary flexibility to confront this diversity. In fact, current communication techniques allow instant interaction between geographically dispersed entities (affiliates) and provide access to the same information, for example, through satellite systems. The decentralisation of production units, marketing and even research, together with a diversification of subcontractors, enables it to take full advantage of this diversity.

Companies increasingly need technological sophistication, maximum flexibility, customised products and extensive supplier networks, as international competition now is largely dominated by micro-electronics and information technology. It has become technically feasible for multinational corporations, banks and service firms as much as industrial concerns, to install captive or intra-corporate worldwide information networks, through which headquarters' management can link together production and marketing facilities around the world. This has largely widened the scope of control and central management. Information technologies are critical in coordinating activities in the whole production line, and in creating synergies between affiliates.

This applies even to more 'traditional' industries, such as textiles and clothing, where design, production and sales of the good are often widely dispersed geographically, but central control can be exercised through advanced communication techniques. Benetton and Levi Strauss use the latest information technologies, including satellites, to spread data to all affiliates to ensure that production closely matches demand in all the countries in which they operate. R&D too, in particular in high tech industries such as aerospace, automobiles, electronics and biotechnology largely depends on the quality and speed of information transfer (UNCTC, 1993).

This implies a new stage for multinationalisation. Firms have gone beyond their traditional practices of exporting to foreign countries and building foreign production facilities to establish intricate networks of research, production and information. Corporations interact on a global scale through a wide range of external alliances, for example, joint ventures, subcontracting, licensing and inter-firm agreements. These flexible webs have not replaced the traditional modes of providing goods and services to other markets, but there is more interaction between trade and foreign investment. To some extent, the global firm can thus become synonymous with a 'network firm', as many companies in different sectors have established complex networks of joint ventures or alliances in one or more parts of the value chain – design, research and development, marketing, assembly of parts and components – thus often turning them into allies and competitors in world wide markets. In particular the automobile industry provides a good example of a sector, where the high degree of mergers and acquisitions, joint ventures, and so on have led to an incomprehensible network of relations. Other examples relate to the computer industry, both for hardware and software, the pharmaceutical industry, aeronautics and telecommunications. IBM, which until the 1980s acted fully independently, has since started developing personal computers with Microsoft, Intel and Lotus. It entered into an alliance with Siemens of Germany to work on microchips and is currently working with Apple, once its archrival, to develop a new type of operating software to work on both companies' machines (*Economist*, 1993).

The globalisation of the goods market is also reinforced by the shortening of the product cycle; this requires firms that wish to remain successful to enter the world market rapidly, in order to amortise the considerable investments required by the development of the highly sophisticated systems necessary to realise this world market entry. Companies may face constraints in expanding, due to geographical, financial, technological or other factors limiting the optimal size of the firm. In those instances, the company can decide to find appropriate control through strategic alliances, networking, joint ventures, and so on, in order to gain access to markets, to exploit complementary technologies and to reduce time required for innovation. Globalisation thus is not strictly confined to the largest and strongest MNCs, but small and medium-sized companies have also access to this mode of operation. A single firm operating at the national level, probably without having all the relevant, complex technological knowledge, and not willing to go down the road of mergers and acquisitions can seek collaborative arrangements or alliances at the international level, thereby also spreading the risks involved. It is now a quite common way of getting access to the international market. Some sectors are less likely to globalise, as they are sometimes bound by strict national rules and regulations, as is the case in certain service industries, while on the other hand constraints posed by the domestic market may give companies an additional incentive to turn global.

Globalisation is directly affecting the traditional paradigm that based a country's comparative advantage on the relative availability of production factors, such as natural resources, labour and capital input. Today, the world's largest corporations look to all nations to gain advantage in production, marketing and research, in effect reducing the comparative advantage of a country to its contribution to their global strategies, for example, through international sourcing. Specialisation now more than ever can occur in one segment of an industry, thus making a country a preferred location for making parts and components for automobiles, semiconductors in electronics or other specialised products. While companies often cooperate with their competitors to gain technological advantages (see also Chapter 4 of this volume), particularly in the intermediate components stage, they still compete keenly in final markets.

Firms often get linked through transnational equity holdings and other arrangements to develop and produce parts and components, including new products, for standards (e.g. in consumer electronics-HDTV and video compact discs, or to meet environmental standards, on emission and so forth, for cars). Such 'strategic alliances' appear as a delicate mix between co-operation and competition, closely linked to the emergence of 'global network' organisations. These may take the form of cooperative agreements in R&D and production, in cross-licensing and in cross-share holdings. They may also take the form of mergers or large-scale acquisitions across national boundaries. The increased concentration through mergers and acquisitions, as well as high entry costs for new competitors in high technology areas, can create oligopolistic or even monopolistic situations, particularly in the case of a limited number of key 'high tech' components which are an essential input in the manufacture of a wide variety of finished products. This again can be particularly observed in the automobile industry, where the largest companies have stakes in each other, or cooperate in R&D, design or marketing of different brands of cars that compete with each other in the same segment of the market.[6]

3.5 International trade within the multinational corporation

International trade in goods has systematically outpaced growth in real output of manufactures since the beginning of the 1980s.[7] This can largely be explained by the growing interdependence of economies and the rapid liberalisation of world markets

6. A very particular case of the mixture between competition and cooperation is provided by rebadging, which illustrates the complexity of the links between firms. It appears that in the United States the 'Big 3' car manufacturers (General Motors, Ford and Chrysler) sell Japanese cars under their own emblems or badges, both direct imports from Japan and cars assembled locally in Japanese plants. Ford, which has a 25 per cent stake in Mazda, sells Mazda models under Ford badges in Japan and other Asian countries, but also produces cars for Mazda in the United States.

7. GATT reports on International Trade, various issues.

in various negotiation rounds. While much of the increase in trade is taking place on a regional level, such as within the EU (Western Europe accounting for 46 per cent of world exports, of which almost 73 per cent is intra-regional), this process was cer tainly not limited to the OECD area *per se*. In particular a number of South East Asian economies, often referred to as the Dragons or Tigers,[8] have been able to position themselves as leading exporters on world markets.

These macro-economic facts and figures hide certain developments taking place on the micro-economic level, such as the prominent role multinational enterprises play, both in their capacity as large firms exporting either from their home economy or from one or several foreign countries, and through their large and growing system of intra-group flows of goods across national borders. It is believed that MNCs are involved in at least 40 per cent of total OECD manufacturing trade. For some countries this figure is considerably higher, such as for the United States and the United Kingdom (each 80%). Nearly a third of these countries' total exports are made up of intra-firm flows. Intra-firm trade (IFT) consists of products sold internationally, but which stay within the multinational enterprise, as opposed to international trade among unrelated parties, also called 'arm's length trade'.

Indeed, the globalisation of economic activities and expansion of MNCs' production subsidiary networks has generated very important flows of goods and services between the different units of a single multinational group. Trade flows basically take place in two directions: vertical exchanges occur between the parent company and its subsidiaries, while horizontal exchanges take place between subsidiaries located in various countries. OECD studies, however, underscore that there is still insufficient knowledge about the way the global operations of MNCs affect the structure of world trade. Goods and services cross borders and are recorded in customs statistics. Yet they do not leave the internal boundaries constituted by the MNCs' organisational structures. The 'internal' market, as discussed earlier, that of the MNCs, exists alongside the 'external' market, which is the only one recognised in orthodox analysis. Goods and services circulating within MNC networks are considered as off-market. For some countries, limited data are available, for instance in the case of the United States. These data are based on a benchmark survey, separated by trade by US-based parent corporations, US affiliates abroad, foreign affiliates based in the United States, and intra-firm trade affecting US imports and exports (whether by US firms within their group structures or by MNCs within theirs). Japan published four benchmark survey reports with respect to foreign affiliates of Japanese companies. In the case of European countries, there are virtually no data available with respect to intra-firm trade, except for some limited information for the UK.

In dealing with the issue of the role of MNCs in international trade, a distinction should be made between two related concepts, intra-industry trade (IIT) and intra-firm trade. Intra-industry trade is defined as the mutual exchange of goods within the same product category, as opposed to inter-industry trade, which is trade between

8. In the OECD these countries are referred to as the Dynamic Asian Economies: Hong Kong, Malaysia, Singapore, South Korea, Taiwan and Thailand.

unrelated product categories (Grubel and Lloyd, 1975; Greenaway and Milner, 1986). Most trade in manufactured goods among OECD countries consists of intra-industry trade, particularly in Europe though somewhat less in North America, thus representing roughly two-thirds of total trade in manufactures. Intra-industry trade is characteristic for trade between economies with a similar state of development, comparable per capita income and relative factor endowments. Products that are typically of an intra-industry nature are automobiles, for example, German consumers buying French cars and vice versa, some French preferring German cars to the French-made cars. It thus represents a two-way exchange of comparable goods, where consumer preference probably is the main factor explaining the trade flow. Intra-industry trade indices for EC and EFTA trade in cars are particularly high, around 90 per cent throughout the 1980s, largely due to the very high intra-European trade.

Intra-industry trade can at the same time consist of intra-firm trade. This is particularly the case in automobile trade between the United States and Canada and between the US and Mexico, particularly in the Maquiladora industry in the North of Mexico: United States parent companies export parts and components and import assembled cars from the affiliates for the American market. According to Michalet (1991), in the case of United States MNCs, for example, 90 per cent of the exports of their Canadian-located subsidiaries go to the United States. Intra-firm trade thus is part of intra-industry trade. It illustrates the pattern of specialisation within the firm and the high degree of internalisation of production and know-how within the company. Companies thus operate on a global scale and can site specific parts of their production process in different geographical locations, while remaining within the company.

Together with the internalisation theory, economies of scale have often been claimed to play an important role in explaining the pattern of intra-firm trade. Intra-firm trade in fact replaces market transactions by internal transactions within the MNC. This is fully in accordance with the internalisation theory, in order to reduce transaction costs or costs resulting from market imperfections, but may also be the result of certain government policies, including tax, tariff or competition policy. Intra-firm trade can be seen as an important, but not the sole, mechanism through which globalisation is currently taking shape.

Inter-industry trade consists of trade flows that are generally explained in international trade theory (Heckscher-Ohlin, Samuelson), thus reflecting differences in comparative advantages between economies and levels of specialisation, given the availability of relative factor endowments in an economy, as explained by classical trade theories. It is often used to explain trade between economies at different stages of development, and is more characteristic for 'North–South' patterns of trade. While consumer preferences again play an important role, this type of trade is explained more in terms of geographical availability, or even scarcity in case of base products, price and degree of specialisation of an economy.

Despite the fact that little accurate information is available on trends in intra-firm trade, some recent OECD studies presented some interesting evidence on IFT (OECD, 1992a). It was found to be particularly important for the United States and represents more than a third of US merchandise trade. The share of US intra-firm trade in total trade, however, remained unchanged between 1977 and the second half of the 1980s.

Almost a third of exports and 40 per cent of imports consist of flows between units controlled by the same group. Thus they have a fairly significant influence on the balance of trade. An exception is US affiliates' imports from their foreign parents, which rose steadily from 19 per cent of total US merchandise imports in 1977 to 26 per cent in 1989. Most of this increase was accounted for by firms from Japan and Korea.

These OECD studies also confirm findings presented in other studies on IFT that US intra-firm trade, both exports and imports, is mostly concentrated in industries which are intensive in technology and human capital, such as machinery, electric/electronic equipment and transport equipment. On the other hand, fuels and minerals represent a large but decreasing share of US imports shipped by foreign affiliates to their US parents. The size of intra-firm flows varies strongly from industry to industry (Table 3.2). The variations are particularly striking in the case of Japan, where the figure for transport equipment stands well above the average, due to the development of sophisticated group policies by Japanese automobile manufacturers. Japanese parent firms export parts and components to their foreign affiliates for assembly abroad. This pattern may change again, with the maturing of fully integrated production facilities abroad. New production techniques now require highly

Table 3.2 Size of intra-firm trade flows by industry for the US, Japan, and the UK

	United States (1982)		Japan (1983)	United Kingdom (1981)	
	Exports	Imports	Exports	Imports	Exports
All industries	32.9	40.8	23.7	27.7	27.0
Petroleum	23.4	24.1	42.4[1]	28.8[1]	....
Mining	....	....	4.5	11.5	....
Manufacturing	38.6	63.0	29.9	20.0	....
Food and Beverage	19.3	22.0	18.3	2.3	27.0
Textiles	....	....	2.7	5.2	....
Wood, paper, pulp	....	....	0.4	22.0	....
Chemicals	36.5	....	19.5	8.0	48.1
Metals	16.7	....	2.2[2]	1.8[2]	21.5
Non-elect. mach.	51.4	74.2	12.8	20.0	....
Elect. mach.	32.5	55.7	24.8	41.9	....
Transport equip.	43.6	....	45.3	42.3	49.8[3]
Precision instr.	....	....	38.7	32.1	....
Other manufact.	36.2	42.8	....	....	18.3
Wholesale trade	12.2	12.8	18.2	30.6	....
Other industries	24.6	49.4	12.3	22.1	21.2

1 Petroleum and coal products
2 Iron and steel
3 Motor vehicles

Source: UNCTC, based on official national sources

sophisticated top to bottom production plants, based on low inventories of parts and components ('just in time' or 'lean production'). This necessitates the establishment of the main subsidiaries for the manufacturing of these parts and components within the region of supply, and may also imply a gradual decrease of intra-firm trade in that sector.

Another striking feature of intra-firm trade between the United States and other OECD countries is that it mostly consists of sales from the parents to affiliates, rather than the other way around. In other words, intra-firm flows between a home-based MNC and its foreign subsidiary are more export-oriented than import-oriented in both the United States and Japan. In contrast to the rest of US intra-firm trade, most imports by US affiliates from their foreign parents are related to distribution, especially in the motor vehicle and equipment industries. Distribution accounted for nearly 80 per cent of total US affiliates' purchases from their foreign parents, with wholesale trade in motor vehicles and equipment accounting for almost 40 per cent of the total. The data on all US imports shipped to US affiliates, not only by their foreign parents, but also by unaffiliated foreign companies, confirm the relative importance of wholesale trade for Japanese companies. Almost 95 per cent of imports by US affiliates of Japanese parents were classified as wholesale trade in 1989. This contrasts with 48 per cent for affiliates of European parents, 31 per cent for affiliates of Canadian parents and 17 per cent for affiliates of other countries' parents.

3.6 International aspects of R&D

With the rapid expansion of economic activities of multinational corporations, R&D has followed suit and internationalised as well. There is evidence (Pearce, 1989) that overseas R&D now plays an important role in the activities of the world's leading MNCs. While decentralisation of R&D activities by MNCs has evolved notably in recent years, it is still not automatically included in the functions of overseas subsidiaries. Overall, the R&D intensity of the affiliates of MNCs is less than that of the parents, but the quality in terms of innovation seems to be gradually improving. This decentralisation of R&D now involves the creation of distinctive product variants in overseas subsidiaries, or the integration of overseas laboratories into centrally coordinated R&D programmes. The extent to which R&D activities have been relocated is hard to assess, because it is not always possible to separate cases where new foreign R&D activities were established from instances where they resulted from takeovers, mergers and acquisitions or other forms of cooperation.

It is generally believed that technological progress – and in particular the rapid growth in telecommunication techniques – has facilitated the process of internationalising R&D since the beginning of the 1980s. A key concern of companies was to keep control over R&D, as it is often a core activity. Moreover, the quality of the research and technology content in the product can affect the competitiveness of the industry as a whole. The development of worldwide telecommunication networks, however, has permitted companies to keep central control over technological know-how. Telematics, computer and data processing industries have thus been leaders in using new methods of control and they have probably seen the greatest development in worldwide organisation of corporate R&D and international sourcing of scientific and technical resources. A prime example derived from the automobile industry is Ford, who, in the development of the world car (Mondeo), have been able to link R&D activities in different countries through advanced communication technologies in such a manner that researchers could interact instantly, thus eliminating geographical barriers. In high tech industries, such as personal computers, where alliances are being formed between competitors, research efforts are often pulled together in different geographical locations, requiring highly performing (tele-)communication techniques to overcome barriers to the physical dispersal of activities.

The networking of large MNCs, through international alliances and cooperation agreements, which has led to oligopolistic structures in some sectors of industry, is noticeable in R&D activities, with companies joining forces in the process of developing a new product. This may have been prompted by rising costs of R&D, and the aim to reduce risks or to strengthen the competitive position of a group of firms *vis-à-vis* a rival. It is particularly noteworthy that this type of inter-firm cooperation can often occur in competing industries, such as the automobile industry, consumer electronics and microelectronics. This confirms the strange mixture of cooperation and competition that can be observed in large industries. Governments can partly be held responsible, in particular when they encourage the creation of joint research programmes that bring industries together in pooling their efforts on a particular project.

The way industries structure their international R&D activities, as well as the extent to which they decide to internationalise R&D, differs markedly between industries. This largely depends on the characteristics of the industry, the type of R&D carried out and the degree to which the industry depends on R&D (OECD 1992). The pharmaceutical industry, for example, has one of the most highly internationalised patterns of corporate R&D as it is the core activity in this industry, with corporate R&D expenditures having grown from 6 per cent to almost 9 per cent of production over the period 1973–88. In particular a small nation like Switzerland, with a very strong pharmaceutical industry, is highly dependent on international markets, both for the supply of its goods and for the inputs and R&D. Pharmaceuticals are constantly in the top four most R&D intensive industries, ranked behind aerospace, computers and electronics. R&D centres have spread out to various countries, and products arriving on the market have increasingly been developed as part of an integrated global, rather than a national or regional, innovation programme.

Empirical evidence (Burstall *et al.*, 1981) suggests that the pharmaceutical industry directs a larger part of its internationalised R&D to basic research than does any other industry. This is probably related to the particular conditions applying to pharmaceuticals: given the responsibilities governments assume with regard to health and safety, regulations in this sector are strict and include testing and inspection procedures. This often requires companies to carry out local R&D, production and processing of drugs in order to comply with the specific standards that apply on the market of supply. In others sectors, such as food processing and the automobile industry, internationalised

R&D is also large, but mainly focused on product development and process adaptation to local market and manufacturing conditions. This is closely related to the customisation of products: local tastes and consumer preferences – which are related to customs and culture – can widely differ between markets. Globalisation of the world economy and new terms of economic competition imply that technological innovation has become a main determinant of industrial competitiveness in different markets and R&D is playing an important role in that process. Companies thus often apply a regional strategy, assuming that there is some degree of homogeneity between the markets within a region.

Views on whether an MNC should centralise or decentralise R&D activities differ widely, with protagonists of centralisation claiming that firms need to keep a close watch on all R&D activities and ensure that they remain close to the head office (Patel and Pavitt, 1991). According to the authors' findings, strategic R&D activities will continue to be concentrated in the home country. A large company could, indeed, benefit from keeping its R&D centralised through synergies generated by the need for constant communication between researchers. It would seem, however, that the establishment of modern communication techniques allows for a continuous exchange of information and personal contact often simplifies matters and shortens communication lines. The antagonistic view (Cantwell, 1989) is that globalisation of production processes also applies to R&D, which necessitates the internationalisation of these activities. The large MNCs will thus carry out their R&D activities on all the major markets in which they are established. Separately, MNCs can be driven by other factors, such as the merits of national scientific capacity, which can play a key role in choosing the location for their foreign R&D activities. The local infrastructure, and in particular the existence of universities, thus providing for a good scientific basis and a highly skilled labour force, may attract subsidiaries of MNCs to conduct their foreign R&D, like Silicon Valley in California for the production of semiconductors.

There probably is not one single answer to the question whether R&D should be centralised or decentralised, as the internationalisation of R&D will again largely depend on the features of the industry and on the market conditions under which the industry operates. Empirical research and fact finding carried out in the OECD (OECD, 1993b), reveals that in those countries for which data are available, the proportion of R&D carried out by foreign subsidiaries is tending to increase steadily. In 1990, the share of R&D conducted by foreign subsidiaries in the United States was equal to 10 per cent of total manufacturing R&D and 15.4 per cent of the total for industry, compared with 3.7 and 6.4 per cent respectively in 1980. It should be observed that, while this finding does confirm the view that the decentralisation of R&D is increasing, it does not prove that foreign firms are relocating their R&D, as the phenomenon may be attributable more to acquisitions of existing laboratories than to the transfer of R&D activities abroad. In addition, the share of R&D carried out by foreign subsidiaries is generally smaller than that of their turnover or production.

3.7 The multinational corporation versus national authority

Public perceptions of FDI and the role of multinational corporations in the host country have evolved considerably over time, particularly in developing countries. Initially, all countries accepted the prevailing international liberal regime for multinational enterprises, based on national treatment. Few restrictions were placed on the operation of foreign investors in the host countries. Latin America was the major exception as it conducted a more restrictive policy. In particular since the 1950s and 1960s, nationalist sentiment developed and multinationals came to be seen as a threat to economic and political independence. In the 1980s, attitudes changed again in favour of multinational corporations, as a more pragmatic approach was adopted, but developing countries continued to closely monitor and control the activities of foreign investors. Multinational corporations gradually were considered less of a threat and more as an opportunity for promoting growth and development. This attitude is prevailing today as controversies about multinational corporations have largely vanished; MNCs are currently seen as a means to attract capital and know-how (Spero, 1990).

An evolution in thinking has occurred and host country governments have become more concerned about the quality of an investment, as they are keen on promoting certain forms of investment that can best contribute to the development of the economy. While nearly all countries now try to attract FDI as a means to stimulate economic growth and welfare, the concern of developing country host governments is particularly related to transfer of capital, technology and the creation of employment, with a view to creating a competitive position on world markets which leads to exports and thus to income. Special incentives are often provided in the form of fiscal advantages, including direct or indirect subsidies, tax breaks, often directly linked to performance requirements imposed on, or negotiated with the foreign investor. This development is not only related to developing countries, but also developed countries have become increasingly concerned with the value added by FDI and its contribution in terms of technology to the local economy. Governments can play a proactive role in attracting FDI, by reducing the costs of market deficiencies, removing entry-barriers and other obstacles, thus encouraging competition in the domestic market and reducing transaction costs for multinational enterprises (see also Chapter 2, Section 2.4). They can encourage the creation of tangible and organisational capabilities that may influence the MNCs' decision on where to invest. Direct incentives are often provided through subsidies or by providing locational advantages. One recent example concerns the future establishment of a Mercedes Benz production plant in Alabama (United States), which the German car manufacturer decided to choose as the location for its American-made brand. While the company publicly denies that local subsidies have been decisive in the investment decision, the fact is that around 30 states have been competing to attract the production facilities and the state of Alabama offered incentives in the order of 253 million dollars (Dickson, 1993).

The European concern about 'screwdriver plants' attracted much public attention, as it illustrated the genuine concern of governments about the quality of the investment in the host country. Governments are increasingly concerned to support so-called 'strategic' industries, which are considered to be those industries that are of fundamental importance to the development of the economic potential of a country. This is because of their technology intensity, and/or the spin-off that the activities of a particular industry can have to related industries. Investments should generate activity in value-adding or 'high tech' industries. Strategic industrial and trade policies aim at securing national advantage in oligopolistic industries (Krugman, 1990). The concern relates to attracting activities that add to the building of an economy's competitive strength on world markets in leading products. Competition is particularly fierce in knowledge-intensive goods, including consumer electronics, computers and telecommunication, as they often have rather short product cycles, and they are generally believed to contribute most to the economy's overall performance, through backward and forward linkages. They often embody the latest state of the art technology. Supporting strategic industries often entails the implementation of a set of complementary measures, aiming at protecting markets, attracting multinationals, securing a competitive environment, but, most of all, attracting technology.

Certain trade policy instruments have been used to ensure that the investment is qualitatively substantial and not merely to circumvent trade measures, but that high-value, high technology operations are transferred or fostered in the host country. Sometimes these objectives are achieved through trade-related investment requirements (Trims), which can vary in nature and are not covered by the rules of the former GATT, but were part of the Uruguay Round package. The most frequently encountered Trims include local content requirements in the value added, export requirements of part of the total output, or conditions with regard to the recruitment of local senior staff as well as, for instance, setting aside part of the capital for local shareholders. Local content is variously defined, but is always a measure of local value-added, that is, the sum of the value of parts and materials procured from domestic sources plus the value of domestic assembly, labour, overhead and mark-ups. Rules relating to local content requirements imposed on foreign investors have been controversial. Most OECD countries do not have mandatory local content requirements, but some negotiate commitments from foreign assemblers in return for location and other assistance.

Related to local content are 'rules of origin', that national authorities apply to confer origin to a product in order to determine the treatment it should receive while crossing a border. They are not designed to be a trade policy instrument *per se*, but should determine the origin of the good. The host country concern, however, is mainly related to the possible circumvention of other trade policy rules. Obviously, a product made within a preferential area (e.g. regional arrangement, free trade agreement) will benefit more from the favourable provisions applying to the goods made within that area than do those coming from outside the region. As the criteria for establishing origin, laid down in the Kyoto Convention, vary, in practice origin rules can be used as trade policy instruments.[9] There are various examples, both relating to the EU and North America. One widely published example relates to the treatment of Honda cars, produced in Canada, that were denied preferential treatment under

9. A thorough discussion on rules of origin can be found in Vermulst and Verwaer, 1990.

NAFTA rules, as US authorities considered they did not meet the local content value of 62.5 per cent required to meet the rule of origin, qualifying the car to be 'North American'. (Under the Free Trade Agreement between the US and Canada, the local content requirement was 50%). Similar disputes have occurred in the EU, relating to automobiles, after the Japanese manufacturers decided to produce their cars in the UK for the European market – given that there would be full freedom of circulation of goods within the EU – since the beginning of 1993. In particular France was keen on a high level of local content in order to confer European (or UK) origin to cars manufactured in the UK. Much confusion has also been caused by the unilateral interpretation of origin rules for televisions and semiconductors, the application of rules of origin in anti-dumping cases and the so-called screwdriver directive.

Despite the fact that all the individual cases have found a solution, this situation is very unsatisfactory for the business community, as this 'discretionary' policy by national authorities creates much uncertainty for producers and investors as to how the final product will be treated. Local content and origin rules are meant to provide an acidity test, but in practice they become a prescription and impose strict conditions on the planned or the realised investment. Host government policies thus have a direct impact on the strategy followed by the MNC including investment, production and siting decisions. Investments are not carried out overnight, but require careful planning, are often very substantial, and are part of an overall business strategy. Also the costs involved are generally considerable and such projects should not be subject to sometimes rather arbitrary decisions, when it comes to the criteria applied in deciding whether origin can or cannot be conferred to a product. Investors need clarity and transparency in the decision-making process, and need to be subject to nondiscriminatory treatment. The Uruguay Round negotiations made a serious attempt to clarify the issue and establish clear rules based on these principles of transparency and nondiscrimination, such as to prevent the arbitrary use of origin rules.

Economically, performance requirements create distortions in investment and trade decisions, and thus are undesirable. They imply a misapplication of economic resources, but at the same time create distortions within the host country, that can also work to the detriment of competing local firms, by bidding up asset and factor prices beyond what they would have been if the trade/investment choice were a policy-neutral one (DeAnne, 1990). They tend to generate economic inefficiencies in the economy and reduce the overall welfare level. Trade policy measures may also be counteracted by the global strategies of enterprises and have unforeseen effects. Trade protectionism can cause firms to substitute investment for exports, thereby creating additional competitive pressures and even excess capacity. Bilateral arrangement to modify flows of imports and exports may encourage collusive behaviour among firms and raise barriers to entry in certain sectors. According to Bergsten and Graham (1992), locational decisions of firms based on incentives provided by host governments must imply an overall net welfare loss, mainly as a result of creation of inefficiencies and the misallocation of resources, as mentioned before. They consider that if a firm structures its worldwide operations in a manner inconsistent with global cost minimisation in order to comply with performance requirements, but also receives incentives to do so, it is conceivable that the value to the firm of the incentives will exceed the value lost due to cost sub-optimisation. For the host government, however, the overall costs necessarily outweigh the benefits, although it presumably believes that its country achieves a net advantage.

The question of multinational corporations versus national authority, is often addressed from the angle of responsibilities of the host government towards its citizens, which include ensuring economic activity and national defence, the latter argument being invoked for justifying the prohibition or regulation of certain kinds of FDI.[10] It is therefore relevant to know to what extent foreign subsidiaries of MNCs contribute to the objective of the government in the host country, or to what extent they undermine achieving domestic policy objectives; related to this is the issue of whether they should be treated on equal footing with national firms. This question certainly is not new, but becomes more pressing as host countries are faced with the prospect of a growing role for non-national firms in their economies, given the rapid surge in FDI in recent years. Home countries must also deal with the challenges that are posed by outward FDI.

Can governments still conduct a national industrial policy in the presence of multinational enterprises that take the globe, rather than a domestic economy, as their field of action? To what extent should affiliates be able to benefit from subsidies and national or regional support, or from R&D programs aimed at strengthening the competitiveness of the domestic industries, or those of regions (EU)? As a result of closer economic integration of national economies, boundaries between economies are gradually blurring, and the scope for governments to confine a domestic policy to national firms is limited. This does not only apply to those countries formally engaged in regional arrangements, but to all economies that have developed close economic ties. In addition, policy instruments themselves become more closely interrelated. In some cases, the distinction between border policies versus domestic policies is becoming artificial; industrial and trade policies, for example, cannot always easily be separated and their impacts cannot easily be isolated. In addition, investment flows easily jump over border protection, thus undermining the conduct of isolated domestic policies.

Also, due to the globalisation of corporate activities, governments cannot be sure of the competitive effects of their industrial policies, when they assume a proactive role. Industrial policy measures to support domestic production may also support foreign production facilities and subsidise foreign subsidiaries. Government aid to research and development may benefit foreign firms through corporate interaction in global technology networks. Programmes to increase domestic production may subsidise goods that have largely been produced abroad through offsets and sub-contracting arrangements. Investment incentives, regional policy schemes and other domestic

10. The national security argument can be widely interpreted, and acquire another dimension, when the threat does not arise from the multinational itself but from the multinational's home government to the host country. The US Export Administration Act of 1979 has been used by the US government to control dealings of foreign affiliates of US corporations, thus implying an extra-territorial application of domestic legislation. American multinational corporations operating abroad were thus obliged to comply with domestic US legislation, which caused incidents with US allies, particularly European governments, who contested the extra-territorial application of US laws.

policies may transfer income to trading partners and help strengthen rival industries (OECD, 1992c).

A fundamental question raised today is: does nationality still matter, now that the largest MNCs are becoming global operators? From a government's point of view and with respect to the national security issue, it would not be realistic to treat foreign and domestic companies alike, but that is probably not the main concern here. The central issue relates to competitiveness and efficacy of government policy in a globalising world. Reich (1990) posed the question in this very direct manner: 'Who is us?' In pursuing efforts to conduct a national policy, this central question is currently at the heart of the policy debate in the US Administration (Wallstreet Journal, 1993). In other words, can one still define the national interest in a context where MNCs site major parts of their economic activities in different parts of the world? What policy should be conducted by the host country? Does an American company doing most of its R&D and product design and most of its complex manufacturing outside the US, thus employing more people outside the US than within the American market, reflect more the American national interest than a foreign company, headquartered abroad, but employing more Americans in the US through its affiliates than foreigners? Reich considers the employment criteria to be decisive. For governments it is control. Whatever the final answer is, it raises the very pertinent question of multinational corporations versus national authority.

It illustrates the consequences of interdependence, that national interest may no longer be confined within the traditional narrow geographic boundaries of the national economy. A growing part of the activity which adds to the wealth of a particular country is taking place beyond its frontiers. Regional cooperation and integration is in part a response to this reality. It reflects a degree of recognition by national governments of the limits to their effective sovereignty and their acceptance that multilateral cooperation is necessary in order to deal more adequately with many of the issues they have to face. Regional cooperation is often easier to establish than multilateral liberalisation, because it involves fewer participants. Moreover, it is more likely to achieve policy convergence on a regional than on a multilateral level, particularly when the economies have a similar level of economic development and are characterised by high levels of intra-industry trade.

Both policy-makers and the business community see a need for adapting national and multilateral rule-making to the new realities, and for ensuring that host government policy cannot be used in an arbitrary manner. Currently, rules are largely based on traditional concepts such as nation states, national industries and national interest. Until now, trade policy issues have mainly been dealt with separately and regardless of the other policy instruments. The globalisation of industrial activities and overlaps between industrial and trade policies necessitate a broader multilateral framework for harmonisation of industrial policies. A good example relates to competition policy rules. Whereas competition policy is strictly confined to the national economy, the application of competition law can have a direct bearing on trade policy and the other way round. While both policies share a common objective, namely the use of the marketplace competition to achieve an efficient allocation of resources and maximum economic growth and welfare benefits, their respective instruments differ and may be conflicting in achieving this objective.[11] A new approach thus requires dealing with these issues in an interrelated fashion.

FDI needs clear and unambiguous rules. A principal rule with regard to FDI is similar to the one that applies to international trade, that is, non-discriminatory behaviour, or equal treatment of foreign and domestic firms. This 'national treatment' principle lies at the heart of OECD principles and aims to ensure that foreign and domestic firms are treated equally.[12] OECD rules lack an enforcement mechanism and apply only to the 24 member countries. A more comprehensive approach with regard to FDI leading to effective multilateral rules has become a necessity, given the economic significance of FDI in the international economy. This should be an important item on the agenda of a next Round on Multilateral Trade Negotiations within the World Trade Organisation (WTO).

An earlier UNCTC report (1992) suggests various avenues to deal with FDI: one relates to enhancing transparency and predictability through improved access to information about international investment policies and the analysis of these policies, for instance through a FDI policy review mechanism, similar to the Trade policy reviews currently being carried out in WTO; in parallel, it would be useful to elaborate international principles and standards and to consolidate them in a global, comprehensive and balanced instrument to ensure the stability, predictability and transparency of the international investment environment. This instrument would have to deal with the main aspects of the relation between MNCs and governments on the one hand, and issues related to their behaviour on the other.

Proposals for new rules on international investment are widely supported by Bergsten and Graham (1992). They consider it to be inevitable that the interplay between differing national policies and different corporate strategies will provoke conflicts of two types: between governments (e.g. between home and host nations, where the firm is caught in the middle), and between a government and a company. In their views, an ideal agreement would grant specific rights to, and simultaneously place certain obligations on, three sets of actors: (a) governments of nations that are host to FDI (including subnational entities), (b) governments of nations that are home to international corporations, and (c) international corporations themselves. The agreement must furthermore provide for an active means to settle disputes both between governments, and between governments and international corporations. It would thus seem that the globalisation of business practices necessitates adapting the

11. Some illustrations of the interface between the two policy instruments are safeguards, grey area measures, anti-dumping practices, subsidies, and so on, that are frequently practised by trade policy authorities, but distort or may distort competition, while a number of private firms' anti-competitive arrangements or practices can undermine trade concessions (restrictive practices in distribution systems, vertical restraints, inter-industry arrangements, etc.).

12. In 1976, OECD member states agreed on a voluntary Code of Conduct for Multinational Corporations. The objective of the Code is to maximise international investment and provide guidelines for corporate behaviour, including disclosure of information and cooperation with the laws and policies of the host country. OECD member states also agreed on guidelines for government policy regarding multinational corporations, including non-discrimination against foreign corporations, equitable treatment under international law and respect for contracts.

rules to new circumstances of economic competition, taking into account the broader scope of action of MNCs, while at the same time coping with the need of governments to assume their national responsibilities and pursue domestic policies.

Bibliography

References

Bergsten, C.F. and **Graham, E.M.** (1992) 'Needed, new rules for foreign direct investment', *The International Trade Journal*, vol. VII, no 1, pp. 15–44.

Buckley, P. and **Casson, M.** (1976) *The Future of the Multinational Enterprise*, MacMillan.

Burstall, M.L., Dunning, J.H. and **Lake, A.** (1981) 'International investment and innovation', in N. Wells (ed.) *Pharmaceuticals among the Sunrise Industries*, Croom Helm.

Cantwell, J. (1989) *Technological Innovation and Multinational Corporations*, Basil Blackwell.

Caves, Richard E. (1971) International Corporations: the Industrial Economics of Foreign Investment, *Economica*, pp. 1–27.

Coase, R.H. (1937) The nature of a firm, *Economica*, vol. 4 new series no. 16, pp. 386–405.

Dickson, M. (1993) 'It's nice to feel really wanted', *Financial Times*, 28 October, p. 14.

Dunning, J.H. (1988) *Explaining International production*, Hyman.

DeAnne, J. (1990) *Global Companies and Public Policy, The Growing Challenge of Foreign Direct Investment*, Royal Institute for International Affairs, Pinter Publishers.

The Economist (1993) Survey on multinationals, 27 March.

Greenaway, D. and **Milner, C.** (1986) *The Economics of Intra-firm Trade*, Basil Blackwell.

Grubel, H.G. and **Lloyd, P.J.** (1975) *Intra-industry Trade: Theory and Measurement of International Trade in Differentiated Products*, MacMillan.

Hymer, S.T. (1976) *The International Operations of National Firms: A Study of Foreign Direct Investment*, MIT Press.

Krugman, P.R. (1990) *Strategic Trade Policy and the New International Economics*, MIT Press.

Michalet, C. (1991) *The Activities of Multinational Enterprises and Their Effects on International Trade*, OECD, July, TD/TC/WP(91)43.

OECD (1992a) *Technology and the Economy, the Key Relationships.*

OECD (1992b) *International Direct Investment, Policies and Trends in the 1980s.*

OECD (1992c) *Globalisation of Industrial Activities.*

OECD (1993 b) *The Impact of Foreign Direct Investment on Domestic Economies of OECD Countries.*

Ostry, S. (1990) *Governments and Corporations in a Shrinking World*, a Council on Foreign Economic Relations.

Patel, P. and **Pavitt, K.** (1990) 'Do large firms control the world's technology?', in K. Pavitt, *What Makes Basic Research Economically Useful?*, paper presented to the Paris TEP Technology and Competitiveness Conference.

Pearce, R. (1989) *The Internationalisation of R&D by Multilateral Enterprises*, MacMillan.

Porter, M. (1986) *Competition in Global Industries*, Harvard Business School Press.

Porter, M. (1990) *The Competitive Advantage of Nations*, MacMillan.

Reich, R. (1990) 'Who is us?', *Harvard Business Review*, January–February, pp. 53–64.

Rugman, A.M. (ed.) (1982) *New Theories of the Multinational Enterprise*, St. Martin's Press.

Smeets, M. (1990) Globalisation and the trade policy response, *Journal of World Trade*, vol. 24, no. 5, pp. 57–73.

Spero, J. (1990) *The Politics of International Economic Relations*, St. Martin's Press.

United Nations Centre on Transnational Corporations (UNCTC) (1992a) *World Investment Report 1992, Transnational Corporations as Engines for Growth*, United Nations.

UNCTC (1992b) *The Determinants of Foreign Direct Investment, A Survey of Evidence*, United Nations.

UNCTC (1993) *World Investment Report 1993, Transnational Corporations and Integrated International Production*, United Nations.

Vermulst, E. and **Verwaer, P.** (1990) 'European Community rules of origin as commercial policy instruments', *Journal of World Trade*, 24 June, pp. 55–59.

Vernon, R. (1966) International investment and international trade in the product cycle, *Quarterly Journal of Economics*, May, pp. 190–207.

The Wallstreet Journal (1993) 'Clinton aides grapple with definition of a US company in a global economy', 2 July.

Womack, J., Jones, D. and **Roos, D.** (1990) *The Machine that Changed the World*, Rawson.

Further reading

Casson, M. (1979) *Alternatives to the Multinational Enterprise*, MacMillan.

Casson, M. (1982) 'Transaction costs and the theory of the multinational enterprise', in A.M. Rugman (ed.) *New Theories of the Multinational Enterprise*, St. Martin's Press.

Dunning, J.H. (1990) *The Globalisation of Firms and the Competitiveness of Countries: Some Implications for the Theory of International production*, Institute of Economic Research.

Dunning, J.H. (1992) 'The competitive advantage of countries and the activities of transnational corporations', *Transnational Corporations*, vol. 1, no. 1, pp. 135–168.

DeAnne, J. (1991) *Foreign Direct Investment: The Neglected Twin of Trade*, Group of Thirty.

EC Commission (1993) *International Economic Interdependence*, discussion paper.

Graham, E.M. and **Krugman, P.R.** (1991) *Foreign Direct Investment in the US*, Institute for International Economics.

Helleiner, G.K. and **Lavergne, R.** (1979) 'Intra-firm trade and industrial exports to the United States', *Oxford Bulletin of Economics and Statistics*, vol. 41, pp. 297–311.

Lall, S. (1978) 'The pattern of intra-firm exports by US multinationals', *Oxford Bulletin of Economics and Statistics*, vol. 40, pp. 209–22.

OECD (1991a) *Technology in a Changing World.*

OECD (1991b) *Strategic Industries in a Global Economy*. Paris.

OECD (1993a) *Economic Studies*, No 20.

Rugman, A.M. and **Verbeke, A.** (1990) *Global Corporate Strategy and Trade Policy*, Routledge.

Transnational Corporations (1992) vol. 1, no. 1, February.

Unido (1981) 'Intra-firm trade and industrial restructuring', *Unido Working Papers on Structural Changes*, no. 20, October.

4 Forms of international cooperation between corporations

4.1 Introduction

The use of inter-firm cooperative agreements has become an increasingly important mode of conducting international business activities. MNCs had previously regarded them as a second-best option to majority or wholly owned affiliates, undertaking cooperative agreements only where absolutely necessary. Even when they did so, generally to overcome entry barriers to access markets or raw materials, they preferred to use equity agreements such as joint ventures to maximise ownership and control. Since the beginning of the 1980s, there has been a shift in trends, with firms undertaking an increasing number of cooperative agreements, especially in high technology sectors. Furthermore, most of these agreements are between firms within the Triad (Western Europe, North America and Japan), who are utilising a wide variety of different modes of cooperative agreements, often simultaneously, that do not involve equity.

The purpose of this chapter is to examine the phenomenon of international inter-firm cooperative agreements. It tries to establish an understanding of cooperative agreements in general and examine the various forms of inter-firm cooperative agreements. Why are firms increasingly using cooperative agreements as a means to conduct international business? What are the causes behind the growing significance of cooperative agreements in the international economy? Why are cooperative agreements regarded as unstable? These are the kinds of questions that this chapter seeks to address.

4.2 What are cooperative agreements?

In order to understand why firms undertake inter-firm cooperation, it is useful to begin with the concept of the value added chain (Porter, 1980, 1985). Essentially, the economic activity undertaken by a firm engaged in production consists of several stages, beginning from acquiring the inputs for production, until a final product is created and sold to the customer. At each stage, value is added to the output of the previous stage, such that the value of the final output has a value equal to the sum of all the values added during the various stages of production. Figure 4.1 illustrates a simplified value added chain for a furniture manufacturer specialising in chairs. The earlier stages of the value chain – as in most industries – involve less value added than do the later stages. The processing of timber, for instance, adds relatively less value to the raw timber than does the production of chairs from plywood. The earlier stages are referred to as *upstream activities*, while those that involve a greater value added activity in a value chain are referred to as *downstream activities.* A firm may seek to undertake all or some of the stages. If it decides to undertake only the manufacture of the chairs, it may make arrangements with a timber plantation to supply the wood, and arrange to sell the finished furniture to a wholesaler, who will take care of the marketing and sales stage. These arrangements represent inter-firm transactions. If it decides to undertake the plywood production itself, it is said to expand upstream along the same value chain. When a firm expands its value added activities along the same value chain either by acquiring an existing operation, or setting up a greenfield subsidiary, it is said to engage in *vertical* integration. When it acquires or sets up another production facility in a related industry, but at the same stage of the value added chain, it is said to undertake *horizontal* integration, for instance, if it establishes a production facility to manufacture tables.

Consider the case where a chair manufacturer is located in Holland, and wishes to buy plywood from Canada. There exists a spectrum of organisational modes through which the firm may conduct such international operations. At the one extreme, the firm can establish a wholly owned subsidiary through foreign direct investment (FDI) such that it has ownership *and* control over its subsidiary operations. Such an arrangement would provide it with complete control over the activities of its subsidiary, but it would also involve some degree of risk, given its unfamiliarity with the Canadian market. All activities are undertaken by the same firm, and all the risks and benefits associated with vertical integration of its operations are internalised within the same firm, thereby creating an MNC. At the other extreme, the Dutch company may decide to import plywood from a Canadian firm, thereby avoiding any risk associated with producing a good with which it has no prior experience, and in a new and unfamiliar environment. There is no expansion of the firm, and it simply engages in an arms-length (or spot) transaction, leaving the risks and benefits associated with the Canadian markets to its Canadian supplier. Between these two extremes lie several other options that represent a compromise between a wholly owned subsidiary that

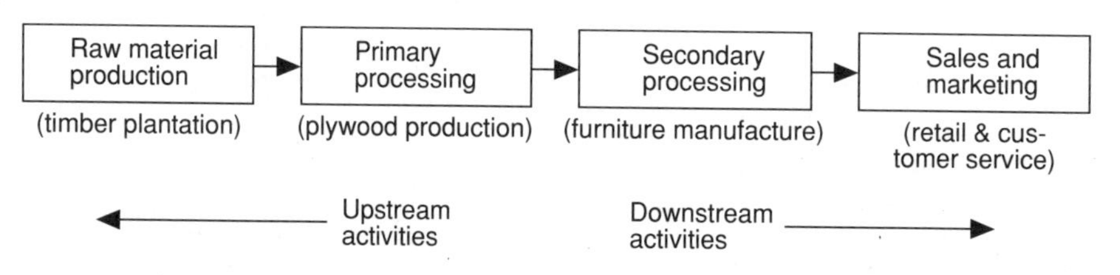

Figure 4.1 A simplified value system for the production of chairs

involves internalising all transactions between two organisationally interdependent affiliates of a single firm, and a spot transaction that involves two separate independent firms. These intermediate options represent varying extents of organisational interdependence between the two firms, and a consequent sharing of the risks and benefits between them. Since they involve two separate firms located in different countries, these organisational modes are referred to as *international inter-firm agreements*. A classification of several of the options, by the extent of organisational interdependence, is presented in Table 4.1.

It is important to note that not all transactions conducted between two firms are inter-firm *cooperative* agreements. Suppose the Dutch firm were to decide to import from an independent Canadian firm, but instead of purchasing discrete quantities occasionally, it decided to make a contract with it as an exclusive supplier, so as to

Table 4.1 A classification of modes of internationalisation and their degree of organisational interdependence

Mode of cooperation	Organisational interdependence
EQUITY	
Majority owned or wholly owned firm	Completely interdependent
Equity joint ventures (e.g. research corporations)	Large
Minority holdings	↓
Cross-holdings	↓
NON-EQUITY	↓
Joint R&D agreement (e.g. joint development agreements)	Medium
Technology exchange agreements 1. Coproduction 2. Cross-licensing 3. Mutual second sourcing	↓
Customer–supplier agreements 1. R&D contract 2. Comakership agreements 3. One-directional technology flows (e.g. second sourcing, licensing, franchise agreements)	Small
Spot (arms-length) transactions	Independent firms

Source: adapted from Hagedoorn, 1990

arrange a discounted price. While they have made an inter-firm agreement, the purpose of their agreement has a purely economic focus: the Canadian firm is interested in acquiring a regular customer and improving its profits, while the Dutch firm is merely seeking to arrange the lowest possible cost for its plywood. In other words, they are both *cost economising*, and there is no organisational interdependence involved. The supplier has complete control and ownership over the product until the point where the buyer acquires it, and after that the buyer has complete ownership and control over the product. Inter-firm cooperative agreements must include some organisational interdependence between the firms involved, such that there is a *strategic benefit* that accrues to either partner as the result of shared capital, technology or other resource. In other words, there must be some expected long-term positive effects of the agreement on the product-market positioning of at least one of the partners (Hagedoorn, 1993a). In reality, inter-firm cooperative agreements are often both strategically motivated as well as cost-economising, although some agreements are clearly biased towards one motivation. The motivations behind inter-firm cooperative agreements will be examined in greater detail in Section 4.5. It should be noted that inter-firm cooperative agreements are not the exclusive domain of firms in the sense of business enterprises; the participants may be charitable foundations, international agencies, government parastatals or individuals.

4.3 Modes of inter-firm cooperative agreements

Although the concept of cooperative agreements has been illustrated using two apparently separate stages of the value chain of a particular industry, the concept of a value chain can be applied to a single firm. The production of a chair or a car consists of several discrete steps, from purchasing through assembly to distribution, and may be done by a single firm, or by several firms. There are also other stages involved that do not directly relate to the production process, such as research and development (R&D) and procurement. These may also be undertaken by a single firm, or be undertaken through cooperative agreements or ventures. Even within a firm, a distinction can be drawn between upstream and downstream activities. Typically, product assembly is considered to be a low value adding activity, while R&D and marketing are considered high value adding activities.

Table 4.1 lists the major modes of cooperative agreements. Joint ventures, research corporations, minority holdings and cross-holdings are equity-based, that is, they involve not just a transfer of control over some of the assets of the partner; they imply some transfer of ownership, through FDI, of at least one of the participating firms to the other. Equity-type cooperative agreements tend, not surprisingly, to have a larger extent of organisational interdependence. By contrast, non-equity based cooperative agreements such as technology exchange agreements, customer supplier agreements and one-directional technology flow agreements result in considerably less transfer of control, since the assets ownership of all the partners remains intact. Non-equity based agreements therefore result in relatively less inter-organisational interdependence. In addition, given the difficulties of identifying whether in fact equity participation represents *de facto* control, the ranking of organisational interdependence presented in Table 4.1 is necessarily ordinal.

It should be noted that more than one mode of cooperative agreement may be undertaken at the same time by the same partners. For instance, it is not uncommon that firms establishing an R&D pact also make a simultaneous agreement for mutual second sourcing and cross-licensing. Such an agreement may indeed result in greater inter-organisational interdependence than a minority holding or even a joint venture. In practice, few inter-firm cooperative agreements can be classified as being of one mode or another. Much of the evidence on cooperative agreements is based on limited information derived from press releases, journals and newspapers; besides, for obvious reasons, collaborating firms tend to provide as little information as possible regarding their agreements. When a joint R&D agreement is undertaken by two firms to develop a new product, they may also make arrangements to cross-license the relevant technology. In addition, the nature and type of cooperative agreements between two firms may change over time. An initial agreement may be a customer–supplier agreement, but after a few years such an agreement may be supplemented with a comakership or coproduction agreement. In other cases, where the prior agreement is aimed at a particular project (such as a joint R&D agreement), after its completion the firms may agree that the output from the first project is produced jointly through a joint venture, resulting in several cross-licensing agreements as well.

A brief overview of the different modes of inter-firm cooperative agreements is presented in the rest of this section. Although it follows the classification suggested in Table 4.1, these definitions are by no means rigid: there exists a continuum of different organisational modes, and the descriptions provided here are only meant to illustrate some of the options available. For instance, comakership and coproduction agreements are sometimes defined as a subset of customer–supplier agreements (Hagedoorn, 1990), but depending on the particular circumstances, they may also be classified as technology exchange agreements, as has been done here.

4.3.1 *Equity-based cooperative agreements*

JOINT VENTURES

Joint ventures represent an alliance of two or more firms which collaborate to form a distinct economic entity in which each of the partners own a sufficiently large proportion of the equity capital to provide them with some degree of control over key areas of decision making (Dunning, 1993). It is important to note that while the ownership of a majority equity share in a joint venture implies *de jure* control, it does not mean that it has *de facto* control. Partners in a joint venture exert control as a function of their relative contribution in other forms of assets apart from equity capital, such as technology or management. As mentioned earlier, cooperative agreements are by definition strategically motivated: some of the partners often contribute equity to a joint venture as a means to generate economic rent, and exert no influence on the operations of the firm. Therefore, a 50–50 joint venture between a 'silent' partner[13] that provides only capital but does not try to influence the operations of the venture (e.g. portfolio investment) and another that provides the management and/or influences the strategy of the joint venture, represents a *de facto* wholly owned subsidiary of the second firm. Although such ventures do not represent cooperative agreements as defined here, it is often difficult to distinguish between them, since the motives of partners are not always apparent, and may change during the lifetime of the joint venture. It is for this reason that most studies on joint ventures necessarily assume that shared equity ownership implies shared control (Prahalad and Hamel, 1990). Joint ventures are undertaken at all stages of the value chain. They may occur between firms with complementary assets, thereby leading to vertical integration: a Chinese tractor manufacturer may arrange a joint venture with a Japanese trading company to market its equipment in Japan. However, joint ventures that combine complementary assets of the partners may also lead to horizontal integration if they are in the same value added stage of the same industry. By undertaking a joint venture that leads to horizontal integration, firms may be able to be more competitive, allowing them to expand into new areas of production because of increased economies of scope. Other joint ventures occur between firms with similar assets, either because each of the partners' share of assets is insufficient to achieve economies of scale, or because partner firms wish to take strategic action against a common competitor.

The nature of joint ventures and their motivation has undergone considerable change since the mid-1970s. Prior to the late 1970s, international joint ventures were primarily in mature industries aimed at seeking markets or access to natural resources, and were often undertaken in developing countries, where government restrictions prevented the establishment of majority or wholly owned subsidiaries. Since that time there has been a growing number of international joint ventures between firms from industrialised nations, with a strong bias towards newer technologies in which economies of scale are present. Joint ventures are generally undertaken across several activities, often including marketing and production, although single activity joint ventures have seen some growth: joint ventures that are formed primarily to conduct R&D are often referred to as research corporations.

MINORITY HOLDINGS AND CROSS-INVESTMENTS

Unlike joint ventures, where a distinct separate firm is created and control over it is shared among the partners, a firm that acquires a *minority holding* that does not provide it with sufficient ownership to be in full control, merely 'participates' in the activities of the firm. Although it may appear that such an inter-firm agreement represents a non-strategic intent given the lack of control, the main advantages of such an action is to provide the minority shareholder with an opportunity to 'assess' the partner and the quality of its technological assets or management; this kind of investment may serve as a precursor to a merger or acquisition (M&A), and minimises the risks

13. Institutional investors, such as insurance companies, pension funds, and banks often play the role of 'silent' partner.

involved in a hasty investment. For example, Daimler initially acquired only 25 per cent of AEG in 1987, before deciding to acquire a majority stake (80%) in 1989. Minority holdings are often taken in frontier technologies such as biotechnology, often by large firms that wish to acquire use of the R&D of a small innovative firm, but remain unsure of the market potential of the new technology that it is developing. Such minority holdings are often coupled with research contracts, or other non-equity agreements (Hagedoorn, 1990). Indeed, the use of minority holdings may also represent a means to enforce compliance of non-equity agreements. For instance, IBM's acquisition of a minority stake in Intel may have helped to make Intel microprocessors, and the IBM PC to become the industry standard in the early 1980s. As this example illustrates, however, minority holdings do not always ensure that the recipient firm will act according to the minority partner's strategic intent: the reluctance of Intel to use IBM standards for its next generation of processors is in part why IBM has begun to divest its equity in Intel.

Cross-holdings or investments involve all partners taking a minority equity share in each other. Unlike minority holdings, cross-holdings are more common among firms of a more equal character in terms of market power and size, although cross-holdings also tend to be undertaken to enforce non-equity agreements; they may also represent a first step towards integration through M&A, or through other more interdependent forms of cooperative ventures.

4.3.2 *Non-equity-based cooperative agreements*

Cooperative agreements are essentially based on the need to control the quality and use of the product that is being exchanged or traded among two or more firms. This product may be proprietary technology or an intermediate good in a vertical value added chain. The use of equity – either through establishing a joint venture, minority holding or cross-holding – generally occurs where one (or more) partner(s) in the firm feels that the ownership of equity will help enforce its control. If the participating firms feel that they can achieve sufficient control over the other partner's use and quality of the product in question, non-equity agreements may be preferred to equity agreements. Once again, there are several different types of non-equity agreements. The main types of these agreements are outlined below.

JOINT R&D AGREEMENTS

Although these are similar to joint ventures in that they require the active collaboration of two or more firms, unlike an equity joint venture, this type of cooperative agreement does not necessarily result in the creation of a separate legal entity. Another major difference is that joint R&D agreements have a prespecified lifetime, during which a prespecified target is to be achieved. Although the activities conducted under the auspices of a joint R&D agreement may be physically located in a facility separate from the existing operations of the partners, this may not always be the case. Instead, the partners may work on their share of the contract independently. As such, there is considerably less inter-organisational interdependence. Although joint R&D

agreements are obviously geared towards conducting R&D type projects, similar non-equity agreements may also be undertaken at other value added stages, although the use of non-equity agreements that result in such a high level of inter-firm organisational interdependence is not very common in other stages. One exception is in the case of large infrastructural projects, such as the construction of a dam or railway line, where a consortium of firms may make an agreement to bid jointly for a project given the high costs and resources needed to undertake such a project. However, even in these cases, the consortium may prefer to set up a separate legal entity such as a joint venture, as in the case of the construction of the channel tunnel between the UK and France, since it provides considerable legal protection against bankruptcy or other legal problems.

Large companies tend to undertake joint R&D agreements (sometimes referred to as research pacts or joint development agreements) as a means to explore possible benefits of further cooperation before entering into closer inter-firm cooperative agreements such as equity joint ventures or cross-holdings (Hagedoorn and Schakenraad, 1990). The level of resources required to develop new technologies may represent too large a commitment for any one firm to undertake comfortably, and by pooling their resources through a research pact, firms pursuing similar innovations may achieve synergies and, at the same time, create or improve industry standards. To give just two examples, Philips and Thomson-CSF have signed an agreement to undertake joint R&D to develop telecommunication hardware that would improve industry standards, and Motorola, IBM and Apple Computer agreed to cooperate in developing a new microprocessor which would make their different proprietary computer systems operate on the same machine, thereby aiming to create a new industry standard.

Joint development agreements may be 'encouraged' or coordinated by national or regional governments as a means to foster competitiveness of firms of a particular nationality. They can do so by providing financial support to participants of an R&D pact, and by relaxing the regulations that prevent cartels and industry collusion. However, funding by governments is often limited to R&D at a precompetitive stage, and it is for this reason that joint R&D agreements are preferred. Examples of such funding projects include ESPRIT (European Strategic Program of Research in Information Technology) and RACE (Research and Development in Advanced Communication Technologies in Europe), both sponsored by the European Union, and Sematech, which represents an alliance of US semiconductor firms,[14] and receives funding from the US government.

TECHNOLOGY SHARING AGREEMENTS

While joint R&D agreements generally result in technology sharing among the participating firms, this is a result of spillovers from joint value adding activities, and is

14. Strictly speaking, Sematech is an equity joint venture and a separate legal entity. However, it has a specific lifetime, with a specific goal, and can therefore be regarded as a contractual joint venture (*Economist*, 1994).

often not the objective of the agreement. In the case of a technology sharing agreement, as the name implies, the sharing of technology is an overt objective. Unlike customer–supplier relations (discussed below), the exchange of technology and information is bilateral or multilateral, rather than unilateral. That is, there is a mutual agreement among firms to make available specific information or technology to each other. This may take many forms, including coproduction, mutual second sourcing and cross-licensing. In general, they result in less organisational interdependence than joint R&D agreements and equity-based cooperative agreements.

Coproduction agreements involve several firms which agree to produce a product, often with a 'lead' company providing some of the technology and taking responsibility for assembling the final product, and other companies manufacturing the sub-assemblies and intermediate products as modules. The Airbus consortium is a good example of a coproduction agreement, with several independent European firms such as Deutche Aerospace, CASA and British Aerospace providing various parts of the aircraft, and the final assembly undertaken by Aerospatiale. The advantage of a coproduction agreement is that the costs of development and production are spread among several manufacturers, thereby making projects with high fixed costs feasible.

Mutual second sourcing involves a mutual transfer of technology that allows all the firms in the agreement to manufacture exact replicas of each other's proprietary products in a particular sub-sector. Such agreements allow for rapid technological development, as each participating firm has the benefit of all the other firms' technologies. Although there is the danger that individual firms may lose market shares to their collaborators, it allows the consortium to develop industry standards and market growth since there are many suppliers. Mutual second sourcing is also undertaken as a defensive move, to prevent other firms or consortia from developing an industry standard, thereby cornering the market. The UNIX computer operating system was developed by a consortium led by AT&T and consisting of several of the largest computer firms in the world. Another example was the aircraft industry consortium set up among the aircraft manufacturers in the US, which allowed all its members to pool their existing and future technologies on airframe design without royalty or patent payments, between 1917 and 1975 (Bitlingmayer, 1988).

Cross-licensing agreements are similar to mutual second sourcing agreements in that there is a mutual agreement to provide to all the participating firms specific proprietary technologies. However, in cross-licensing agreements, the value of each firm's technology that is to be shared is calculated, and they are exchanged on this basis between the firms involved. Royalties are only paid when the technology 'packets' that are exchanged are of unequal value. Cross-licensing is often undertaken among firms working on R&D in similar products, and because of the similarity of their work, they may tend to duplicate each other's innovations. By cross-licensing, they avoid the risk of patent infringement, which can be costly and difficult to resolve for all firms concerned.

CUSTOMER–SUPPLIER AGREEMENTS

Unlike the other two types of non-equity cooperative agreements discussed, customer–supplier agreements primarily represent vertical agreements between firms at different stages of the same value added chain. A majority of customer–supplier agreements involve relationships along a value added chain between a firm in one country and that in another (Dunning, 1993). Customer–supplier agreements may take many forms, including R&D contracts, licensing, management contracts and franchise agreements. Each of these involve varying degrees of cooperation between the participating firms. R&D contracts, licensing, management contracts and franchise agreements tend to involve a uni-directional flow of technology or assets, where the customer provides specifications of the kind of product it needs, and the supplier firm undertakes to meet this demand within the terms of the contract. The product supplied to the customer may be an intermediate good, management know-how, production technology or market information, and it may be sold outright to the customer, as in the case of an R&D contract, or it may be used by the customer for a specified time in a manner agreed upon by the parties involved, as is the case with most licensing and franchise agreements.

R&D contracts represent a means for one partner to subcontract particular research projects to another. Large firms often prefer to make an R&D contract with smaller, more specialised firms that have expertise in fields in which the large firm does not have sufficient resources to undertake in-house R&D. However, it is not always the case that R&D contracts are between small and large firms; they can also exist between two large firms in unrelated fields of technology, for instance chemicals and electronics.

Comakership agreements are similar to coproduction agreements, except that they establish long-term contracts between users and suppliers.

Licensing agreements are unilateral technology flows that involve the right to use technology that is proprietary to a particular firm (known as the licensor) under conditions agreed in a contract. The technology may be a trademark, product or process patent or equipment. The firm that acquires the licence (the licensee) is responsible for exploiting the technology, and its use is generally restricted by the licensor to prevent loss of its technology, as well as to prevent the licensee from competing with the licensor or other licensees. The restrictions often include controls on the manner in which the technology is used, including production methods, quality control and markets served. The licensee usually pays for the licence through a royalty payment based on the value or quantity of the output which utilises or embodies the technology. When the technology that is licensed is embodied in the employees of the licensor, such as specific management or engineering skills, it is often referred to as a *management contract*. In general, however, management contracts are associated with other forms of cooperative agreements, such as franchise or licensing agreements. Licensing agreements are generally undertaken in industries and technologies which are relatively mature, and for which property rights, such as patents and trademarks, are well defined and easily enforceable (Mowery, 1989).

Franchise agreements are similar to licensing agreements, but are generally associated with service sector industries, such as hotel and restaurants. Franchise agreements usually involve the transfer of a 'package' that includes management know-how, equipment, trademarks, and so on, all the components necessary for the franchisor to operate a duplicate of other franchisees. For instance, MacDonalds restaurants are generally franchises, in which MacDonalds provides the franchisee with the recipes for hamburgers, kitchen equipment, training facilities for managers, uniforms for employees and quality control guidelines, as well as specifying the prices of the items sold. Even more so than licensing agreements, the contractor has considerable control over the use made of the technology transferred.[15] MacDonalds retains the right to inspect the franchise facilities, and revoke the franchise agreement if its conditions are not met. The franchisee pays for the franchise through a lump sum payment and a royalty fee based on gross or net sales.

4.4 Trends in international cooperative agreements

The evidence on international cooperative agreements is considerably scattered and fragmentary, for several reasons. First, there are problems with data collection, because national governments and international agencies tend to monitor broad and historically more significant areas of international economic activity such as exports, imports and foreign direct investment. Even though several forms of cooperative ventures are equity-based, little systematic and detailed data is publicly available, with the possible exception of the United States. Secondly, it is difficult to identify the motives behind cooperative agreements, and especially to differentiate between agreements that are purely cost-economising and those that involve some strategic intent, since firms do not readily reveal their agenda to the public.

Much of the data on cooperative agreements has been collected by universities, research institutes and financial firms, and tend to rely on publicly available information, such as trade journals, newspapers, press releases and books. Given the limited resources of these organisations and the various purposes they are designed for, each of these databases tend to concentrate on particular sectors, regions, countries and specialities. Several of the databases are project-specific – that is, they are compiled for a specific task, and are no longer updated once the task is completed.

One of the difficulties associated with this fragmentation is that each organisation uses a somewhat different definition of inter-firm cooperative agreements. While some exclude equity agreements, others exclude customer–supplier agreements. However, while they are not strictly comparable, they all broadly illustrate the same general trends. One of the most complete databases on cooperative agreements is the Cooperative Agreements and Technology Indicators databank (CATI) of the

15. Although licensing agreements are often quite specific as to the use of the technology provided, because of the complex and disembodied nature of the technology provided, it is often more difficult to enforce them. In franchising agreements a complete package identical to that produced by other franchises is produced, and it is easier to assess whether the conditions are being complied with.

Maastricht Economic Research Institute on Innovation and Technology (MERIT) at the University of Limburg in the Netherlands. This databank provides information on nearly 5,000 technology-based cooperative agreements since 1980, and is continually being updated. Despite its focus on technology agreements, it is indicative of the overall trends associated with inter-firm cooperative agreements.

Traditionally, firms have preferred to undertake, wherever possible, much of their international value added activity through wholly owned or majority owned subsidiaries, rather than through arms-length transactions. Even when the use of wholly owned subsidiaries has not been possible, either because the assets that the firm needs have been internalised by another enterprise or because of government restrictions on wholly-owned subsidiaries, there has generally been a marked preference for undertaking equity-based cooperative agreements (such as joint ventures) over non-equity cooperative agreements. Another feature that has traditionally been associated with international cooperative agreements has been that these often took place between firms from industrialised countries and those from developing countries. Firms from developing countries have utilised cooperative agreements with industrialised country firms as a means to acquire technological and managerial know-how, preferably on a non-equity basis. Industrialised country firms, on the other hand, have preferred to use equity arrangements in their agreements with developing country firms, since this provides them with control over the use and dissemination of their know-how, while ensuring maximum benefits from it. Another important trend has been for MNCs to use cooperative agreements to achieve access to protected markets or essential natural resources. However, even where markets have been 'open', foreign firms may seek a local partner so as to overcome their lack of familiarity with local conditions. Such agreements were primarily of a cost-economising nature rather than being strategically motivated.

Since the beginning of the 1980s, there has been a marked shift in these trends. A large (and increasing) percentage of cooperative agreements are now being conducted between firms from the industrialised world. The decline in the share of cooperative agreements undertaken between industrialised country firms and developing country firms is due in part to the relaxation of the import-substituting policies of the developing countries, and a shift towards policies that allow majority ownership of firms by foreign-owned MNCs. Not surprisingly, agreements between firms from the industrialised world tend to be in sectors which are relatively technology intensive. Even more significant, while in the past agreements were geared towards accessing either markets for finished goods or necessary inputs for production, there has been a considerable growth of agreements to develop technology or engage in R&D or production, especially in new technologies that represent the cutting edge. Figure 4.2 illustrates the growth in the number of strategic technology agreements worldwide, based on the MERIT-CATI databank. Over the period 1980–89 as a whole, 41 per cent of all such agreements were in information technologies, 10 per cent were in new materials and 20 per cent in biotechnology. Agreements involving older and more mature technologies – such as automotive equipment, aviation, chemicals, instruments, food and beverages and electrical equipment – also grew in number over this period, increasing from 447 agreements during the 1980–84 period, to 710

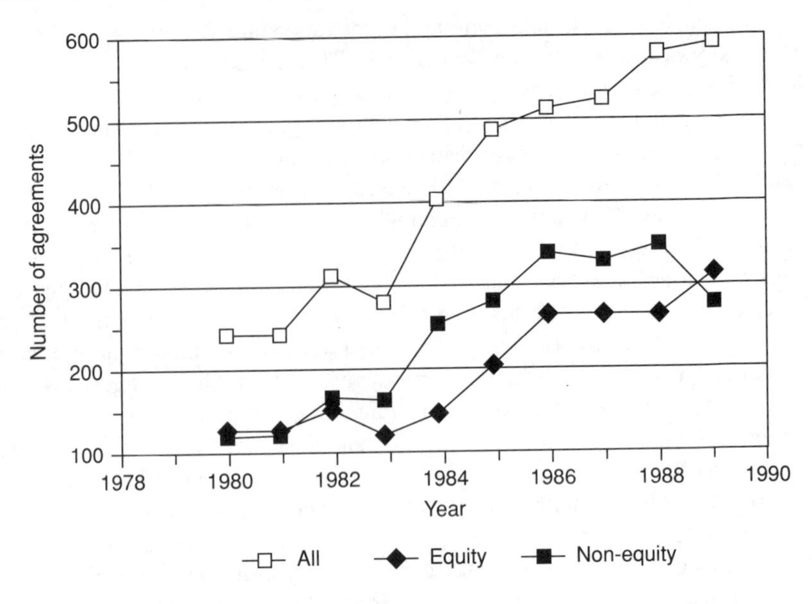

Figure 4.2 Growth of technology inter-firm cooperative agreements, 1980–89

Source: MERIT-CATI databank

between 1985–89, but in relative terms were dwarfed by the newer technology sectors, which accounted for 56 per cent of all alliances between 1980 and 1984, and over 73 per cent by the second half of the 1980s.

Figure 4.3 illustrates the regional distribution of technology agreements over the 1980s. Over 90 per cent of technology agreements are between firms within the Triad. Agreements involving US firms tend to dominate technology agreements: about two-thirds of all agreements between 1980 and 1989 in the CATI databank involve at least one US firm, while about a quarter of all agreements are between US firms. This domination is a result of several factors: the immense size of the US market, the traditional dominance of US MNCs in international commerce, and the competitive advantages of US firms, especially in biotechnology and in some information technology sectors. These factors are particularly exaggerated by the database used because of its focus on technology cooperative agreements. Nonetheless, the relatively low share of intra-European and intra-Japanese cooperative agreements would tend to indicate that US firms may have a higher propensity to engage in cooperative agreements. Preliminary analysis of more recent data suggests that this trend has continued, and that European and Japanese firms prefer to set up wholly owned subsidiaries or engage in arms-length transactions wherever possible.

An interesting feature in the new trend for cooperative agreements is that the use of non-equity alliances has become increasingly common, compared with the traditional inclination towards equity agreements (Figure 4.2). Figure 4.4 shows the distribution of all technology cooperative agreements by type between 1980 and 1989. Equity

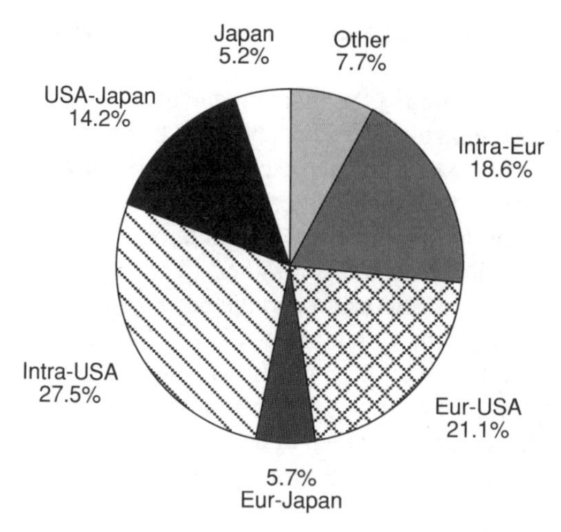

Figure 4.3 Distribution of inter-firm cooperative technology agreements by region, 1980–89.

Source: MERIT-CATI databank

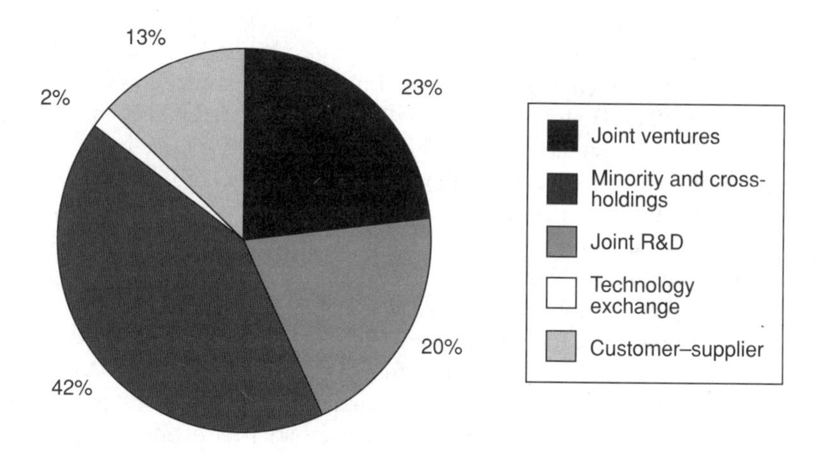

Figure 4.4 Distribution of inter-firm cooperative technology agreements by type, 1980–89.

Source: MERIT-CATI databank

agreements account for almost 43 per cent of all agreements. The most common form of equity agreements are equity joint ventures, which account for more than half of all equity agreements, while equity cross holdings are the least common, accounting for less than 1 per cent of the total.

4.5 Why do firms undertake inter-firm cooperative agreements?

The preceding section examined the main modes of international inter-firm agreements, and while illustrating the differences between them reference has been made to the most common scenarios under which each type of cooperative agreement is generally undertaken. Much of the existing literature on the internationalisation of firms is concentrated on explaining why firms prefer to internationalise their overseas operations through foreign direct investment rather than using the market mechanism. These arguments have been centred around the need for firms to circumvent market imperfections and market failure, and essentially emphasise that where the firm finds it more cost effective to use hierarchies rather than markets, they will engage in foreign direct investment, preferably using a 100 per cent owned affiliate.

Cooperative agreements are regarded as being the result of the inability of firms to internalise assets either because (a) they are owned by another firm (and are therefore firm-specific) (b) there are barriers to entry such as government restrictions on wholly owned subsidiaries (c) there are other cost-economising reasons, such as economies of scale or scope, which can be achieved by combining the assets of several firms, and not by a single firm. While this argument is fundamentally sound, it has two important limitations. First, it primarily emphasises the transaction cost economising argument, and does not pay sufficient attention to the strategic reasons for undertaking a cooperative venture. As explained earlier, an inter-firm cooperative agreement is one in which there is usually both a cost-economising intent as well as a strategic motivation that affects the long-term perspective of the companies involved. Second, it does not help in explaining why firms may prefer one form of cooperative venture over another. Both these issues will be discussed in this section, using once again the two extreme modalities of international business transactions, the wholly owned subsidiary and spot-market transactions, as the backdrop for understanding the motivation behind cooperative agreements.

What do we mean by a cost-economising motivation? When two firms make a transaction, there are certain costs involved with the transaction itself, such as the expenses incurred in negotiating the transaction, legal fees, costs of monitoring and enforcing the terms of the transaction. For instance, if the Dutch furniture company in the earlier example orders some plywood from a Canadian supplier, it must negotiate a price, and continually check whether the supplier is providing the type and quality of plywood that they have agreed upon. These costs are *transaction costs*. Firms also have *production costs* which are a function of several factors, such as the nature of its technology and its scale of operations. In a cost-economising scenario, a firm's decision regarding the manner in which it transacts with another firm is based on the criterion of minimising the sum of its production and transaction costs (Kogut, 1988). If the Dutch firm finds that the transaction costs associated with monitoring its spot transactions with the Canadian firm are high, such that the transaction costs of relying on a outside supplier are higher than the production savings that might occur if it has control over the Canadian supplier, it will seek to establish some form of agreement. A similar argument can also be made for horizontal agreement. If a computer firm X wishes to make use of a more efficient manufacturing technology that is proprietary to firm Y, it can make arrangements to license the technology. However, the transaction costs (which include the royalties) may outweigh the production cost savings associated with the use of the new technology, and firm X may then attempt to reduce the transactions costs by making an agreement with firm Y. It could also make an R&D contract with firm Z to develop a similar technology, if the costs of making an R&D contract was lower than the net present value of its future transaction costs.

A strategically motivated agreement is based on improving the competitive position of the firm relative to that of its competitors. Although one of the objectives of a firm is to maximise its profits – and it can be argued that by improving its competitive position *vis-à-vis* its competitors its profits should improve – this does not necessarily imply that it is maximising its profits, in the short run at least. For instance, if two firms make a cooperative agreement to block a large and more powerful competitor from gaining further market share, they may decide to have a mutual second sourcing agreement and agree on a lower price than they might otherwise have done. Therefore, in the short run they may experience lower profits than they might have made otherwise, but they gain some market share. If they are successful in gaining sufficient market share at the expence of their common competitor, the increase in sales volume may make up for the loss of profit margin in the long run. Strategically motivated agreements may be both offensive and defensive. If two firms make a horizontal agreement to protect their market from a large (and more cost-efficient) competitor, they may do so by mutually agreeing to lower their prices to gain market share, or exchanging technologies to become more efficient. Such an action would lower their profitability in the short run, but if they succeed in increasing their joint market share, there may be long-term benefits. If the firm participating in an agreement simply intends to maximise profits, a cost-economising motive is more likely to achieve this.

Most inter-firm cooperative agreements are both cost-economising as well as strategically motivated, and it is often difficult to distinguish between agreements which have no strategic motivation (and are therefore simply cost-economising inter-firm agreements) and those which have a strategic intent. For obvious reasons, companies do not make public all the motivations behind the agreements they engage in. Nevertheless, certain agreements such as customer–supplier agreements tend to be primarily cost-economising in nature, whereas equity and contractual joint production are generally more strategically motivated.

There are at least six overlapping reasons why firms engage in cooperative agreements. These are:

1. *Risk reduction*. Firms can reduce the risk (and uncertainty) associated with a project by spreading the risk among several firms through a cooperative agreement. A company wishing to enter into a foreign market in which it has no prior experience can face high risk, especially when the socio-political climate is unfamiliar. It can reduce its risk by cooperating with another firm which has prior experience in that market. Cooperative agreements to reduce risk can also be horizontal, where several firms may combine their resources to develop a new product. R&D costs for developing new products in industries such as pharmaceuticals, automobiles,

information technology and aircraft can be very high, deterring individual companies from undertaking projects, either because of the high cost of development, or because of the long payback period to recover their capital investment. Development costs of a new aircraft, for instance, can run to several billion dollars, and it may take more than 10 years to recover the initial investment, if the product is successful. The Boeing 767 was designed and developed by Boeing, Aeritalia and a Japanese consortium, and although it has been in production since 1983, in 1994 it had yet to make a profit. Sometimes, where the risks of development are too high, even for a cooperative agreement between large firms, governments supply some of the financing. Very often, horizontal alliances are between firms with unequal technological expertise, not only to share the financial risks involved in a large project, but also to divide a project to take advantage of complementary technologies associated with each of the partners.

2. *Reducing innovation time span.* The product life cycle of certain technologies such as in the information technology and consumer electronics industry is considerably short – within one or two years of the introduction of a new product, lower cost imitators enter the market, destroying the profit margins of the initial innovator, and preventing it from recovering from the high costs of developing the product. Imitators develop similar but sufficiently different products, making patent protection ineffective. Cooperative agreements between several competing firms to develop products jointly can significantly reduce the time and cost it takes to develop a new innovation, thereby allowing either imitating firms to compete with the initial inventor, or allowing the initial inventor to develop the next generation of the product faster.
3. *Access to markets.* This can be facilitated by cooperative agreements in three ways.
   (a) Firms with limited international experience are often hesitant to engage in overseas production activities, and may prefer to use an equity joint venture so as to acquire the benefit of another firm's experience in – and knowledge of – the market. This is typically the case where the culture and socio-political environment of the host country are very different from that of the home country. As the firm develops its expertise in that market, it may later decide to acquire its partner firm, or set up its own operations. The use of cooperative agreements to internationalise operations allows a firm to develop its international competitive presence at a significantly faster rate than if it tried to do so independently. Quick access to overseas markets may be important, especially where the product life cycle is short.
   (b) There may be government mandated restrictions on wholly owned subsidiaries in foreign countries. Japan, for instance, actively discouraged wholly owned subsidiaries of MNCs in the 1950s and 1960s, insisting that domestic firms use non-equity agreements such as licensing, or equity agreements such as minority holdings to acquire technology, and at the same time limiting the participation of foreign firms through majority or wholly owned subsidiaries (Dunning and Narula 1994). Government policy may restrict entry in some or all sectors, except where the foreign firm undertakes an alliance with a local firm. This practice is widespread among developing countries, which wish to

protect weak domestic sectors from being overwhelmed by strong foreign competition. Generally speaking, firms from industrialised countries possess more efficient technologies, and by encouraging cooperative agreements, governments can help domestic firms acquire some of these technologies, thereby making them more able to compete on an international basis. The alliance between McDonnell Douglas and China's Shanghai Aircraft Industrial Corporation is such an alliance, with McDonnell Douglas providing the bulk of the technology, and the Chinese partner providing the access to the large Chinese market. The agreement requires that Chinese scientists and engineers work with the American company on new aircraft design (Hladik, 1988).

(c) Cooperative agreements can be used as a means to enter a new *product* market. In other words, a firm can expand into a new or related industrial sector, but avoid the high cost of entry in two ways. It can either do so by collaborating with another firm that is already in that new sector or by cooperating with another firm that also wishes to enter the new sector, and whose technological capability is complementary to its own; in this case, the combination of their technologies can provide them with a competitive advantage in the new market.

4. *Access to technology.* By engaging in a cooperative venture, partner firms avail themselves of technological expertise which would be too expensive and time-consuming to develop independently. By doing so, the participating firms can continue specialising in the areas in which they have a competitive advantage, and avoid the costly process of developing an expertise in a field in which they have weak competitive advantage. Companies usually have limited resources, and by concentrating on a few areas of specialisation, their resources can be utilised more efficiently. These agreements can be unilateral, as is the case with customer–supplier agreements, or multilateral, such as in technology exchange agreements. Such agreements can be between firms with complementary technologies, vertically along the same value added chain, or horizontally between firms with similar assets.
5. *Economies of scale and production rationalisation.* Cooperative agreements can lead to product rationalisation. If two firms producing a similar product combine their production activities together, a reduction in the average cost per unit may be realised, because higher production volumes in a single plant may result in economies of scale. A firm that undertakes product rationalisation will seek to locate the production of its various components to take advantage of the locations with the highest comparative advantage, thereby lowering its overall cost of production. A car manufacturer that undertakes to rationalise production would locate its glass manufacturing facility wherever the comparative advantage of glass production is lowest (say, Morocco), and its axle production wherever the comparative advantage of axle production is lowest (say, Taiwan), and so on. The traditional approach would be to produce all the components in or around one location, where the final assembly would be done. Product rationalisation also leads to benefits associated with economies of scale; because the car company would now produce all its axles

for all its models in the same location, it would have a higher volume requirement, and therefore even lower costs. Unfortunately, the cost of setting up in so many different locations may be prohibitively expensive, a problem tackled by setting up cooperative agreements with other firms, most often through an equity agreement. In fact, this motive is almost always associated with the establishment of joint ventures.

6. *Co-opting or blocking competition.* Cooperative agreements are very often used as a means to co-opt competitors by making agreements with them, or to block competition by teaming up with one or more competitors to form a united front against a particular firm. For example, the agreement between Philips and Matsushita, aimed at sharing technology on digital audio tapes, is an attempt to prevent Sony from making minidisc technology the standard in the music industry. Not coincidentally, such agreements also allow the cooperating firms to acquire each other's technological secrets, and eventually to compete more successfully with each other after the demise of the partnership. When such cooperative agreements involve firms with large (and dominant) shares of the market, they may also try to set artificially high prices by establishing a cartel. While such arrangements are generally illegal, they are often hard to monitor when firms from different countries are involved. The Organisation of Petroleum Exporting Countries (OPEC) is an example of such a cartel between the major oil exporting countries which was very successful in raising the price of petroleum during the mid-1970s.

It is important to re-emphasise that several motives can underlie any particular cooperative agreement, and that participating firms do not necessarily have the same motives for undertaking a cooperative agreement; some of these motives may be more strategic, while others are more cost-economising. Furthermore, certain motives are associated with particular types of cooperative agreements, for instance, when the primary motive is to overcome government regulations on foreign ownership in order to achieve market access, a joint venture is the preferred mode.

Table 4.2 shows the motives for technology-based cooperative agreements. Although the results given in the first column are across all industries and sectors, some variation is expected to be covered up by such a broad generalisation. First, the motives for undertaking any particular agreement may be different for different groups of firms, depending upon their relative bargaining power, size and other characteristics. Secondly, it is to be expected that there will be some variation of motives between industries, depending upon the nature of the industry, which includes such factors as its R&D intensity, the effectiveness of patents, the degree of competition, and the market structure.

The last two columns of Table 4.2 show the motives for two sectors which differ considerably in nature. The Food and Beverage sector is a mature, low R&D intensive sector, which is marked by a very competitive market structure, whereas the Biotechnology sector is a new, highly R&D intensive sector dominated by relatively few firms. These two sectors reveal considerably different results, highlighting the fact that there are considerable inter-industry differences in motivations behind cooperative agreements. The most important motive for Food was co-opting and

Table 4.2 Motives for inter-firm cooperative technology agreements, 1980–89

Motive	All Sectors	Food and Beverage	Biotechnology
Risk reduction	10%	1%	14%
Access to markets	11%	7%	15%
Access to technology	36%	17%	45%
Reducing innovation time span	28%	10%	31%
Co-opting and blocking competition	32%	43%	13%

Notes:
1. The total of motives do not add up to 100% because each agreement may have more than one motive.
2. The fifth motive described, economies of scale and product rationalisation, is primarily associated with joint venture activity, and is therefore not included.

Source: MERIT-CATI databank

blocking competition, with 43 per cent, compared with the Biotechnology score of 13 per cent, while the most important motive in the Biotechnology industry was access to technology with 45 per cent, compared with the Food and Beverage score of 17 per cent.

4.6 Causes of growth in inter-firm cooperative agreements

Although the evidence on international inter-firm cooperative agreements is fragmented, the general picture is unambiguous. It is important to ask why these agreements have begun to play an increasingly significant role, especially among firms from within the Triad. Gugler and Dunning (1992) suggest there are three main reasons behind this trend, which are associated with the changing technological and economic environment that firms are faced with: technological innovation, the convergence of technologies, and globalisation.

Since the mid-1970s, there has been a shift in the process of technological innovation. Technological innovation has become increasingly capital intensive, requiring very large investments to develop new ideas and make them commercially exploitable. This is true not only for new areas of technology such as new materials, information technology and biotechnology, but also for more mature sectors such as pharmaceuticals, automobiles and aerospace. Not only are the costs of R&D very high, but there is considerable uncertainty involved in whether the product will be commercially feasible, especially when the innovation is a radical one and there is little or no existing demand for the product. However, it is not just the invention of a new product or process that can be costly: once an innovation is made, the innovator must commercialise the product, and capture a large market share before it is imitated or a better product is created by a competitor. This is made even more difficult by the fact that new products are faced with increasingly shorter product life cycles, making it essential for the innovating firm to recoup its high R&D costs in a relatively short time, before its competitive advantage is eroded. Developing a new car or computer can cost anywhere from half a billion dollars or more and provide a firm with a competitive advantage of less than one or two years before a competitor develops a similar or better product. The use of property right protection such as trademarks and patents does not act as a guarantee against loss of competitive advantage, especially in complex technologies, where legal action against imitators is often difficult and expensive. It is not always possible to sell the product at a price which would defray its cost of innovation in a short time, since relatively few customers would be able to afford it: the firm also has to maximise its market share and set industry standards, and therefore cannot use monopoly pricing even if it dominates the market. For instance, Intel initially charged $900 for its new Pentium microprocessor, but within a year of its release the PowerPC developed jointly by Motorola, IBM and Apple began to compete with it, forcing Intel to lower its price to $450.

Industrial sectors are becoming increasingly interdependent, and new products often require the combination of innovations in a wide range of disciplines. This is true not just within related technological sectors such as consumer electronics and information technology, but also between technological sectors hitherto regarded as separate disciplines. For instance, automobiles require not just expertise in mechanical engineering, but utilise a considerable amount of microelectronics and are one of the largest potential consumers of new materials such as ceramics. Cooperative agreements allow different technologies to be utilised by a manufacturer at the same time, which, if all the technologies involved were developed by the firm independently, would make the costs of developing products much higher. The world's largest robot manufacturer, GMF, is a joint venture between the world's largest automobile manufacturer, General Motors and Fanuc, a spin-off from Fujitsu. Such cooperative agreements allow each company to specialise in the core area in which it has a competitive advantage, and at the same time create opportunities for synergistic technologies to be developed. In the case of GMF, for example, GM was able to concentrate on automobile design and manufacturing, and Fanuc was provided with a large customer, as well as a collaborator to design new robots for automobile production.

There are two ways in which globalisation has influenced the growth of international cooperative agreements. First, firms from countries in the triad have become increasingly similar in the kinds of technology and competitive advantages they possess. Technological innovation used to be dominated by large MNCs, primarily from the United States. Over the two decades since the mid-1970s, European and Japanese MNCs have been able to catch up technologically with US firms, and now are able to compete directly with them. They can now contribute as equals in international cooperative agreements, and in many instances they have superior technologies to the US firms which used to dominate. Most, if not all, of these firms have international production facilities, and thus can compete directly with each other, creating a global marketplace. One of the effects of this is that there is a greater number of competitors with similar products competing directly, thereby increasing the pressure on individual firms to maximise their market share as well as to continually develop new products. Needless to say, this development increases the scope for firms to engage in cooperative agreements as a way to minimise the risks and costs of maintaining or improving their competitive advantages.

Second, there has been an increasing homogeneity in consumer needs and preferences among the countries of the Triad as markets become global. This has encouraged firms to collaborate in order to develop worldwide standards. For instance, Philips and CSF-Thomson are collaborating to develop and establish a new European standard for high-definition television. Even where industry standards are not an issue, cooperative agreements become necessary in order to enter as many new markets as possible both to spread the costs of innovation and to defend existing markets.

4.7 The instability of cooperative agreements

Inter-firm cooperative agreements provide an alternative to the use of spot-transaction and majority owned subsidiaries, and provide unique opportunities to share the assets and capabilities of several partners. Most cooperative agreements tend to have a limited lifetime, and although non-equity type cooperative agreements are often designed for a specific project or task to be achieved within a specific time frame, some estimates suggest that the failure rate of all cooperative agreements may be as high as 70 per cent (*Business Week*, 1986). While some types of cooperative agreements have a natural lifetime which may be just a few years, premature termination of an agreement is quite common. In a study of 895 cooperative agreements, Harrigan (1988) found that only 45 per cent of the agreements studied were judged to be successful by all the participants. Of the successful agreements, 50 per cent lasted less than four years. Even if there is no predetermined objective or time frame, as is the case with most equity agreements, the cooperative agreement may be concluded either by one of the participants acquiring the majority control over the joint venture, or by one of the partners acquiring majority control over the other. Such an event is often implicit when a large firm takes a minority holding in a small start-up firm, as indicated in the earlier discussion. In such a case, because the participating firms are of unequal size and hence have unbalanced bargaining power, the small firm may not have a choice, even if it were unwilling to be acquired. As Harrigan (1988) points out, successful agreements are not necessarily indicated by long-lived agreements. However, it is important to realise that agreements which are prematurely terminated are not necessarily mutually unsuccessful; one partner may achieve some or all of its motives, and an often implicit (but secondary) motive may be to frustrate the other partner's objectives. Some of the main reasons why one or more of the participating firms may terminate an agreement prematurely are presented below.

1. *Unfulfilled expectations.* One of the major causes of cooperative agreement failure is that one or more partners find that the agreement does not fulfil their expectations. This can be for several reasons. First, because one firm may not trust the other(s), and provides only the minimum amount of resources to the agreement, to

prevent loss of proprietary technology. Such a situation would result in relatively little cooperation, thus frustrating the possible synergies that might otherwise have resulted from the agreement. Second, one or more participating firms may have expected quicker, larger or more significant benefits than actually accrued from the agreement. This is particularly common in cooperative agreements geared towards the development of new technologies, where practical applications of the research may take longer than the partners may have anticipated, leading one of the partners to decide that it cannot continue to invest resources in the project.

2. *Lack of trust and asymmetric learning*. This may occur because one of the firms in an agreement feels that it is contributing more than its share to the agreement, or that the other partner is contributing too little. The over-contributing firm may feel that, by continuing the agreement, the partner may acquire all of its competitive assets and may then start to compete directly with it. However, the imbalance in the agreement may not be noticed until it is too late, and the over-contributing partner discovers that it has lost its competitive advantage to the partner. Even if there is no multilateral flow of technology, such as in unidirectional cooperative licensing agreements, the licensee may be able to utilise the technology to develop its own version of the technology and compete with the licensor. For instance, Intel had licensed the technology of its earlier microprocessor designs to several firms including Cyrix and AMD in an effort to make them the industry standard, but these firms have now developed their own versions of processors which compete directly with those of Intel.
3. *Incompatibility*. Another major reason for cooperative agreement failure is that the partners may be incompatible. For example, they may have different business cultures, making it exceedingly difficult for the two organisations to work together. When IBM acquired a minority holding in Rolm, a telecommunications manufacturer, it had hoped to develop new applications for its computers and acquire technological expertise in a new area. However, Rolm was a small company with a relaxed, informal business culture and IBM tried unsuccessfully to impose its own style of management on it. Less than three years later, IBM sold its share in Rolm to Siemens.
4. *The division of control and responsibilities*. In the case of a cooperative agreement between two firms, there is often a conflict based on each firm's desire to control the use of its resources, and in cases of a joint venture or joint R&D agreement, further conflict arises from identifying who has control over the mutually owned assets. A firm participating in a cooperative agreement will try to coordinate the activities of the cooperative agreement within the scope of its other activities and, because the character of the cooperative agreement generally reflects both partners, making the agreement fit the bureaucratic nature of both organisations will cause considerable friction. Both partners may want to ensure, for example, that the jointly developed product conforms to their own product lines, and to avoid developing a product that competes or takes away market share from its existing products (Hladik, 1988). This is especially common among agreements where the partners have had no prior experience with cooperative agreements or when they have used majority control over their previous international activities.

5. *Government policies and regulations.* Governments can put legal barriers on certain types of agreements. This can be for a number of reasons, but most commonly it is to protect domestic infant-industries from foreign competition. Most of these limitations are associated with equity-type agreements – most countries place limits on foreign ownership of equity in particular industries. This is not just associated with developing countries – to a lesser extent, the industrialised countries also restrict foreign ownership. For instance, the United States restricts foreign ownership of equity in the defence industry. Even where there are no legal barriers, governments can 'discourage' joint ventures or other cooperative agreements by withholding subsidies or contracts from the domestic partner, or setting up complex bureaucratic procedures for approval.

   Another important government policy influencing cooperative agreements is the use of antitrust or antimonopoly laws, which discourage a few firms from dominating the market either through collusion to fix prices or through offensive action to eliminate other competitors. Such restrictions, however, are generally not applied to R&D agreements, provided the cooperative agreement is limited to the precompetitive phase.

Bibliography

References

Bitlingmayer, G. (1988) 'Property rights, progress, and the Aircraft Patent Agreement', *Journal of Law and Economics,* vol. 31, pp. 227–48.

Business Week (1986) 'Corporate odd couples: beware of the wrong partner', 21 July, pp. 98–103.

Dunning, J.H. (1993) *Multinational Enterprises and the Global Economy*, Addison Wesley.

Dunning, J.H. and **Narula, R.** (1994) 'Transpacific direct investment and the investment development path: the record assessed', *Essays in International Business*, March.

Economist (1994) 'Uncle Sam's helping hand', 2 April, pp. 91–93.

Gugler, P. and **Dunning, J.H.** (1992) 'Technology-based cross-border alliances', *Rutgers Graduate School of Management Working Paper Series 92-03*, Rutgers University, Newark.

Hagedoorn, J. (1990) 'Organizational modes of inter-firm cooperation and technology transfer', *Technovation*, vol. 10, no. 1, pp. 17–30.

Hagedoorn, J. (1993a) 'Understanding the rationale of strategic technology partnering: interorganizational modes of cooperation and sectoral differences', *Strategic Management Journal,* vol. 14, pp. 371–385.

Hagedoorn, J. and **Schakenraad, J.** (1990) 'Strategic partnering and technological cooperation', in B. Dankbaar, J. Groenewegen and H. Schenk (eds) *Perspectives in Industrial Economics*, Kluwer.

Harrigan, K. (1988) 'Strategic alliances and partner asymmetries', in F. Contractor and P. Lorange (eds) *Cooperative Strategies in International Business*, Lexington Books.

Hladik, K. (1988) 'R&D and international joint ventures', in F. Contractor and P. Lorange (eds) *Cooperative strategies in International Business,* Lexington Books.

Kogut, B. (1988) 'Joint ventures: theoretical and empirical perspectives', *Strategic Management Journal*, vol. 9, pp. 319–32.

Mowery, D. (1989) 'Collaborative ventures between US and foreign manufacturing firms', *Research Policy,* vol. 18, No. 1, pp. 19–32.

Porter, M. (1980) *Competitive Strategy*, The Free Press.
Porter, M. (1985) *Competitive Advantage*, The Free Press.
Prahalad, C. and **Hamel, G.** (1990) 'The core competence and the corporation', *Harvard Business Review*, May–June, pp. 71–91.

Further reading

Cainarca, G., Colombo, M. and **Mariotti, S.** (1992) 'Agreements between firms and the technological life cycle model: evidence from information technologies', *Research Policy*, vol 21, no. 1, pp. 45–62.
Contractor, F. and **Lorange, P.** (1988) 'Why should firms cooperate? The strategy and economic basis for cooperative ventures', in F. Contractor and P. Lorange (eds) *Cooperative Strategies in International Business*, Lexington Books.
Ghemawat, P., Porter, M. and **Rawlinson, R.** (1986) 'Patterns of international coalition activity', in M.E. Porter (ed.) *Competition in Global Industries*, Harvard Business School Press.
Hagedoorn, J. (1993b), 'Strategic technology alliances and modes of cooperation in high technology industries', in G. Grabher (ed.) *The Embedded Firm*, Routledge.
Hamel, G. (1991) 'Competition for competence and inter-partner learning within international strategic alliances', *Strategic Management Journal*, vol. 12, pp. 83–103.
Mowery, D. (1992) 'International collaborative ventures and US firms' technology strategies', in O. Granstand, L. Hakanson and S. Sjolander (eds) *Internationalisation of R&D and Technology*, John Wiley.

5 Trade in services

5.1 Introduction

Services are playing an increasingly important role in the economies of all industrialised and most developing countries. Services account for about 60 to 70 per cent of GDP and employment in OECD countries and represent about 20 per cent of world trade, and almost 50 per cent of annual flows of foreign direct investment (Hoekman and Sauvé, 1993, p. 2). In 1992, international trade in commercial services amounted to US $1,000 billion (some 22 per cent of world trade; GATT, 1993, p. 1).

The main exporters in services are the United States, France, Italy, Germany, United Kingdom and Japan, which together accounted for 50 per cent of world exports of services in 1992; the same countries are also the main importers, representing together more than 50 per cent of world imports of services (GATT, 1993, p. 5).

Given the considerable importance of services in the world economy as well as in international economic relations, services have become an increasingly important issue in international economic policy (Gaudard, 1989). For the first time in the history of GATT, services have been negotiated under the auspices of the GATT in the context of the Uruguay Round (see also Section 5.2.3). Furthermore, in the recent negotiations on regional agreements – which used to concentrate on goods – the attention to the liberalisation of international transactions in services has been prominent (e.g. Canada–USA Free Trade Agreement, NAFTA, EC-1992, EEA, Australia–New Zealand Closer Economic Relation trade agreement, etc.).

In this chapter, attention will be paid to the specificities of trade in services, and the recent progress towards liberalising international trade in services in the GATT framework (Section 5.2), followed by a characterisation of the main service sectors and their recent developments: banking (Section 5.3), insurance (Section 5.4), telecommunications (Section 5.5), transport services (Section 5.6), and other service sectors playing an important role for economic growth (Section 5.7). In this way, an overview is given of recent developments in the internationalisation of the various service sectors.

5.2 Specificities of trade in services

5.2.1 *Nature of trade in services*

Most of the theoretical and conceptual interest in international trade in services dates back no further than the 1970s. Before then services were commonly considered as typical *non-traded* activities, involving production for the domestic market, and by domestic factors only (Ruane, 1990, p. 3). In a similar vein, many economists (such as Hill, 1977) defined services as necessarily involving consumption and production in the same location, thereby defining away the possibility of an internationally tradeable service product. However, more recently economists have increasingly extended Hill's definition. Service trade is now commonly considered as involving the international movement of factors of production, products and consumers.

Defining trade in services involves defining both *services* and *trade*. Defining the services concept is a rather difficult task. Some definitions are based upon characteristics such as tangibility, visibility, portability and storability to mark the dividing line between goods and services. Some definitions are based on standard statistical sectoral disaggregation and simply describe services as activities other than agriculture, mining and manufacturing. Still other definitions are based on an exhaustive list of activities which can be considered as services. In the latter tradition, services will here be simply defined as categories of intangible goods, including (but not limited to): business services (e.g. professional services, computer and related services, research and development services, real estate services, rental/leasing services); communication services (e.g. postal services, courier services, telecommunication services, audiovisual services); construction services; distribution services (e.g. commission agents' services, wholesale trade services, retail trade services, franchising); educational services; environmental services; financial services (e.g. banking, insurance); health-related and social services; tourism and travel-related services; recreational, cultural and sporting services; and transport services (e.g. maritime transport services, air transport services, and road transport services).

As far as international trade is concerned, there are significant differences between trade in services and trade in commodities. For example, while international trade in commodities involves either product or factor trade, international trade in services may involve both channels. In this respect, it may be interesting to note that evidence suggests that, although the quality aspect and the variety of services vary more than those of goods, the demand for services, for example, between consumers from different countries at a given level of income, is likely to be less heterogeneous. This helps to explain the current trend toward the globalisation of some services, such as investment banking, insurance, hotels, advertising and airlines (Dunning, 1989, p. 8).

In Box 5.1 the four modes of international delivery of services have been distinguished.

5.2.2 *Obstacles to trade in services*

Services providers are facing various obstacles with regard to international trade in services. This may help to explain why services account for about 60 per cent of GDP in most developed countries, but for only about 20 per cent of world trade.

Box 5.1: Modes of delivery of services

Cross-border trade: the service is supplied through telecommunications, mail and services embodied in goods (e.g. a computer diskette) and does not imply any movement of factors of production.
Consumption abroad: trade in services can also take place through the supply of a service in the territory of one country to a consumer of another (e.g. tourism, ships repaired abroad).
Commercial presence abroad: due to the limited tradeability of many services, foreign direct investment is one of the main vehicles for the delivery of services abroad.
Movement of natural persons: the service providers (natural persons who are themselves service suppliers, as well as natural persons who are employees of service suppliers) move across the border in order to provide a service (e.g. management consulting specialists, medical specialists, etc.).

Barriers to trade in services may affect not only the use of the modes of supply but also the decision as to which mode of supply to use. Some examples may serve to illustrate how barriers to trade may affect the modes of supply. For example, common barriers to cross-border trade include residency requirements and commercial presence requirements. Impediments to movement of consumers are often linked to cultural barriers or exchange transaction restrictions. Examples of measures affecting commercial presence are: the participation of foreign equity ownership, the juridical forms allowed, and the regulations on activities performed by foreign entities established in the country. Barriers to movement of personnel are linked to immigration laws and international differences in the recognition of diplomas, and so on.

In addition to any service transaction, an economic agent's preference in deciding between these modes of delivery will obviously depend on the feasibility and relative costs of employing alternative modes of delivery.

Regulatory impediments are in general important barriers to international trade in services. However, a substantial reduction in regulatory impediments may not necessarily lead to a significant increase in the internationalisation of service markets due, for example, to the dominating impact of the remaining cultural and linguistic differences and the transaction costs involved.

Several impediments to trade in services may be distinguished: (a) quantity-based measures (quantitative restrictions such as needs tests); (b) price-based measures (implying a tax on foreign suppliers); (c) measures that require physical or corporate presence in a market in order to supply a service; (d) measures relating to standards; and (e) measures relating to government procurements and subsidisation (Hoekman and Sauvé, 1993, p.7). These barriers may be classified in the following four groups:

- *quantitative non-discriminatory barriers* which restrict market access irrespective of whether suppliers are domestic or foreign (e.g. via concessions, quotas, needs tests, etc.);
- *quantitative discriminatory measures* such as limitations on the number of foreign service providers;
- *qualitative non-discriminatory measures* such as quality or security standards or specific requirements related to professional knowledge and experience;
- *qualitative discriminatory measures* such as nationality conditions or requirements relating to diplomas in order to be entitled to provide a service.

There seems to be some confusion and uncertainty about how and to what extent liberalisation of trade in services can be achieved, due *inter alia* to the complexity of services (many kinds of sectors, several modes of delivery, obstacles due to an internal regulation). However, as one increasingly recognises that liberalisation of trade in services promotes economic growth and competitiveness of nations, several procedures have been followed, either unilaterally, bilaterally, or multilaterally to achieve this liberalisation. Because multilateral liberalisation of trade in services has become an increasingly important issue, it will be the focus of the next sub-section.

5.2.3 *Multilateral liberalisation of trade in services*

In the eighth GATT round of multilateral negotiations – launched in Punta del Este in September 1986 and finalised on 15 December 1993 – for the first time, liberalisation of trade in services was formally placed on the multilateral negotiating agenda. This was to achieve a General Agreement on Trade in Services (GATS), which is an integral part of the Uruguay Round's results (signed in Marrakesh by more than 120 countries on 15 April 1994). Indeed, the GATS will be one of the three pillars on which the newly established World Trade Organisation (WTO) is founded, along with the existing GATT for trade in goods and the Agreement on Trade-related Aspects of Intellectual Property Rights (TRIPs), which is also new.

GATS covers the universe of services and applies to all measures affecting trade in services. The Agreement[16] contains three elements: a framework of general rules and disciplines, national schedules of initial commitments, and annexes addressing special considerations relating to some service sectors/modes of delivery. These elements will be highlighted in this order.

GENERAL RULES AND DISCIPLINES

General obligations are formulated in Parts I and II of the framework; they aim at achieving progressively higher levels of liberalisation of trade in services, and at

16. See 'Final Act embodying the results of the Uruguay Round of Multilateral Trade Negotiations', GATT Secretariat, MTM/FA, 13–12–1993. The Final Act also contains Ministerial Decisions or provisions with regards to negotiation on basic telecommunications, maritime transport, labour mobility and financial services which will be held during the following months for a period of time indicated in each of these decisions or provisions.

providing more predictability and stability in this type of trade. The most important articles are:

Art. II (most-favoured-nation treatment); this requires that every GATS Member (hereafter 'Member') shall accord to services and service suppliers of any other Member, treatment no less favourable than that it accords to like services and service suppliers of any other country;
Art. III (transparency) which requires that all laws and regulations should be made public and easily accessible to all service providers;
Art. IV (increasing participation of developing countries) which provides for flexibility in the initial application of rules in order to permit developing countries time to assume obligations;
Art. V (economic integration) which allows economic integration under certain conditions;
Art. VI (domestic regulations) which indicates that in sectors where commitments are undertaken, each Member shall ensure that all measures affecting trade in services are administered in a reasonable, objective and impartial manner;
Art. VII (recognition of licences and certifications) which allows for the establishment of procedures for the recognition of licenses, education and experience granted by a specific Party.

NATIONAL SCHEDULES OF SPECIFIC COMMITMENTS

Part III of the framework contains three articles, Art. XVI–XVIII, dealing with market access, national treatment and additional commitments, respectively. These articles apply only to the services sectors and sub-sectors where commitments on market access and national treatment have been undertaken by Members individually, and which are therefore included in the schedule of the Member concerned. Such a schedule of commitments is required for each Member which is intending to sign the GATS; it will bind Members to ensure that national regulatory regimes are consistent with the schedules in regards to the sectors/sub-sectors to which they apply.

THE ANNEXES

The Agreement has eight annexes which may be divided into three categories: first, an annex on MFN (most favoured nation) exemption (enabling a member to add exemption to Art. II prior to the entry into force of the Agreement); second, annexes covering specific sectors or modes of delivery (air transport, financial services, telecommunications, movement of natural persons supplying services under the Agreement); third, annexes providing the modalities for continuation of negotiations on financial services, basic telecommunication services and maritime transport services.

According to the GATS, a Member shall not apply a regime more restrictive than the regime inscribed in the national schedule without being required to grant compensation. The content of national schedules at the conclusion of the Uruguay Round will therefore represent an effective initial stage of multilateral liberalisation of trade in services. However, according to GATS Art. XIX (progressive liberalisation), liberalisation of services is meant to continue under the auspices of future negotiations: existing barriers to services trade should be reduced, a process of ongoing liberalisation should be established and no new barriers erected.

One should underline that forums other than GATS are also dealing with the liberalisation of international trade in services, such as is reflected in the OECD Codes for capital movement and for invisible operations, or in liberalisation programmes in regional trade agreements (e.g. EC-1992, NAFTA) and in specific bilateral agreements (e.g. Swiss-EC Agreements on non-life insurance and on road transport transit).

5.3 Banking

Banking involves interaction with a broad range of economic activities and agents through its role in credit, monetary and payments systems. Banks also have close relationships with public policy, and their operations are strongly influenced by the regulatory environment of the economy.

Banks' international activities have been expanding at an extraordinarily fast pace since the beginning of the 1960s, and have become a major component of overall banking activity in many countries. The changes affecting competition in financial markets have increased considerably since the mid-1970s, under the pressure of an accelerating and self-reinforcing process of technological innovation, domestic deregulation and international liberalisation. No undisputed comprehensive measure of international banking activity is available, but proxies and indicators suggest that banks' international activities may have advanced at an average annual rate of some 25–30 per cent since the 1960s (OECD, 1983, p. 16). Indeed, the volume of international financial transactions has increased tremendously since the mid-1960s, and trade in financial services is assumed to be among the most dynamic components of world trade in services (Hoekman and Sauvé, 1991, p. 2).

International trade in banking services encompasses six broad product categories (Walter, 1988, pp.16–20):

1. Deposit taking in onshore markets abroad and in offshore markets (demand and time deposits of residents and nonresidents in foreign onshore accounts as well as Euro-deposits in offshore accounts).
2. International trading and dealing (*inter alia* in foreign currencies, deposits, financial futures and options).
3. Traditional international trade and cash management services, which encompasses international documentary collections, letters of credit, and acceptance financing.
4. International lending, which encompasses loans to local corporations, banks, governments and individuals not domiciled in the bank's home country (either in local or foreign currencies).
5. International securities business, which involves underwriting and trading or dealing in domestic and international securities issues as well as futures, options and equity shares.

Table 5.1 Deposit banks' cross-border claims (US$ bn)

Country	1980	1989	1993
UK	356	924	1,053
Japan	66	842	919
US	204	658	543
France	148	359	515
Switzerland	137	356	359
Hong Kong	38	355	446
Netherlands	63	146	173
Italy	32	84	113
Spain	n.a.	54	117
Canada	25	49	43
Sweden	9	38	26
Denmark	5	36	45
World total	1,823	6,585	6,465

Source: Hoekman and Sauvé, 1991; Bank for International Settlement, 1994.

6. Other merchant-banking activities, including international mergers and acquisitions, interest-rate and currency swaps, parallel loans and private placements.

Table 5.1 reflects the total value of foreign assets held by deposit banks (such as commercial banks) in the major exporting countries at the end of 1980, 1989, and 1993. Cross-border claims of deposit banks grew at around 14 per cent per year during the 1980s whereas world merchandise trade increased at an average annual rate of only 4.5 per cent during the same period, and that of services trade at a rate of 6.5 per cent (Hoekman and Sauvé, 1991, p. 5). The share of inter-bank claims in total cross-border claims is very high for most countries, frequently accounting for two-thirds to three-quarters of the total.

5.4 Insurance

The insurance industry is indispensable for the functioning of modern economies. It is one of the largest industries in the world with premiums for most developed countries equivalent to about 5 per cent of GNP. The main markets are concentrated in North America, Europe, and Asia (Table 5.2).

The insurance industry is composed of:

- enterprises (insurers and reinsurers) that act as professional risk-bearer in providing insurance services;
- intermediaries who act as agents of the buyers of insurance and reinsurance services;
- suppliers of other services associated with insurance (such as legal services, risk management consultants, etc.).

Table 5.2 Distribution of world's total insurance premiums (1990)

Continent	Total premiums (US$ mln)	Total premiums (as % of total)
North America	513,937	37.9
Latin America	9,428	0.7
Europe	459,998	33.9
Asia	334,035	24.6
Africa	14,387	1.1
Oceania	23,944	1.8

Source: Schweizerische Rückversicherung-Gesellschaft, *Sigma*, March 1992

Insurance business can be sub-divided into life insurance, non-life insurance and reinsurance. Life insurance includes conventional life insurance contracts, annuities, unit-linked insurances and private insured pension schemes, whereas non-life insurance embraces a broad residual category of insurances, such as insurance related to the loss of physical assets, insurances against negligence, transport insurances and credit insurances. Reinsurance, finally, represents life and non-life insurance contracts between insurance companies which allow them to spread the risks that they face.

Like other financial services, the insurance industry is facing a period of rapid change due to innovation in information technology. This has profound effects on the administration as well as on the development, marketing and distribution management of insurers. Also, the interrelationship between banking and insurance services has been increasing during the last few years.

The degree of the competition between insurers and its characteristics depend upon the normal competitive forces, such as market structure, and the extent of the regulatory constraints on such aspects as market entry, contract terms, investment choice and marketing practices.

Apart from a few exceptions, domestic insurance markets are capable of meeting the demand for insurance from most potential buyers. So international insurance transactions represent only a very small share of the total world premiums, particularly for life insurance. It has, for instance, been estimated that overall foreign insurers write about 5 per cent of worldwide life insurance premiums and about 11 per cent of worldwide non-life insurance premiums. Indeed, international trade in reinsurance is largely concentrated in non-life business. Since the mid-1960s the share of worldwide reinsurance premiums written by foreign reinsurers has risen to about one-third of world total.

International reinsurance markets represent one of the major insurance activities traded abroad. The world supply of reinsurance was estimated at around $100 bn. in 1989, 65 per cent of which was provided by professional reinsurers and the rest by direct insurers. European reinsurers have a very high international profile, unlike US and Japanese reinsurers, who write most of their business in the domestic market. About 80 per cent of the demand for reinsurance relates to non-life business. As for

Table 5.3 The main markets for reinsurance in 1990 (as % of world demand)

Country	Non-life	Total
USA	31.7	33.7
Japan	21.0	17.4
Germany	14.5	14.9
UK	4.7	6.0
France	5.5	5.4
Rest of OECD	18.0	17.9
Total OECD	95.4	95.3
Rest of the world	4.6	4.7
Total	100	100

Source: Schweizerische Rückversicherung-Gesellschaft, *Sigma*, March 1992

direct insurance, the demand for reinsurance is concentrated in the OECD area, which accounts for around 95 per cent of total demand (Table 5.3).

International trade in insurance services is subject to so many restrictions that insurance is one of the world's most highly protected industries. The main reason for this protection are protecting consumers, avoiding the excesses of competition, developing a domestic market, the retention of funds, reduction of balance of payments costs, and dependence on foreign suppliers in general.

5.5 Telecommunications[17]

Telecommunication services include: voice telephony, mobile communications, data communications, image communications, videotext, and integrated system digital network (ISDN). Telecommunication services regroup into two main categories: basic services and value-added services. In spite of the growing importance of value-added services, basic services are predominant: in Europe, for instance, they are responsible for about 85 per cent of the telecommunication revenues in almost every European country (Seabra, 1991, p. 1).

As shown in Table 5.4, an important increase in the infrastructure development has taken place since the beginning of the 1970s. The table also shows that telecommunication infrastructures are now somewhat less concentrated in OECD countries than in the past.

17. Telecommunication is the exchange of information at a distance with the use of electrotechnical devices. A telecommunication service is the provision of an opportunity to (tele)communicate. Telecommunications services can be supplied on the market, but they differ from other services because they are provided via networks consisting of wires, optical fibres or radio waves transmitted via terrestrial towers or via satellites (Blankart, Schwandt and 1993, p. 2).

Table 5.4 Telecommunications infrastructure development: number of main lines (mln)

Area	1971	1980	1990
OECD	150	250	360
Africa	2	3	8
Latin America	5	13	27
Asia	7	17	42

Source: OECD, 1993a

The telecommunication services sector has shown a revolutionary development since the mid-1960s. Until the 1960s, only a limited range of basic services (telegraph, telephone, telex) was available to business and resident users. Telecommunication services were traditionally provided by government-owned and operated public telecommunications organisations (PTOs). Also the telecommunication service sector has traditionally been protected in domestic markets, usually by allowing monopoly positions in infrastructures and services and through a range of regulations. The justification of such protection of national markets was based on universal service considerations. This original border protection placed limits on the internationalisation process of the telecommunication industry.

However, as a result of the globalisation of service activities (e.g. in financial services), there has been an increasing demand for a more liberal regulatory framework. Significant technological changes have created additional pressure for structural and regulatory changes in the telecommunication services sector. These changes in telecommunications – a market which expands at a rate of 10–15 per cent a year – are based on three main factors: privatisation, deregulation and globalisation. To illustrate:

- the PTOs have increasingly been split into separate telecommunication and post administrations, with the telecommunication part being sold to the private sector;
- traditional monopoly rights are being abolished or at least limited;
- freed from government control at home and with new opportunities growing abroad, the telecommunication companies have started to expand globally.

The liberalisation process in the international telecommunications sector – with an annual turnover of some $300 bn – has taken place at the multilateral level as well as at the regional or bilateral level. Due to the abolition of monopoly rights in countries such as the United States, newly privatised telecommunication groups have begun to follow their multinational business customers and started expanding globally, through acquisitions and strategic alliances, or as stake-holders in consortia for new operating licences. However, protection of basic services was usually left intact, whereas advanced services are generally open to competition.

Today, PTOs are playing an important role in international trade in the telecommunication industry, although international telecommunication services did exist in the past. The PTOs activity in this respect was to interconnect domestic networks in different countries without competition between PTOs in international telecommunications. Nowadays, many PTOs are extending geographical coverage of service provision beyond national boundaries. For example, AT&T announced in its annual report 1991 its intention of enhancing its international businesses: while 15 per cent of AT&T's revenue was generated from its international activities, the objective was to obtain 25 per cent of the sales in 1995 from these activities and 50 per cent by the year 2000 (OECD, 1993a). PTOs are thus increasingly competing with each other in international markets.

5.6 Transport services

The main transport services are maritime transport services, internal waterways transport, air transport services, space transport, rail transport services, and road transport services. These services are usually classified under three main groups: maritime, air, and land transport services.

5.6.1 *Maritime transport services*

Three main concepts have to be explained in order to understand international trade in maritime transport services: flagging, the categorisation of cargoes, and conferences.

1. International conventions require that ships have a home country of registry. 'The concept of flagging allows a categorisation of trade in international shipping services that has similarities with trade in goods. To the extent that a country grants incentives so that shipments to or from its shores are carried in vessels flying its own flag, this is roughly equivalent to a measure (tariff or quota) protecting the domestic production of goods. Citizenship requirements for crewing on, and ownership of, national-flag vessels are similar to immigration and foreign investment restrictive measures (White, 1988, pp. 5–6).
2. Ocean shipping cargoes, including the ships and companies that transport them. They fall into three broad categories:
   (a) liner cargoes: regular trade routes according to fixed, pre-announced schedules (the liner companies function as common carriers);
   (b) dry bulk cargoes: freight transportations are usually on demand rather than on a fixed sailing schedule. Dry bulk cargoes are either owned or chartered by the exporter or by an independent shipping company; and
   (c) tanker cargoes: these are similar to dry bulk cargoes but concern crude petroleum and petroleum products.
3. Liner companies, which are generally organised into shipping conferences that cover one or more trade routes. The conferences are cartels that have arrangements with regard to freight rates and sailing frequencies.

The distribution of the world fleet by country groupings as indicated in Table 5.5

Table 5.5 Distribution of world tonnage by group of countries of registration 1992

Flags of registration by groups of countries	Tonnage in gross registered tonnes (mln)	Tonnage in deadweight tonnes (mln)
Developed market-economy countries	142.3	216.6
Open-registry countries	153.0	257.2
Countries in Central and Eastern Europe (incl. the former USSR)	33.7	39.0
Socialist countries of Asia	15.1	22.6
Developing countries	94.6	149.9
Other, unallocated	6.2	9.4
World total	444.9	694.7

Source: UNCTAD, 1993, p. 16

shows that the developed market-economy countries and open-registry countries constituted the dominant groupings in the world merchant fleet in 1992 (by flag of registration). However, the share of developing countries has increased during the last decades: in 1991, this share was 20.9 per cent in terms of million grt (gross registered tons), whereas its share was only 6.7 per cent in 1970 (UNCTAD, 1993, p. 8). At the end of 1991, the controlling interests of nearly 94 per cent of the world deadweight tonnage was located in 35 countries and territories. Shipowners of the four leading countries (Greece, Japan, the United States and Norway) controlled about 46 per cent of the world fleet, while the ten most important countries and territories (the four countries mentioned above and Hong Kong, the former USSR, China, United Kingdom, South Korea and Germany) controlled 69 per cent of world tonnage (UNCTAD, 1993, p. 10).

5.6.2 *Air transport services*

Air transport services are a key component of the enormous travel and tourist industry. The $2,000 billion spent on travel and tourism each year accounts for 12 per cent of the global GNP (Airbus Industrie, 1993). The falling costs of air travel associated with economic growth and affluence has increased the demand for air transport even further. Scheduled airlines account for about 90 per cent of passenger transport (Table 5.6).

Table 5.7 shows the regional distribution of traffic: the main shift has been the decline in importance of airlines based in Europe on the one hand, and the rise of airlines based in Asia and the Pacific on the other hand.

Table 5.6 Traffic of commercial air carriers 1983, 1988 and 1992 (tonne–kilometers performed by type of service)

Type of carrier	Millions of tonne-kilometers performed		
	1983	1988	1992 (prel.)
Scheduled Airlines			
Scheduled services:			
– international	73,780	113,180	142,780
– domestic	72,620	98,930	101,240
Non-scheduled services (international and domestic)	5,620	10,040	11,590
Total	152,020	222,150	255,610
Non-scheduled operators (international and domestic)	8,040	13,060	14,790
All carriers total	160,060	235,210	270,400

Source: ICAO world statistics, 1992

Table 5.7 World airline traffic, by home region of carrier 1983 and 1992 (as % of passengers–kilometers performed by region)

Region	1983	1992
Europe	32.6	28.3
Africa	2.9	2.3
Middle East	3.2	2.7
Asia and Pacific	16.0	20.8
North America	40.2	41.3
Latin America and Caribbean	5.1	4.6
Total	100.0	100.0

Source: ICAO world statistics, 1992

The international commercial aviation system is governed by agreements between airlines and states. These agreements are based on several packages of norms, often called 'freedoms' (OECD, 1993b, p. 91):

- 1st freedom: permission granted to a civil aircraft to fly over the territory of another country without landing, provided the overflown country is notified in advance and approval is given;
- 2nd freedom: allows a civil aircraft of one country to land in another country for technical reasons (e.g. refuelling or maintenance) without offering any commercial service to or from that point;
- 3rd freedom: allows an airline to carry traffic from its country of registry to another country (e.g. Swissair carrying traffic from Zürich to Rome);

- 4th freedom: allows an airline to carry traffic from another country to its own country of registry (e.g. Swissair carrying traffic from Madrid to Zürich);
- 5th freedom: provides for the right of an airline to carry traffic between two countries outside its own country of registry as long as the flight originates or terminates in its own country of registry;
- 6th freedom: deals with international traffic that originates from behind a carrier's homeland (e.g. from South America to Europe via New York on a US carrier). Such traffic is not considered a right, and no bilateral air transport agreement refers to '6th freedom' traffic;
- Cabotage rights allow air transport services within the boundaries of a country to foreign carriers (e.g. Swissair carrying traffic from Nice to Paris).

The fundamental principle in aviation trade and the basis of much in the regulation of aviation – that of national sovereignty over territorial airspace – had been firmly implanted as a principle of international law at the beginning of the Second World War. This principle was reconfirmed at the Chicago Convention (1944), which is the basic charter of aviation and forms the constitution of the International Civil Aviation Organisation (ICAO).

The Chicago Convention provides recommended standards and practices for every aspect of the operation of aircraft and air services, both in the air and on the ground. However, its existence has not yet been able to establish a multilateral framework regulating the exchange of air traffic rights (or freedoms of the air), the control of fares and freight tariffs, and the control of frequencies and capacity. The development of a bilateral system was a response to this failure: about 1800 bilateral agreements now govern international air transport services between states.

Since the late 1970s, liberalisation of air transport services has been progressing. Deregulation of air transport services is part of new developments occurring in this sector such as: the increasing density of traffic, the increasing number of competitive airlines, the use of vertical integration in the tourism sector, the increasing role of the computer reservation system (CRS) as a strategic tool for carriers, the development of new long-distance flight aircraft, the trend toward privatisation, the emergence of megacarriers, and the recognition of the importance of networking.

Domestically, many countries have privatised their nationally owned airlines whereas liberalisation of international trade in air transport has become a steady preoccupation and a source of much debate at the bilateral, as well as the regional (e.g. in the EU) and multilateral level (GATS).[18] The liberalisation of the first four freedoms is mainly covered through bilateral agreements. However, the fifth freedom as well as cabotage and multilateral ownership of airlines are mainly achieved through regional agreements such as in the EC-1992 programme.

At the level of airline carriers, the response to the pressures for liberalisation and the increasingly competitive aviation operating environment has been through an

18. However, the coverage of the GATS is limited: the GATS' Annex on Air Transport services practically excludes from the GATS air transport services scheduled, non-scheduled, and ancillary services except for aircraft repair and maintenance services, selling and marketing of air transport services, and computer reservation systems (CRS) services.

internationalisation and globalisation process. New and innovative forms of strategic alliances, partnerships and limited equity swaps have emerged in recent years, not only for the operators but also for computer reservation systems (Gugler, 1992). Indeed, liberalisation has also brought some significant changes in the carriers' activities, such as in the development of hub-and-spoke networks. These allow carriers to combine passengers for various destinations on flights bound for the hub, and to combine passengers from various points of origin on flights outbound from the hub (OECD, 1993b, p. 10).[19]

5.6.3 *Road transport services*

Road transport services are more regionally than globally oriented. International trade in road transport services therefore mainly involves continental trade. For example, only 18 per cent of the transport (tonkm) within the EU involves international transport and about 80 per cent of all goods are transported over a distance of less than 100 kilometers (Carlen, 1993, p. 2).

However, it has been observed for all EU member states, except for Italy and Greece, that in the 1980s the growth of international transport was significantly higher than that of domestic transport (Sleuwaegen, 1991, p. 8). This may be explained by the ability of the lorry to offer quick door-to-door transport with great flexibility in time and space. The competitiveness of road transport has been strengthened through technical development with increased loading capacity as a result, as well as through an extension of the road network (Carlen, 1993, p. 2). Changes in the production mix of European countries have also worked in a positive way for road transport: indeed, heavy manufactured goods are often shipped by rail and sea, while the increasing share of intermediate and finished merchandise is preferably transported by road.

The completion of the internal market has led to a new market environment, which now also covers the European Economic Area (EEA). The resulting main developments are: a fully liberalised market of international road transport; free access to the national markets; harmonised taxation; and harmonised prices of productive inputs, with the exemption of labour. The liberalisation of cross-border traffic and the progressive introduction of cabotage are expected to increase the efficiency of road transport services within the EEA. For example, every fourth lorry passing Switzerland on the North–South axis is now empty!

5.7 Services: infrastructure for economic growth

Services industries facilitate social, political and economic activities and thus play an important role in national economic growth. Indeed, the provision of physical

19. A hub airport is a central location where several in-coming flights can be connected conveniently on-line with several out-going flights (of the same company) within a reasonable period of time. In order to maximise the number of on-line connections of these 'spokes' at a hub, carriers try to schedule arrivals from several different places of origin at approximately the same time (Weisman, 1990, p. 21).

infrastructural services such as telecommunications and transport, together with social infrastructures such as health, housing and education, as well as the availability of financial services is an integral part of national development processes. Thus, policies with regard to these sectors are strongly influenced by considerations of national security, the attainment of particular strategic objectives, ensuring the widest possible access of the population to essential services, and providing the necessary infrastructure for many economic activities. These considerations have led governments to play a major role in services markets as well as in regulating them.

It is important to examine three sectors not already mentioned above in order better to understand the role of services in a country's economic growth: professional services, construction services, and tourism.

5.7.1 *Professional services*

Professional services have been described as services that may cater to producers of commodities and other services, or that directly serve the needs of final consumers (Mallampally, 1990, p. 94).[20]

Most professional services are intangible, non-storable and intensive in human capital or skills. Their delivery often requires close relationships between the producer and the customer. Therefore, international transactions in professional services involve more than pure cross-border trade. Some professional services, such as education and entertainment, can be embodied in goods (tapes, books, computer discs) and traded across borders: this could be classified as trade in goods. Some other cross-border trade in professional services may be conducted through transborder data flows on international information channels (telecommunications), such as consultant services. In many cases, however, international trade of professional services is realised through the establishment of a commercial presence and/or through the movement of individuals across borders.

The quality of statistical information about the international trade of professional services is rather poor. However, some statistics are available for a few sectors such as consulting and engineering design services (these are professional services linked to construction services). According to this information the international design-related billings of the top 200 international design firms totalled $8.8 bn in 1990. In 1990, developing countries accounted for 58 per cent of the international design market compared to 87 per cent in 1986. In 1990, the markets in Asia and Europe showed an increase of 17 per cent and 32 per cent respectively, and represented the two strongest regional markets, each bringing in $2.3 bn of design billings (Table 5.8).

20. According to the GATT classification of services, professional services are mainly: legal services, architectural services, engineering services, accounting, auditing and bookkeeping services, taxation services, medical and dental services, veterinary services, services provided by midwives, nurses and para-medical personnel.

Table 5.8 Regional distribution of foreign billings of the top 200 international design firms (1986–90, US$ mln)

Region	1986	1987	1988	1989	1990
Africa	855	949	824	938	894
Asia	982	1,134	153	2,000	2,340
Latin America	321	435	322	444	648
Middle East	907	742	809	803	1,210
Europe	314	532	622	1,770	2,340
North America	161	231	4,292	1,434	1,370
Total:	3,540	4,023	7,022	7,389	8,802

Source: United Nations, 1993, p. 6

5.7.2 *Construction services*

The construction services sector plays an important role in the economies of all countries. It accounts for about 8 to 10 per cent of GDP in the industrialised and middle-income countries to about 3 per cent on the average in the least developed countries (United Nations, 1993, p. 1).

Trade in international construction involves firms from one country building under contract in another country. The construction industry is highly fragmented and in many cases concentrated in home markets. Compared to other services sectors, international trade of construction services is rather limited. However, due *inter alia* to technical changes and to deregulation of public procurement, the construction industry has become more and more internationalised, particularly as far as large projects are concerned.

The value of international construction contracts amounted to $120 bn in 1990. The trend since the mid-1980s shows that the growth of the international construction market has generally been slow. Developing countries accounted for 57 per cent of this market in 1990, compared to 70 per cent in 1986, and 85 per cent in the beginning of the 1980s (United Nations, 1993, p. 13). In terms of regional distribution of foreign construction contracts, Europe constitutes the fastest growing market: its value of international construction business grew by about 27 per cent per annum between 1986 and 1990 (Table 5.9). The rapid expansion of this regional market may be due, in part, to the achievement of the EC internal market and the realisation of the EEA (European Economic Association).

In 1990, there were 108 European and 63 US firms among the top 250 international contractors; these 250 contractors controlled more than 80 per cent of the construction services' export market. The US is the leading exporter, accounting in 1990 for 36 per cent of this market, followed by Japan (14%), Italy (11%), the United Kingdom (10%), France (9%) and Germany (8%) (United Nations, 1993, p. 16).

Table 5.9 Regional distribution of foreign construction contracts awarded to the top 250 international contractors (1986–90, US$ bn)

Region	1986	1987	1988	1989	1990
Africa	13.2	9.0	10.1	14.3	15.2
Asia	17.3	15.5	20.5	24.5	27.1
Latin America	5.2	7.4	7.5	7.6	5.8
Middle East	16.1	13.4	17.4	17.8	19.9
Europe	11.9	17.2	19.4	25.4	30.4
North America	10.4	11.5	19.2	22.7	21.6
Total:	73.9	73.9	94.1	112.5	120.0

Source: United Nations, 1993, p. 15

5.7.3 *Tourism*

It is not easy to define tourist services. According to the World Tourism Association, the term 'visitor' covers two categories: (a) tourists and (b) excursion visitors or transit passengers (any person staying in the country less than 24 hours).

Tourism services encompass activities such as the organisation of tourist activities (travel agencies, tour-operators, guides), the transport of tourists (rail transport, air transport, sea transport and road transport), accommodation (hotels, flat rental, secondary residence, camping, etc.), and supplementary activities involving leisure facilities, recreational facilities, and so on.

Tourism has become an important service activity and a powerful factor for economic development in many countries, particularly in developing countries. Tourism may have an important effect on several key aspects of the national economy of a country: it may account for a large part of the domestic production in many countries; it generates directly and indirectly productive activities and jobs; it may be an important factor of infrastructure development; and it may increase the surplus in the balance of payments of countries.

Trade in tourism services occurs when a supplier from one country sells a service:

(a) in the supplier's home country to a visitor (consumer) who is a resident of another country or to a supplier of another country, either through cross-border movement of the foreign supplier or through the foreign supplier's commercial presence or establishment in this country;
(b) in another country to a supplier or resident of, or visitor to, that country.

As indicated in Table 5.10, total international tourism receipts represented in 1991 1.5 per cent of world GNP, 9.0 per cent of total world exports and 18.6 per cent of world services exports. Slightly less than one quarter of total international tourism receipts is registered in the developing countries, where tourism services are playing a comparatively more important role in the national economies than in the developed countries' national economies.

Table 5.10 Importance of trade in tourism

		World				Developing countries			
		1980	1989	1990	1991	1980	1989	1990	1991
Gross National Product (GNP)	US$ billion	10,219	19,294	20,899	21,584	1,584	2,745	2,829	2,872
Total exports	US$ billion	1,864	3,013	3,392	3,482	403	699	779	827
Services exports	US$ billion	745	1,331	1,598	1,694	87	155	170	176
International tourism receipts	US$ billion	102	211	255	261	26	55	64	63
International fare receipts	US$ billion	18	40	48	54	4	6	8	7
Total international tourism receipts	US$ billion	120	251	303	315	30	61	72	70
Total international tourism receipts as:									
% of GNP	%	1.2	1.3	1.4	1.5	1.9	2.2	2.5	2.4
% of total exports	%	6.4	8.3	8.9	9.0	7.4	8.7	9.2	8.5
% of services exports	%	16.1	18.9	19.0	18.6	34.5	39.4	42.4	39.8
International tourism receipts as:									
% of services exports	%	13.7	15.9	16.0	15.4	29.9	35.5	37.6	35.8
International fare receipts as:									
% of services exports	%	2.4	3.0	3.0	3.2	4.6	3.9	4.7	4.0
		Annual Growth Rate							
		89/80	90/89	91/90	91/80	89/80	90/89	91/90	91/80
Gross National Product (GNP)	%	7.3	8.3	3.3	7.0	6.3	3.1	1.5	5.6
Total exports	%	5.5	12.6	2.7	5.8	6.3	11.4	6.2	6.8
Services exports	%	6.7	20.1	6.0	7.8	6.6	9.7	3.5	6.6
International tourism receipts	%	8.4	20.9	2.4	8.9	8.7	16.4	–1.6	8.4
International fare receipts	%	9.3	20.0	12.5	10.5	4.6	33.3	–12.5	5.2
Total international tourism receipts	%	8.5	20.7	4.0	9.2	8.2	18.0	–2.8	8.0

Source: World Tourism Organisation, 1994

5.8 Summary

The international development of services transactions has become a major policy issue since the 1980s. This issue has been pushed to the fore by the Uruguay Round multilateral negotiations on services, as well as by the various regional integration agreements which increasingly include liberalisation of trade in services in their programmes.

It has been indicated that the conceptual distinction between services and goods is not easy. The intangibility character of services, in contrast with the tangibility of goods, immediately comes to mind. Services are usually considered as intangible, invisible and perishable, requiring simultaneous production and consumption. Goods, in contrast, are tangible, visible and storable, not requiring direct interaction between consumers and producers. The fact that the supply of services requires direct interaction between providers and consumers is an important determinant of the form taken by most trade in services. Therefore, some services sectors are more tradeable than others. However, due partly to technological changes, many services sectors have become much more tradeable than in the past.

As far as international transactions in services are concerned, four modes of delivery are distinguished: cross-border trade, consumption abroad, commercial presence, and movement of natural persons providing services.

It has been shown that international transactions of services differ from one sector to the other, depending *inter alia* on the tradeability of the activities involved. For example, international trade in the construction sector is far less developed than international transactions in the banking sector.

Many services sectors such as telecommunication, transportation and professional services as well as financial, health and education services play an important role in national economic growth. Indeed, the efficient supply of services is increasingly perceived as a critical factor in the development process. As technological change expands the scope for international transactions in services, the role of these transactions in improving development opportunities is receiving special attention. Thus liberalisation of trade in services constitutes a major challenge for government policies, particularly in sectors traditionally highly regulated and/or under national monopolies such as in telecommunication and air transport.

Bibliography

References

Airbus Industrie (1993) *Market Perspectives for Civil Jet Aircraft*, Toulouse.

Bank for International Settlements (1994) *International Banking and Financial Market Developments*.

Blankart, C.B. and **Schwandt, F.** (1993) *Telecommunication in Switzerland*, University of Humbold.

Carlen, B. (1993) *Road transport in EFTA Countries*, Paper prepared for the EFTA Secretariat.

Dunning, J.H. (1989) 'Multinational enterprises and the growth of services: some conceptual and theoretical issues', *The Service Industries Journal*, vol. 9, no. 1, pp. 5–39.
GATT (1993) *Le commerce international.*
Gaudard, G. (1989) 'L'ouverture du marché des services', *Revue économique et sociale*, no. 4, pp. 205–13.
Gugler, P. (1992) *Strategic Alliances in Services: Some Theoretical Issues and the Case of Air Transport Services*, Working Paper No. 212, University of Fribourg, Switzerland.
Hill, T.P. (1977) 'On goods and services', *The Review of Income and Wealth*, vol. 23, pp. 315–38.
Hoekman, B. and **Sauvé, P.** (1991) *Integration and Interdependence: Information Technology and the Transformation of Financial Markets*, Atwater Institute project on 'the impact of telecommunication and data services on commercial activity and economic development'.
Hoekman, B. and **Sauvé, P.** (1993) *Regional and Multilateral Liberalization of Services Markets: Complements or Substitutes?*, Internal Paper, GATT, 23 April 1993.
ICAO world statistics (1992) *Civil Aviation Statistics of the World.*
Mallampally, P. (1990) 'Professional services' in: P.A. Messerlin and K.P. Sauvant (eds) *The Uruguay Round: Services in the World Economy*, The World Bank and UNCTC, United Nations.
OECD (1983) *The Internationalisation of Banking: The Policy Issues.*
OECD (1993a) *Communications Outlook 1993.*
OECD (1993b) *International air transport: the challenges ahead.*
Ruane, F. (1990) *Internationalisation of Services: Conceptual and Empirical Issues*, EC Commission.
Schweizerische Rückversicherung-Gesellschaft (1992) *Sigma*, 4/92.
Seabra, C. (1991) *Telecommunications Services in the EEC: Present Situation and Evolution*, paper prepared for the Directorate-General for Economic and Financial Affairs and for Employment and Social Affairs of the EC.
Sleuwaegen, L. (1991) *Road Transport: The Effects of the European Single market*, mimeo. Paper prepared for the EC Commission for the project on the effects of EC-1992 on services sectors.
UNCTAD (1993) *Review of Maritime Transport 1992*, United Nations.
United Nations (1993) *Information Technology and International Competitiveness: The Case of the Construction Services Industry.*
Walter, I. (1988) *Global Competition in Financial Services: Market Structure, Protection, and Trade Liberalization*, Ballinger.
Weisman, E. (1990) *Trade in Services and Imperfect Competition: Application to International Aviation*, International Studies on the Service Economy, Kluwer Academic Publishers.
White, L.J. (1988) *International Trade in Ocean Shipping Services: The United States and the World*, Ballinger.
World Tourism Organisation (1994) *Tourism and the General Agreement on Trade in Services (GATs).*

Further reading

Ascher, B. and **Whichard, O,G.** (1987) 'Improving services trade data', in O. Giarini (ed.) *The Emerging Service Economy*, Pergamon Press, pp. 255–81.
Carlisle, C.B. (1991) *Remarks on the Uruguay Round Negotiations*, The Geneva Papers on Risk and Insurance Issues and Practice, no. 61, October, pp. 401–4.
Findlay, C. (1990) 'Air transport', in P.A. Messerlin and K.P. Sauvant (eds.) *The Uruguay Round: Services in the World Economy*, The World Bank and UNCTC.
Hirsch, S. (1989) 'Services and services intensity in international trade', *Weltwirtschaftliches Archiv*, no. 1, pp. 45–60.
Lohéac, F. (1991) *Deregulation of Financial Services and Liberalization of International Trade in Services*, The Geneva papers on Risk and Insurance, vol. 16, no. 61, pp. 406–13.

McGowan, F. (1992) *Air Transportation*, paper prepared for the EC Commission.
Nicholaides, P. (1989) 'The problem of regulation in traded services: the implications for reciprocal liberalisation', *Aussenwirtschaft*, 44 Jahrgang, Heft 1, pp. 29–47.
Richter, C. (1987) 'Tourism services', in O. Giarini (ed.) *The Emerging Service Economy*, Pergamon Press, pp. 213–44.
Riddle, D.I. (1987) 'The role of the service sector in economic development: similarities and differences by development category', in: O. Giarini (ed.) *The Emerging Service Economy*, Pergamon Press, pp. 83–104.
Pipe, G.R. (1990) 'Telecommunication', in P.A. Messerlin and K.P. Sauvant (eds.) *The Uruguay Round: Services in the World Economy*, The World Bank and UNCTC.
Ultman, Ch.W. (1992) 'Regulation of international banking: a review of the issues', *Journal of World Trade*, vol. 26, no. 5, pp. 79–92.

6 Exports: risks, insurance and finance

6.1 Introduction

It is clear that a number of risks arise with exporting that either do not figure with domestic trade, or do so to a much lesser degree. First of all, the transactions will generally be larger and significant amounts of money will therefore be involved. Secondly, in many cases the exporting party will have difficulties ascertaining the financial standing of the counter-party. Thirdly, a wide range of government measures or political events abroad may hamper smooth export operations. Finally, the goods will have to be transported over long distances (sometimes by sea).

The risks arising from all these factors can be divided into the following categories:

(a) Risks connected with payment: this type of risk relates to the risk of foreign buyers failing to comply with their contractual commitments, either for reasons attributable to them or *force majeure*.
(b) Transport risks: this means the loss of – or damage to – goods during transport.
(c) Exchange-rate risks: these occur if exporters invoice in a currency other than their own.
(d) Legal and administrative risks.

The legal risk only arises if the commercial contract is subject to foreign regulations. This risk can prove particularly important in the case of transactions with non-European countries, as foreign regulations may differ fundamentally from domestic regulations. Any disputes will then be resolved in accordance with rules of law with which the importer or exporter is not fully familiar, and in a foreign court. What is more, even if the dispute is decided in the exporter's favour, enacting the judgment may cause serious problems. In an attempt to avoid legal risk to both parties, it is sometimes required that in the event of failure to reach agreement, the dispute will be submitted to a Council of Judges, to be appointed in accordance with the method stipulated in the commercial contract.[21]

21. A point to note here is that there exists a Court of Arbitration at the International Chamber of Commerce in Paris; this may be authorised by both parties to resolve any disputes between them. An arbitration procedure does carry the drawback, however, of being slow and expensive, and it is therefore only used for contracts that are large in scale.

The administrative risk is in fact a collective term, as every transaction with another country entails some degree of red tape. All these formalities – such as obtaining import and export licences and customs procedures – serve to raise the price. Furthermore, failure to comply with these formalities may lead to claims for damages, if for example, the goods are declared inadmissible for import or if funds cannot be transferred.

Technical problems may arise by the following factors entering the equation elsewhere: different standards, different systems of weights and measures, specific health rules, and so on. Packaging (e.g. to take account of specific label regulations) and communication difficulties (the use of foreign languages in commercial documentation, correspondence, telephone calls, etc) may also cause problems.

The first part of this chapter deals mainly with the issue of non-payment of an export contract and with related financing and insurance problems. In Part 2, the traditional export-financing techniques are examined. Rapidly evolving export markets and increasing competition, however, have forced banks to develop new, alternative financing techniques. Part 3 discusses some of these techniques.

PART 1: EXPORT RISKS

6.2 The various risks

This section pays particular attention to the problem of non-payment of an export contract and the associated financing and insurance problem.

All sales transactions carry risks of loss if the purchasers or debtors fail to comply with their commitments for reasons for which they are responsible or on account of *force majeure*. Depending upon the criterion adopted, the risks may be classified in various categories: according to the time at which the risk presents itself (Section 6.2.1); according to the cause of the risk (Section 6.2.2); or according to the status of the debtor (Section 6.2.3).

6.2.1 *Risk according to the time at which it occurs*

THE RISK OF BREACH OF CONTRACT

Exporters, regardless of whether they are manufacturers or agents, incur costs before receiving payment from their customers. In most cases they will therefore incur a loss if the purchaser breaches the commercial contract prior to delivery. If the goods are from stock or have a wide market, resale to other customers will be relatively easy. If, however, the exporter manufactures a 'tailored' item, in accordance with very precise specifications, resale will generally be impossible and the loss will be all the greater.

RISK OF PAYMENT

After delivery, the risk assumes concrete form if exporters fail to receive payment to which they are entitled by virtue of fulfilling the contract.

6.2.2 *Risk according to cause*

DEFAULT ON THE PART OF THE DEBTOR

If debtors are in default, they are unable to meet their commitments. In the case of a private debtor (natural persons or legal entities with articles of association under private law), this risk assumes concrete form in the event of the customer's insolvency. This insolvency can be established in law after bankruptcy, legal settlement or legal procedure of the same tenor. Insolvency may also exist in fact, that is, if the debtor's status makes any payment unlikely and enforced implementation or application for bankruptcy would actually increase the risk of loss. This whole spectrum of risks regarding private customers is termed the commercial risk.

It is evident that a government debtor may be in default as well, but this point will be discussed later.

THE POLITICAL RISK

Political risks relate to circumstances, where political or other events in the debtor's country or measures taken by foreign authorities render it impossible for debtors to comply with their commitments. These are instances of *force majeure*. Examples to consider are political events such as war, revolution and insurgency, or disasters such as earthquakes, volcanic eruptions or tidal waves. It may also be the case that as a result of diplomatic tension, a country decides to take certain measures against imports from a particular country or exports to a particular country, for instance via an embargo, boycott, import ban, withdrawal of import licences, not permitting exchange authorisations or subjecting to licences certain products which hitherto could be freely imported. This is termed 'autonomous behaviour on the part of a country' (*le fait du prince*).

The political risk also spans economic and monetary difficulties that may trigger a currency shortage in a particular country, which means that the country is unable to meet its commitments towards other countries and transfers overseas are delayed or halted. This is called the transfer risk. In such cases debtors are solvent in the sense that they make payment or are in a position to make payment in the local currency; the central bank of the country in question will not, however, be in a position to supply the requisite currency.

6.2.3 *Risk according to the status of the debtor*

The name given to the risks covered differs according to whether the foreign debtor is a government body or a private individual. When we are dealing with private customers, we talk about the commercial risk on the one hand and the political risk on the other. As far as government debtors are concerned (the state, regional or municipal authorities, companies with public-law status), the purely political risk and default on the part of the debtor are regarded as a single political risk and denoted by the summarising term 'risk of a governmental customer'. In view of the political nature of governmental institutions it is in fact difficult to make a distinction between the various causes of non-payment.

6.3 Cover against the risks of non-payment

There are various techniques to which exporters may resort to cover themselves against these risks. The most commonly used techniques are credit insurance (6.3.1 and 6.3.2) and documentary credit (6.3.3). Bank guarantees (6.3.4), forfaiting (6.3.5) and factoring (6.3.6) are also discussed below.

6.3.1 *Export credit insurance via public insurers*

All the OECD countries and an increasing number of newly industrialised countries (including the countries of Central and Eastern Europe) have set up organisations to promote exports. The cornerstone of an export-oriented policy is called a public credit insurance institution or ECA (Export Credit Agency); these include private companies acting on the government's behalf. Official support from an ECA may be restricted to 'pure cover', which means insurance or guarantees given to exporters or lending institutions without financing support. The following are examples in various European countries:

- NDD or Nationale Delcrederedienst (Belgium);
- NCM or Nederlandse Credietverzekeringsmaatschappij (Netherlands);
- COFACE or Compagnie Française d'Assurance pour le Commerce Extérieur (France); and
- ECGD or Export Credits Guarantee Department (United Kingdom).

Alternatively, official support may be given in the form of 'financing support', which is defined as including direct credits, refinancing and all forms of interest subsidies. The following are some examples:

- EXIM Bank or the Export–Import Bank of the United States;
- JEXIM or Export–Import Bank of Japan; and
- EXIMbank of Turkey.

Box 6.1 presents an overview of the principles underlying public credit insurance.

6.3.2 *Export credit insurance via private insurers*

A number of private insurers also provide cover against the risks of exporting. In contrast to the ECAs, they do not require any globalisation of the risks, the goods may

Box 6.1: Principles of public credit insurance

The main principles underpinning public credit insurance are as follows:

- Origin of the goods: in principle, cover is only extended to export contracts where the goods originate from the ECA country itself. What this means in practice is that where the insurance lasts at least one year, the national added value must be at least 80 per cent. If, however, the suppliers originate from a member state of the EU, the cover provided by a European ECA may be extended to these sub-contracts provided that they do not exceed between 30 per cent and 40 per cent of the total contract (see section 6.4.3 on this point).
- The residual risk: exporters will only be insured up to a certain percentage of their receivables from other countries (up to a maximum of 95%). They will therefore have to bear a residual risk themselves. There are, however, major exceptions to this rule: the US EXIMbank, the JEXIM and the UK's ECGD will cover up to 100 per cent of the risk.
- Globalisation policy: exporters must undertake to insure their global sales or part thereof, as determined on the basis of objective criteria (for example, certain countries, certain categories of products).
- Globalisation risks: the commercial and political risks are covered jointly, in other words, separate cover for one risk or another is not possible, unless the commercial risk is not acceptable to the ECA, for example on account of doubts about the debtor's financial strength or because the debtor is a subsidiary of the insured party.
- Setting the premium: the premium that the insured party has to pay for the cover extended is determined mainly by:
  (i) the degree of risk attached to the debtor's country;
  (ii) the nature of the risks covered;
  (iii) the duration of the risk; and
  (iv) the intensity of the risk.
- Waiting period: if a claim arises, the exporter or the bank or both will only be reimbursed after a more or less significant waiting period (which may range between a few months and a year, according to the risk).
- Risks covered: both the risk before and after delivery may be covered, but the exporter may agree with the ECA that only the risk of non-payment will be covered.

come from any source, advance payment of 15 per cent is not necessarily required, and the premium is calculated on the basis of the risk amount and not the contract amount. The policies of private insurers also have some drawbacks: premiums are rather high, the risks covered are less comprehensive, the period of cover is often shortened (three to five years with the possibility of roll-over), and the waiting period is longer.

There is also some complementarity between the ECAs and private insurers. This may take the form of co- or reinsurance. In the case of the latter, insured parties negotiate with single insurers, who act as the front and will reinsure themselves in whole or in part. In recent years a number of ECAs have sold their short-term export-credit insurance activities (maximum one to two years) to the private sector (for example, NCM taking over short-term business from ECGD) or they have taken a stake in a private company via capital participation (for example, NDD and COBAC) aiming at the joint development of this branch of insurance. (For a comparison of public and private insurers, see Box 6.2).

Box 6.2: Comparison between public and private insurers

	ECA	Private insurers
Globalisation	Yes	No
Positioning of claim	In principle a claim by the ECA country against a foreign debtor	Nationality of creditor or debtor irrelevant
Origin of the goods	In principle the same nationality as ECA	Not relevant
Duration of the risk		
– consumer goods	180 days from date of arrival; 210 days from date of dispatch	The limits of 180 days and 210 days may be changed
– capital goods	Actual duration of transaction	3 to 5 years with possibility of roll-over
Advance payment	In principle 15% for transactions with a duration of more than 1 year	No commitment
Amounts to cover	In principle, contract amount	The risk amount
Deductible franchise	Yes	Yes (except with some underwriters)
Waiting period	Usually 6 months	180 to 370 days according to country

6.3.3 *Documentary credit*

A documentary credit is an agreement whereby the bank granting the credit undertakes, at the importer's request, one or more of the following:

- to make cash payments, or pay by an agreed deadline;
- to accept bills of exchange; and
- to negotiate to the exporter's benefit against production of compliant documents within the valid duration of the credit.

The documentary credit was developed to reconcile the conflicting interests of importers and exporters. Importers do not wish to pay until the goods have reached their destination. Exporters do not want to dispatch the goods until they have received payment. These interests are reconciled by the intermediary of a third party, the bank opening the credit.

The exporters will not dispatch until they possess a documentary credit, whereby it is not the importer but a banker who gives an undertaking. Importers are aware that the bank opening the credit will only perform its undertaking if it possesses all the documents that satisfy the requirements laid down via the documentary credit.

The documentary credit is not a credit in the sense that certain liquidities are made available, but it is in the sense that the bank gives its signature or provides its guarantee to the beneficiary (credit against signature). It is called a documentary credit because the credit is given against submission of documents. As with a bill of exchange, the documentary credit leads a life of its own, in that it stands apart from the underlying commercial transaction. (For characteristics of the documentary credit, see Box 6.3).

Box 6.3: Characteristics of a documentary credit

As an instrument to cover the risk of non-payment, the documentary credit displays the following characteristics:

- The documentary credit is mainly used for short-term transactions, i.e. 1 year or less.
- Exporters are guaranteed from the time the documentary credit is raised, i.e. they are wholly or partially covered against the risk prior to delivery.
- In contrast to export credit insurance, there is no waiting period or residual risk. From that point of view the documentary credit certainly offers benefits to the exporter.
- The exporter/beneficiary of an irrevocably confirmed documentary credit is not exposed to any payment risks, at least in so far as the confirmed bank is solvent and is in a country free of political risk.
- The documentary credit is a relatively expensive product and is mainly used if the country or debtor risk or both are high. If only a debtor risk is involved, one should certainly check whether export credit insurance might not be a cheaper option.

6.3.4 *Bank guarantees*

Exporters can also resort to bank guarantees to cover their risks. This guarantee is issued by the purchaser's bank and counter-guaranteed or otherwise by the banker of the beneficiary–exporter. The issuing bank will issue the guarantee in accordance with the requirements set by the client. Bankers provide a credit against signature, that is, they give their name and good reputation to ensure payment of a monetary sum under certain conditions.

The risks associated with the issuing of a bank guarantee are so important that exporters/beneficiaries have everything to gain from seeking their banker's recommendations so as to minimise the risks. Much will depend upon the law that is applicable, the wording and duration of the guarantee.

There are a substantial number of similarities between the documentary credit and the bank guarantee. Both are credits against signature. The documentary credit is abstract in nature, and the same applies to certain bank guarantees. In both cases, the banker will only proceed to make payment in so far as the beneficiary submits documents which comply with the requirements of the letter opening the credit or the bank guarantee. As in the documentary credit, which carries a high degree of formalism, the client should pay the greatest heed to the actual wording of the bank guarantee. Payment or non-payment by the issuing bank will in many cases depend upon the correct wording of the bank guarantee.

There is, however, one fundamental difference between them: in a documentary credit, the banker will only pay in so far as the beneficiary submits documents that provide confirmation that the commercial contract has been fulfilled, while a banker who has issued a bank guarantee will only pay on the basis of documents that give rise to suspicions of non-fulfilment of a commercial transaction. If there is an unconditional guarantee, the banker will pay upon the initial request, without the beneficiary being obliged to prove that the client is in default.

In the United States banks are not permitted to issue guarantees. Instead, US banks issue stand-by letters of credit, which are usually subject to the uniform rules and practices of documentary credits.

The stand-by letter of credit is a letter of credit raised to guarantee the fulfilment of a contract or undertaking; it is a support credit. And herein lies an essential difference with the documentary credit: the primary purpose of the latter is to guarantee payment of a commercial transaction relating to goods, the stand-by letter of credit is simply designed to guarantee an undertaking. This implies that the stand-by letter of credit is only triggered in cases of failure to perform on the basis of a contract agreed between the parties. When calling upon the guarantee, beneficiaries should submit one or more documents to support their call upon the guarantee (for example a bill drawn by the beneficiary against the bank opening the credit and an affidavit from the beneficiary indicating that the client failed to comply with commitments).

6.3.5 *Forfait discount*

Forfait or discount without recourse is when the bank or forfaiter purchases either bills or promissory notes acquired by an exporter from its foreign clients to represent the deferred payment that it has granted to them. In concrete terms, this purchase by the bank takes the form of a 'forfait discount', that is, the bank or a forfaiter discounts the bills without recourse against the exporter. As a result, the risk of non-payment by the buyer or the guarantor is fully taken over by the bank or forfaiter.

This technique, which also allows the risk of non-payment to be covered, exhibits the following characteristics:

- the political and commercial risks are covered;
- exporters are only guaranteed once they issue accepted bills for discounting: since they only receive these bills at or following delivery, this technique does not offer any cover against the risk prior to delivery; and
- as with the documentary credit, there is no residual risk or waiting period.

6.3.6 *Factoring*

The essential point of this technique is that the factoring company assumes responsibility for collecting customer receivables in a way which means that it pays the vendor the countervalue of the said receivables a few days after the due date, without recourse, that is, regardless of whether the receivables have been paid. Factoring companies only operate in industrialised countries.

Factoring is therefore a combination of collection (termed debtor administration) and export credit insurance. As most factors take over claims against foreign clients, factoring as such can be regarded as a means of cover against the risk of non-payment with exports. Compared to credit insurance, factoring offers the advantage that there is no residual risk. This technique, however, does not offer any cover against the political risk. Furthermore, vendors must commit their entire sales or certain categories of clients to the factoring company.

6.4 International aspects of public credit insurance

ECAs do not enjoy full freedom of operation, but have to take account of various commitments that are international in nature. These commitments were either undertaken as part of regulations via international organisations (for example, the OECD or the EU) or entered into voluntarily by the ECA in the context of the Berne Union (with the approval of the supervisory authorities), and their main role is to avoid the various ECAs outbidding one another. In periods of economic decline in particular there is of course a tendency to foster exports via favourable credit or insurance conditions or both.

6.4.1 *The Berne Union*

The International Union of Insurers of Credit and Direct Investment was set up in 1934. The Union is subject to Swiss law; its head office is in Berne, but the secretariat is currently in London. The 40 members of the Union, from 32 countries, are either public institutions (for example, NDD) or private companies which insure political risks for the account of governments (for example, NCM).

The Berne Union aims to promote healthy competition in the field of export-credit insurance and direct investment, to establish or maintain a discipline on credit conditions and to bring about a climate which is favourable to investment. In order to emphasise cooperation between its members, the Berne Union has developed a number of procedures for exchanging information (including notification of claims) and introduced a number of standards to regulate credit conditions. In order to limit the credit period, the Union has developed a goods classification (Box 6.4).

Apart from this goods classification, the Berne Union has also accepted a credit period which in the case of capital goods is dependent upon the relevant contract value. In addition, some types of goods are subject to special regulations under sector-specific agreements, for example, breeding animals, fertilisers, insecticides, pesticides, paper and paper pulp, lorries and chassis, coaches and containers.

6.4.2 *The OECD*

Most of the OECD members participate in the 'Arrangement on Guidelines for Officially Supported Export Credits', also known as the Consensus, which came into effect in April 1978. The main purpose of this Arrangement is to provide the institutional framework for an orderly export credit market and thus to prevent an export

Box 6.4: Goods classification and credit period according to the Berne Union

- Raw materials, semi-manufactured goods and consumer goods with a maximum credit period of six months; any cases of this period being exceeded must be notified to the secretariat.
- Consumer durables, that is, goods sold to consumers and designed to remain usable for a relatively long period and not to be used in a manufacturing process; these goods are usually sold on short-term credit. In case of large orders, however, credit of up to two years (and even longer in exceptional cases) is accepted.
- Parts or components (goods in an interim stage); these are completed products, usually with a low unit value and designed to be processed into light or heavy capital goods. Delivery of these goods is usually backed by short-term credit, although credits of up to two years or more may be involved with large orders.
- Light capital goods: sales of such products may be backed by credit periods of up to five years.
- Heavy capital goods: credits for these goods are subject to the same conditions as light capital goods, although the amount of the payments often justifies a credit period of more than five years.

race in which exporting countries compete on the basis of who grants the most favourable financing terms rather than on the basis of who provides the highest quality and the best service for the lowest price.

The most important terms and conditions set by the Consensus for export credits with a duration of two years or more that are officially supported (i.e. insured, guaranteed, extended, refinanced or subsidised by or through ECAs) are as follows:

(a) at least 15 per cent of the contract is to be covered by cash payments;
(b) the maximum 'repayment term' is eight-and-a-half years, which may be extended to ten years for relatively poor countries and for a limited number of intermediate countries; and
(c) minimum rates of interest are set for periods of up to five, up to eight-and-a-half and up to ten years.

Since October 1983 the minimum rates, known as the 'matrix', have been adjusted every six months in accordance with an automatic mechanism based on the weighted average of the yields on government bonds falling due more than five years in the future in the five countries whose national currencies constitute the basket of Special Drawing Rights (SDR). A margin of 0.50 per cent is added to this average. Each year, in January and July, these conditions are automatically modified if the weighted average of the interest rate prevailing during the last month of the previous term differs by at least half a percentage point from the interest rate that was the basis for the previous change.

However, matrix minimum rates are no longer available for Category I or relatively rich countries (since July 1988) and for Category II or middle income countries (since January 1991). For those countries all participants in the Arrangement lend at market rates or at Commercial Interest Reference Rates (CIRRs), which are subject to monthly adjustment to reflect market rates.[22] For export credits to low income countries, any participant may lend at the Consensus rate or at the CIRR (in any currency) whichever is lower. If the Consensus rate is offered, the differential between the market rate and the Consensus rate is covered by the authorities of the country of the exporter, for instance in Belgium the Ministry of Foreign Trade (Copromex), or in the Netherlands the Ministry of Economic Affairs.

In September 1994, the OECD decided to abolish the matrix completely by the end of August 1995, also for the 'poor' countries of the third category (the so-called Schaerer Agreement). By that date, all participants would lend to all countries at market rates or at CIRRs. Table 6.1 presents the minimum annual interest rates applied (in %) between 1 January 1995 until 31 August, 1995.

Within the above-mentioned limits certain 'derogations' from the rules and some 'deviations' from what is considered normal practice are possible. These must be notified to all other participants in the Arrangement, however, who can then 'match' the deviation or derogation.

22. The CIRR is based on the yield on the secondary market for government bonds with a residual maturity of the Swiss franc: 2%.

Table 6.1 Minimum annual interest rates of export credits (1 January 1995–31 August 1995)

	Interest rate	Duration
Category I	market rate or CIRR	5 years
Category II	market rate or CIRR	8.5 years
Category III	7.35	10 years

Except for export credit activities, the Arrangement also covers tied or partially untied aid financing, that is, credits or grants that are wholly or partly based on public funds for development purposes and that are tied to purchases from the donor countries. A number of governments combine development aid with export credits to create 'mixed credits' or soft loan facilities. According to the latest Arrangement guidelines (the so-called Helsinki Agreement, dated 15 February 1991) the following conditions are applicable for mixed credits:

- they can only be granted for development projects which are not commercially viable and which are executed in developing countries with a yearly per capita income not exceeding $2,465; and
- the concessionality level of the mixed credit is at least 50 per cent for poor countries and 35 per cent for other less developed countries.[23]

For a more extensive survey of the modalities of the OECD regime with respect to mixed credits, the reader is referred to Chapter 7 of this volume.

6.4.3 *The European Union (EU)*

The EU also has an ongoing focus on export credit and credit insurance policy. As long ago as 1960 a 'Group responsible for coordinating policy on credit insurance, guarantees and financing credits' was set up, with the following objective:

- to be a contact point for public credit insurers;
- to coordinate policy and techniques on credit insurance; and
- to develop appropriate solutions to creating common European transactions.

One of the few concrete results produced by the Group is the automatic inclusion of certain sub-supplies from other EU countries in European export contracts. This means that European ECAs also insure these foreign sub-contracts, if they do not exceed:

- 40 per cent for contracts with a value less than 7,500,000 ECU;
- 3,000,000 ECU for contracts with a value between 7,500,000 and 10,000,000 ECU;
- 30 per cent for contracts with a size over 10,000,000 ECU.

23. The concept of the concessionality level or grant element can be explained as follows: the grant element of a grant is 100 per cent; that of an export credit at market rate 0 per cent. In case of a soft or mixed credit, the grant element is calculated as the difference between the nominal value of the future debt service payments to be made by the borrower, expressed as a percentage of the nominal value of the loan. The discount rate used is also determined by the OECD Arrangement.

However, if due to the risk of the transaction being particularly heavy, the principal contractor's credit insurer is unable to cover the whole transaction, consultation between the interested ECAs shall take place to resolve the problem by means of joint insurance or, if possible, reinsurance.

With the Community's internal market coming into force on 1 January 1993, fresh life was injected into an old dream, namely to harmonise policy on export credits within the EU. This, it was claimed, would make the opportunities for insuring exports to countries outside the EU the same for every exporter, regardless of nationality. In addition, it would make the costs of this insurance identical in every EU country.

In concrete terms, this means that for export credits with a minimum term of two years there are proposals for:[24]

- assigning the countries into six risk categories on the basis of a common methodology;
- introducing a common premium system;
- harmonising the various components of the insurance policy, for example adopting a universal maximum of 95 per cent cover (in Great Britain the figure is 100 per cent for example);
- common rules on bank provisioning and capital adequacy cover; and
- common rules for the proportion of foreign components that can be covered.

Advocates of harmonisation consider it a particularly good opportunity to enforce European consortia to compete with the powerful US Eximbank and JEXIM (Japan). Opponents, however, believe the proposal is completely unfit, because:

- the envisioned trans-European ECA in which the European Commission would have considerable decision-making power would play too important a role; and
- European exporters would have a disadvantage if compared to their counterparts from other industrialised countries (especially the US and Japan) to whom the new set of rules would not apply.

These critical remarks are expected to hinder the harmonisation proposal of the European Union. Meanwhile, the OECD is becoming involved in the discussion on an increasing scale. By the end of 1994, the OECD mandate was extended (with respect to the duration, interest rates, and mixed credits) to include credit insurance as well.

24. For more details, see 'Report to the Policy Coordination Group for Export Credits on the formulation of common principles for premium systems and cover policy' or Tuffrau Report, dated 4 May and 11 June 1993.

PART 2: EXPORT FINANCE IN THE MEDIUM AND LONG TERM

6.5 Basic principles

6.5.1 *Capital goods and services*

Only capital goods can be financed in the medium (one to five years) and long term (five years or more). What is lacking, however, is a tight definition or well-defined list of goods that are to be regarded as capital goods. The term 'major export' includes simple machinery and coaches, as well as telephone exchanges ready to go straight into operation. Services include transfers of know-how, activities under management contracts, or technical assistance, preferably but not exclusively relating to exports of capital goods.

Two basic criteria in financing exports of capital goods and services continue to apply:

- the economic life of the goods must be equal to or longer than the term of the credit; and
- the goods or services to be financed must be national in origin: it is generally assumed that the national added value must be at least 70 per cent.[25]

6.5.2 *Credit terms*

Apart from the aforementioned basic rule governing financing terms, they are also determined as a function of the scale of the export contracts. By way of illustration, the following figures are usually applied in Belgium:

- from 3 to 6 million BEF: three years;
- from 6 to 12 million BEF: four years; and
- from 12 million BEF upwards: five years or longer.

A specific arrangement has been developed in the OECD with a view to limiting or extending the financing period for certain products. For example, there is a maximum period for coaches and agricultural machinery (five years); for ships, nuclear power stations and aircraft, by contrast, longer periods than the normal term (eight-and-a-half years) are provided.

6.5.3 *Interest rates*

If financing is expressed in the vendor's currency, the interest rate to be applied is in principle the market rate. According to the Consensus (see Section 6.4.2), governments may, however, also grant an interest supplement or subsidy if the market rate is above the Consensus rate established by the OECD.

25. If the foreign added value originates from sub-suppliers from EU member states, this percentage may fall to 60 per cent in certain cases (see also 6.4.3).

In cases where financing is in a currency other than the national currency, the interest rate to be applied is the 'Commercial Interest Reference Rate' (CIRR) for rich and middle-income countries (Categories I and II), and the CIRR or the Consensus rate if the latter is lower for poor countries (Category III).

6.5.4 *Advances*

Export credits are only provided under the Consensus up to 85 per cent of the export contract, that is, the buyer has to pay 15 per cent in advance, and at least 5 per cent with the order. Nevertheless, many buyers also seek financing for the advance, which is usually in the form of a Euro-currency commercial loan or via a soft loan. The latter are credits advanced under particularly attractive (or soft) conditions and are subject to the OECD rules for mixed credits (see also Section 6.4.2).

Euro-currency loans, it should be noted, are usually provided in the form of rollover credits, in other words loans with a fixed amount and term but with a floating interest rate (usually LIBOR six months + spread). The term is usually shorter than that for parallel export credit. These credits are of course not eligible for credit insurance or interest supplements. It is only the banks, therefore, that bear the risks of debtor insolvency or transfer risk or both. Hence, these credits are usually syndicated among various international banks.

6.6 Financing schemes

6.6.1 *Manufacturing credits*

In order to finance the costs of manufacturing the equipment ordered, exporters may use the traditional credit lines available from their bankers. These include cash loans, supplier discount credit for payment of the raw materials, and acceptance credit for the prior financing of purchases in other countries. In each individual case the choice will be determined by the suitability and, above all, the cost price of the various forms of credit. A cash credit that may only cause a debtor position for a few days may be cheaper than any other form of credit on account of its flexibility for a short-term transaction.

There does, however, exist a form of credit specially designed for the financing of manufacturing costs, namely discounting promissory notes signed by exporters to the order of their bankers. The total amount of the credit embodied by the promissory notes will be determined as part of financial planning of manufacture, in which income (advance payments received) on the one hand and expenditure (wages, suppliers and other expenditure incurred during the manufacturing process) on the other are offset. A manufacturing credit may therefore be taken out for the difference between the two.

A manufacturing credit is usually repaid by funds raised from the instalment credit (see also 6.6.2). Naturally, in the case of an export contract with cash payment, payments received directly from the buyer will be used to clear the manufacturing credit.

One other route available to the exporter to finance activities during the manufacturing period is to obtain stage payments from the buyer, quite apart from the traditional advances. This possibility arises as part of the financing of the instalments by a buyer's credit (see also 6.4.2), where the buyer will be able to deduct from the export credit prior to delivery the amounts that agree with the payments. This formula, known as stage or progress payments, offers the advantage of freeing exporters from the financial charges they would have to bear under classical manufacturing credit, and where interest rates fluctuate in line with the market. With progress payments, the interest rate borne by the buyer may be fixed, but subject to the condition that the credit satisfies the characteristics of 'instalment credit' described below.

6.6.2 *Payment term credits*

Figure 6.1 clearly illustrates the central role of the exporter in the organisation and throughout the life of the supplier's credit.

The supplier's credit has the following characteristics:

1. It is the seller who grants the payment terms to the foreign buyer and who therefore has to negotiate and define these terms in the commercial contract. In this contract, the other contracting party will not only agree on the technical and commercial characteristics of the goods and services it is going to acquire but also on the payment and financing conditions.
2. Being the only party granting the credit, the exporter:
   - must carry out all the formalities with the ECA to obtain cover of the credit risks;
   - is the direct beneficiary of the insurance policy; and
   - bears all the risks not covered by credit insurers as well as the treasury cost for the delay between the date of a claim and the date of indemnification by the credit insurer (which currently amounts to, for instance, 6 months for OND and NCM).
3. The exporter will approach the authorities to obtain the interest subsidies if, according to the Consensus, a lower rate than market rate or CIRR can be offered to the buyer. The exporter will be the beneficiary of the subsidies and bear the charges related to late payment of these subsidies.

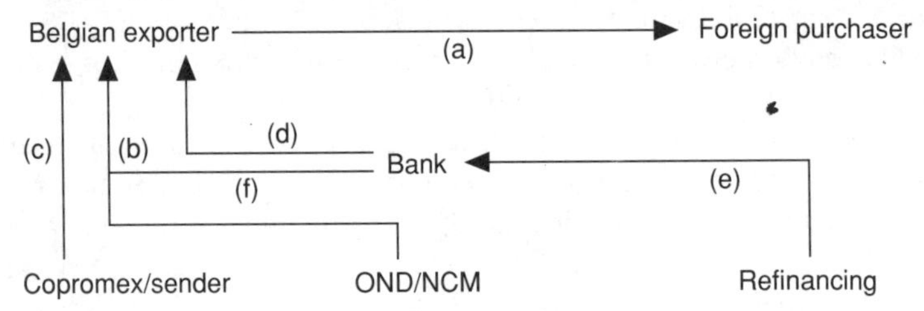

Figure 6.1 The supplier's credit scheme

(a) one single contract: the commercial contract;
(b) insurance;
(c) subsidy;
(d) refinancing of trade bills;
(e) refinancing;
(f) transfer of the benefit of the insurance policy.

The bank itself has no direct contact with the foreign buyer. Its credit is granted to the exporter according to the following scheme:

- the bank opens a credit line in favour of the exporter, who can use it to discount the trade bills representing the payment terms granted to the foreign buyer;
- the bank refinances it with the appropriate refinancing institution or in the market for the same periods and the same amounts; and
- to cover the risks on its customer, the bank will normally require a transfer of the benefit of the insurance policy issued by the credit insurer in its favour.

The use of the supplier's credit technique brings significant administrative charges and risks for the exporter, which is often a small- or medium-sized company, not properly equipped to tackle major export problems and risks. This leads to the somewhat contradictory situation where, because of the size of their contracts, such small- and medium-sized companies cannot enjoy the benefits of the buyer's credit technique, and share with their bank the risks and administrative burden related to their exports. To remedy this situation, banks have developed a forfaiting scheme or a technique of discounting trade bills or promissory notes in the framework of the export financing system (see also Section 6.3.5).

With respect to the relationship between the exporter and the foreign buyer, forfaiting is very similar to a supplier's credit, since the exporter will stipulate all the financial arrangements in one single agreement: the commercial contract. However, there are several differences in comparison with the supplier's credit as is seen in Figure 6.2.

The main characteristics of this type of financing may be summarised as follows:

- the bank discounts, without recourse to the exporter, the bills (drafts or promissory notes) representing the payment terms granted by the exporter to the foreign buyer under the terms of the commercial contract;
- as the bills are discounted at the time of shipment, the bank relieves the exporter of all credit risks from that moment on and pays the exporter the net proceeds of the discount;

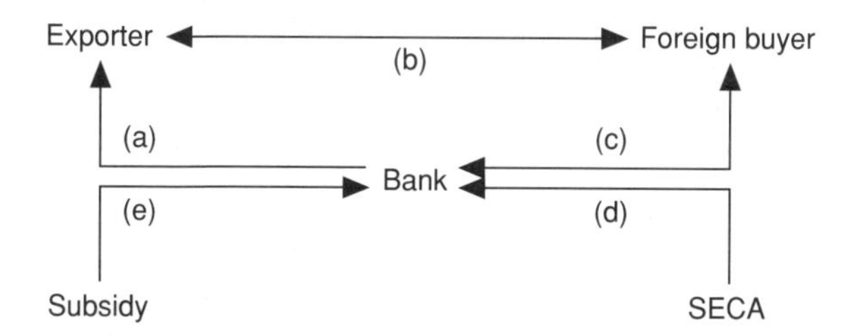

Figure 6.2 Forfaiting scheme

(a) discount at subsidised rate and without recourse;
(b) commercial contract;
(c) risk relationship;
(d) insurance;
(e) subsidising (if applicable).

- the bank obtains cover for part of its risks from credit insurers (ECA or private insurers); and
- the bank applies for the necessary subsidies to be able to discount at a rate allowing the supplier to compete with foreign suppliers.

6.6.3 *Financial and buyer's credits*

The technical and commercial complexity of major export transactions and the increasing amounts of money involved has induced banks to develop an export financing technique which dissociates the financing of the transaction from the technical and commercial negotiation. This is the 'buyer's credit', which is granted by the bank to the buyer. (Sometimes a buyer's credit is granted to the bank of the buyer; then the export credit is called a financial credit.)

The introduction of buyer's credits has been very successful since they meet the exporters' wish to be discharged of the financial aspects of their export contracts, with regard to both the purely administrative work and the balance sheet implications. In addition, this financing technique is well adapted to public foreign buyers that only handle the commercial and technical aspects of the contract, whereas the Ministry of Finance is at the same time negotiating its financial aspects.

This financing technique makes it possible to transfer the organisation and management of the credit and the corresponding risks to the bank in a relatively straightforward manner. This is shown in Figure 6.3.

In the case of financing through a buyer's credit, the commercial contract between the exporter and the foreign buyer can be limited to the technical aspects of the transactions and to the 'cash' payment conditions (see Box 6.5).

Figure 6.3 The buyer's credit scheme

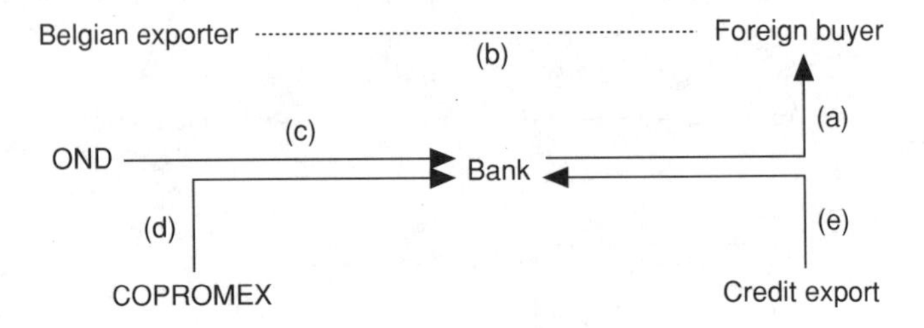

(a) credit agreement;
(b) commercial contract;
(c) insurance;
(d) subsidising;
(e) refinancing.

Box 6.5: The characteristics of the financial credit

The main characteristics of the financial credit are as follows:

- The bank enables the foreign buyer, through a credit agreement which is separate from the commercial contract, to pay for purchases of foreign goods and services in cash.
- Since the bank extends the credit, it bears the foreign risk (except for the part of the risk that is not covered by the ECA and that the bank is allowed to transfer to the exporter) and will therefore be the direct beneficiary of the ECA's insurance policy.
- The exporter will remain the beneficiary of the insurance against arbitrary cancellation of the contract since this covers, by definition, the portion of the contract not yet paid by the buyer.
- The exporter and its bank will therefore apply simultaneously to the ECA, but the bank will assume the overall supervision of the repayment of the credit by the foreign debtor (supervision of incoming funds, claims filed with the ECA, etc.).
- Together with its exporting customer, the bank applies for interest subsidies. The exporter provides all the technical data and details on its position regarding competitors and on the origin of goods of the contract, in order to justify the necessity of subsidies that reduce the rate of interest paid by the purchaser.
- Since the bank provides the credit, it will also receive the subsidy. Possible delays in the payment of the subsidies will sometimes be borne by the bank, to the extent that the delay exceeds a specific period agreed upon for which the exporter remains liable.
- As in the case of a supplier's credit, refinancing by the bank will occur in the market or with the appropriate institution.

6.6.4 *Buyer's credit or supplier's credit?*

The various aspects that play a role in the selection of either credit type can be summarised as follows:

- The size of the contract. By way of illustration, most Belgian banks take the point of view that a transaction involving less than 50 million BEF is not worth the cost of setting up a buyer's credit (negotiation of agreements, travel, etc.).
- The comparative cost of both techniques. The interest rate, credit insurance, commissions and other charges are the same in both cases. The only additional cost attached to the buyer's credit is the management fee of the bank. This commission is, in principle, payable by the foreign buyer.
- The main incentive for choosing the buyer's credit alternative is certainly the exporter's wish to pass to the bank not only the problems of negotiating the credit conditions but also part of the risks and the entire administration of the credit.

- The approval by the ECA of the credit term and of the maximum portion of the contract to be financed (generally 85 per cent of the contract value) does not depend on the financing system chosen.
- As against that, the use of the 'progress payments' formula or release on 'instalment credit' with a view to financing payments falling due during the manufacturing period (excluding advances, of coursc) can only be achieved easily in the context of a buyer's or financial credit. One should bear in mind that 'instalment credit' at a fixed interest rate and with an interest supplement prior to despatch of the equipment is only possible if the foreign buyer has agreed to make larger payments than the customary 15 per cent advances during the period of manufacture. The ECA only permits such credits in so far as they will not result in any over-financing or, if when added to the advances collected, do not exceed the total expenditure incurred during the period of manufacture in connection with expenditure for goods not yet despatched.

6.6.5 *Export finance in foreign currencies*

REFINANCING

In the case of export financing in the national currency, the banks refinance by resorting to the money or capital market (in the Netherlands for example) or to a specialised institution (such as Creditexport in Belgium). In the event of financing in foreign exchange, however, the banks are compelled to refinance on the international foreign exchange market. However, in view of the specific problems entailed in financing large export contracts (uncertainty as to the contract coming into force, the time of drawing down the credit, the time of starting repayments, etc.), it is impossible for the banks in most cases to refinance the credit for the entire term. In most cases the bank will have to refinance on the Euro-currency market, short term and on the basis of a floating interest rate.

To give the banks the possibility of offering the buyer a fixed interest rate (the CIRR, or the Consensus interest rate if it is lower), the national governments responsible for exports have set up a mechanism for stabilising interest rates. The way the mechanism works is that the government (in Belgium Compromex, and in the Netherlands Senter) covers the difference between (floating) financing costs on the one hand and the (fixed) lending interest rate on the other, if the latter is lower. If the bank's financing costs, including its margins, are lower than the lending interest rate, the bank pays the difference to the government. This settlement takes place every six months on the day on which the export credit falls due on the basis of the six-month LIBOR rate (London Interbank Offered Rate) of the particular currency.

INSURANCE OF THE EXCHANGE RISK

In addition to the various risks covered by the ECA examined above, the ECA may provide cover against the various types of exchange risks that the exporter or the bank faces at the various stages of a project.

Exchange risk for the exporter during the tender period. The exporter is exposed to a direct exchange-rate risk during the tender period. The selling price has been converted into a foreign currency, and any fall in its value will incur exchange-rate losses.

It is not possible to eliminate this exchange-rate risk during the tender period by means of a forward transaction, as the exporter is not certain of being awarded the contract. The risk can be covered, however, by taking out an option contract in the currency of financing.

Exchange-rate risk for the exporter during the period of manufacture or construction. As soon as the export contract has been signed and the period of manufacture or construction commences, the exporter could in principle take out forward cover. However, that raises the risk of substantial exchange-rate losses as a result of non-compliance with or breach of contract, resulting in the claim not being paid. In this case, the loss occurs where there is a rise in the currency rate. The fact is that exporters must themselves buy the requisite currency in order to be able to honour their forward sales, and at a higher purchase price than the rate at which they sold the foreign currency. The term used here is a reverse exchange risk. If exporters fail to cover themselves against this, they are running a direct exchange-rate risk as they do during the tender period.

Exchange risk for the bank/exporter during the reimbursement period. During the reimbursement period there is also a reverse exchange risk for the exporter or bank, depending upon whether it is a supplier's or buyer's credit. If reimbursement fails to be made, the lender will of course be obliged to purchase the necessary currency to clear the credit.

PART 3: EXPORT FINANCING TRENDS IN THE 1990s

6.7 General

The traces left by the debt crisis since the start of the 1980s on the international credits market are slowly beginning to fade. Restructuring programmes accompanied by debt restructuring or write-offs, or otherwise tighter country-risk analysis and more rigorous policy on the part of financial institutions and by bank supervisory authorities, are part and parcel of this. The net result is that there only remain certain financing techniques that can be applied to some 'difficult' countries (for example, pre-financing). In addition, the growing trend towards privatisation is expanding the operational area of project finance and related techniques (for example, co-financing). It is not just in Central and Eastern Europe, but also in Latin America, Asia and some African countries that the conviction is growing that private initiative and market forces should be given or restored to economic sectors, as is their natural right.

The reduction in public export support, both internationally (OECD) and nationally (by such means as budget cuts) is also leading exporters and bankers to search for new, creative solutions. Finally, there is the internationalisation of export and investment projects caused by the growing interdependence of business life. This is creating more and more 'multisourced' export transactions, with international consortia placing orders for the supply of goods and services in various countries where various forms of export financing and possibly government support are available. As a result of this internationalisation, public credit insurers are also being compelled to cooperate more closely, co- and reinsurance being just two examples. The financing of international projects, with exporters taking a significant capital stake or otherwise, is inducing the ECAs and banks to take other risks than with classical export financing.

6.8 Alternative export-financing techniques

6.8.1 *Export leasing*

Regardless of the form it takes, leasing entails one party (the lessee) making use of a good that belongs to another party (the lessor), to whom the lessee pays a fixed or variable rental agreed in advance. The following characteristics are important:

- leasing always relates to items that can be individualised;
- transfer of usage rights lies at the heart of the agreement; and
- there is always some relationship between the contract term and the usability period of the lease item.

Apart from these common characteristics, leasing may relate to two very different transactions, both in terms of structure and contractual provisions: financial leasing and operational leasing.

Under financial leasing, a leasing company or bank purchases an item on the basis of the future lessee's specific instructions. The lease item is rented to the lessee for a fixed period, which corresponds to the economic life of the item. The lease contract cannot be terminated during that period and the rental sums enable the item to be written off in full. In most cases the lessee also wishes to become the owner of the item after the contract has expired. For the lessee, the lease contract terminates with the transfer of ownership against payment of the residual value of the item. The investment risk is borne by the lessee, who is thus liable for maintenance, repair and insurance costs.

Operational leasing is a rental agreement under which the owner of an item assigns the right to use it for a certain period against payment of a rental. The total value of the rentals contractually paid by the lessee does not permit the lessor to reassemble the invested capital in full. Operational leases may take several forms: fixed-term contracts shorter than the economic life of the lease item, or redeemable contracts. Operational leasing is usually accompanied by a wide range of attendant services, such as insurance, maintenance and repair.

Export leasing, sometimes termed cross-border leasing, is a special form of international leasing, with the lessor and lessee being of different nationalities. As with classical export financing, export leasing is also subject to international rules (Berne Union, OECD Consensus): a maximum of 85 per cent of the contract value can be financed, there are restrictions on the term, and foreign incorporation.[26] (For the possible benefits of export leasing, see Box 6.6).

As against that, in certain cases the ECAs are prepared to adopt a more flexible stance on the requirement that at least 15 per cent of the contract value must be paid in cash as an advance. Financial leasing of the full 100 per cent of the proportion of the export amount that can be repatriated is permitted, but the ECA cover will only relate to the 85 per cent proportion.[27]

Box 6.6: Possible benefits of export leasing

Export leasing is generally based on financial leasing and can be very attractive in some cases:

1. The 'off balance sheet' effect. Export leasing is not recorded in the foreign debt of the country concerned (which can substantially reduce the country risk and make it easier to obtain credit insurance). The same principle applies to private debtors in certain countries, i.e. the absence of a commitment under book-keeping regulations to include the item in the balance sheet.
2. To public debtors in particular, leasing offers the additional advantage of writing off against the current budget and not the investment budget. This accelerates and smoothes the approval procedure (which explains why leasing was very successful in Germany, for example, at least in the period from 1980–89).
3. In addition, the way leasing is dealt with in fiscal terms in the leesee's country (for example, import duties only being levied on the residual value of the item, exemption from or deferment of payment of import duties, total interest deductible i.e. principal plus interest); and the difference in fiscal regime between the country of the lessor and that of the lessee (reflected, for example, in the possibility of double writing-off) provide grounds for choosing export leasing over export financing for certain export transactions.
4. Ownership of the rented item can in some cases be wholly or partially included in the payment guarantee package. This is certainly the case with 'international movable assets' such as coaches, lorries, aircraft and ships.

26. The Consensus actually makes a concession regarding lease practice: equal half-yearly rentals comprising the capital and interest instead of fixed half-yearly redemption of the capital with degressive half-yearly settlement of interest are permitted.

27. If ownership of the item represents a genuine guarantee to the lessor which can readily be made good in practice, the ECA will be prepared in some cases to extend the scope of the cover to 100 per cent of the rental amounts.

The bank or leasing company acting as lessor purchases the capital goods from the manufacturer solely with a view to the export-leasing operation. This means that the technical characteristics of the good and the price were agreed in advance between the exporter and lessee and the bank does not enter into any undertaking whatsoever. The term of the lease agrees with the economic life of the item; usually three, five, or seven years (maximum). The sum of the rentals under a full pay-out lease will be equal to the value of the item and reimbursement to the lessor; in the event of a non-full pay-out lease a relatively substantial residual value remains after payment of all rentals at the end of the contract.[28]

At the end of the lease the lessee has the option of buying the item at the residual value agreed in advance or of returning the item to the lessor at the lessee's expense. The lessor then remains the legal owner of the item, but beneficial ownership is transferred to the lessee. This means on the one hand that the lessee is entitled to claim certain investment incentives in its own country, but also that the lessee must insure the item against all damage. If the lessee fails to do so, it is obliged to pay all outstanding rentals and to return the item.

6.8.2 *Prefinancing foreign exports*

Agreements on prefinancing of exports (usually commodities) from foreign vendors by their customers have been familiar for some time in the form of a 'red clause' in a documentary credit. Under this clause, the vendor-beneficiary of the documentary credit is permitted to draw down a certain amount against the documentary credit prior to delivery of the goods. The red clause can therefore be regarded as an advance payment, granted by the buyer to the vendor, which will be deducted from the invoice amount at the time of shipping the goods. The economic objective of this 'advance', which generally speaking does not yield any interest, is to provide the vendor with the necessary funds to produce the goods covered by the documentary credit. A red clause in a documentary credit, pertaining to the sale of agricultural products for example, allows the harvest to be financed in whole or in part: purchasing seeds, fertilisers, spare parts for machinery, and so on.

The technique of prefinancing the vendor by the buyer, used on a relatively modest scale until a few years ago, has resurfaced recently, largely on account of the debt problems of developing countries. The fact is that prefinancing is currently the only means available for some countries to obtain financing in foreign currency. In some cases the amounts are so large that a bank syndicate has to be put together. In that event, the technique of refinancing without recourse of an advance under a red clause is usually replaced by a direct credit, granted by the bank syndicate to the vendor. This credit is interest-bearing in contrast to the general red-clause practice. This credit (plus interest) is repaid using the amounts owed by the buyer to the vendor, which are paid directly by the buyer to the banks under an irrevocable instruction given by the vendor.

28. This formula is usually restricted to items carrying a significant value on the existing second-hand market. The bank does not take any risk on the residual value of the item, however, and will take out cover with the exporter or a third party in advance.

The advantage of prefinancing lies in the nature of the risk itself: the risk of non-fulfilment of a particular commercial transaction. This is a risk that differs markedly from a purely financial risk with credits to cover deficits on the balance of payments. Prefinancing, it should be noted, has been repaid as a priority to date and did not come under debt restructuring.

Failure to repay the advance implies that the vendor is in default of delivering the goods to the buyer. This default, which also results in losses for the buyer (for example, the goods to be received have already been bought by a future option), will result in the vendor in future having difficulty in finding buyers for its products, thus cutting off access to the last sources of foreign currency available to it.

Prefinancing constructions may sometimes be used to finance the importing of capital goods in the country of the exporter. The funds advanced to the foreign supplier are used in that case to pay for purchases that this borrower wishes to make in the country of sale. The prefinancing technique therefore makes it possible to finance exports to developing countries which in many cases are not eligible for classical financing methods such as documentary credits or export credits.

The term of such prefinancing is admittedly usually shorter than that of export credits in the medium term, but in some cases comparable terms can be obtained, sometimes by cover from a public credit insurer. Setting up such prefinancing for export purposes naturally demands excellent knowledge of both the international goods market and export financing. This technique can also be combined with project financing and may lead to buy-back operations, but repayment of the project is then effected by sale of the goods produced by the project itself.

6.8.3 *Project finance*

If they are to maintain a presence on certain markets, or penetrate new markets, exporters often have to invest themselves, via a joint venture with local partners or otherwise, particularly in the case of services, when presence in the foreign market is often necessary (see also Chapter 5). In arriving at such a decision, the company usually wishes to find a way of reducing the risks and consequences for the balance sheet from financing the investment project. In other cases, the exporter is not compelled to invest itself, but to sell to a foreign company set up specially to implement a particular project (for example, the construction and operation of a private telephone network) and which either cannot or does not wish to benefit from payment guarantees by the state or a local bank.

These are both instances of project financing: it is not the state, the bank or the buyer's parent company that serve to reimburse and repay debts but simply the cash flow of the project. Project finance can therefore be defined as follows: a financing of a particular economic unit in which a lender is satisfied with looking initially at the cash flows and earnings of that economic unit as a source of funds from which a loan will be repaid and at the assets of the economic unit as collateral for the loan.

As the bank cannot resort to the 'sponsor's' balance sheet (strong or otherwise), this usually increases the risk, for two reasons. First, the uncertainty as to whether the project will actually be implemented: if not, there will be no cash flow at all from which to repay the debts incurred. Secondly, if the project does come about, the actual returns must agree with the expected return.

The pre-completion risks of the project are as follows:

- The technical and technological risk: this is connected with the quality of the licences, procedures, engineering studies, the capital goods to bc supplied and related services (transport, assembly and the like);
- The financial risk: this is connected with possible cost over-runs, delays with financial repercussions, or price adjustments, penalty clauses, rising interest per centages, and so on; and
- The political risk, including *force majeure*.

As regards the post-completion risk, the initial financial risk is now replaced by a cash-flow risk: internal factors (management, labour, maintenance and the like) and external factors (supplies of raw materials, sales outlets, decisions by local governments, etc.) can adversely affect the level of the cash flow.

The project sponsor or its financial advisor or both (in many cases a bank working on the basis of a mandate to provide consultancy, which usually stands separate from the financing itself) have to identify and analyse these risks and bring them to the attention of potential lenders. This is done on the basis of a memorandum of information. There is a descriptive part, a market study, a section on the legal structure of the financing, and a feasibility study with supporting figures. In addition to a computer model with basic data and assumptions, the latter also includes a number of variants that take account of fluctuations in the key parameters (known as a sensitivity analysis).

The sponsors and their advisors should therefore ensure that they set up an adequate security package. Prior to completion of the project, efforts must be made to ensure a balanced distribution in terms of efforts and undertakings between the various intervening parties (see Box 6.7).

Following completion of the project, securities should be created within the project company and beyond. Within the company, the project company's balance sheet is a major source of security:

- The assets: fixed assets may be mortgaged and current assets pledged.
- The liabilities: the company shares are also pledged, such that the company can be taken over as a going concern if major problems arise.
- The sponsors may be invited to retain a certain percentage of the shares until all credits have been repaid. Finally, restrictions may be imposed on dividend payments and on the scope for additional investment and lending.
- Information commitments are usually imposed within the company. There are also contracts that continue after completion of construction, mainly management, licence and insurance contracts: such agreements are usually pledged to the lenders.
- The viability of the company naturally also depends on having a profitable process for processing raw materials or other inputs into saleable products. Therefore, the existence of long-term commitments with suppliers or buyers or both is also a major source of security. The sponsor of a project is sometimes a supplier or buyer itself.

Box 6.7: The parties involved in project finance: inputs and commitments

The sponsor(s): the sponsor's financial commitments, apart from providing capital, range from undertakings on resources (doing everything possible to ensure project completion by a certain date) to formal guarantees whereby, until a wide complex of conditions and tests has been satisfied, credits are guaranteed by the sponsors (the completion guarantee) and/or with cost over-runs being exclusively or jointly financed by the sponsors.

The contractor(s) (who have usually undertaken to deliver a turn-key project): apart from the technical risks, they also bear financial risks by issuing guarantees of good performance (termed performance bonds) and by accepting penalties in the event of failure to comply with contractual commitments.

The end user or its government or both: in some cases they may influence the timely completion of the project; in such cases it is therefore logical that they should shoulder some of the risks.

The financial world: the banks and other financial institutions granting the credits and the insurers covering the various risks (including fire and similar risks).

The project company itself: the operating assets are also included in the security package from the outset. In most cases their value is not rated very highly until the project-completion stage, since it is determined more by the capacity of the project to generate cash flow than the acquisition value of the assets.

6.8.4 *Build-operate-transfer (BOT)*

The BOT financing technique is a special form of project financing, where private capital is invested in public infrastructure such as in the case of energy (electricity generating plants, hydraulic power plants, oil pipelines, gas pipelines, etc.), water, telecommunications, and transport (metros, motorways, tunnels, etc.). The BOT technique is mainly used in the privatisation of infrastructure projects and public utilities which traditionally were created and operated by the public sector.

Although there are numerous examples of BOT techniques in OECD countries (motorways, Eurotunnel and others), the technique has not yet really been launched in non-OECD countries. The reason lies in the complexity of the legal and financial constructions and the commitments demanded of the various partners. What is required is the setting up of a company holding and a concession by a group of entrepreneurs and exporters, based on contracts signed with project developers on implementation, financing and management of the project. Following an operating period determined in advance, generally 25 to 30 years, the project is handed over to the local government.

The success criteria for projects organised as BOTs are as follows:

- The project must be economically credible and financially profitable;
- A BOT technique in practice is only feasible in industrialised countries or countries where industrialisation has sufficient momentum, and which have sufficient political stability, sufficient currency resources, and so on;
- The project must have the backing of the local government, which must provide the legislative framework for the project;
- The project must satisfy a real need among future users (i.e. there must be a clear definition of buyers); and
- The project must lend itself to independent management.

A BOT project offers the following benefits to the importing country:

- It avoids any increase in the government's visible external debt;
- It guarantees proper management of the infrastructure created;
- It includes a guarantee of successful completion and contains a performance bond for the entire operational life;
- It avoids any growth in the public sector and leads to greater competition; and
- The presence of an experienced operator from the company holding the concession, who commits for a long period and shares in the profits, is also vital.

The BOT construction is partial in nature if the party granting the concession retains a proportion of the risks attached to the project, for example by guaranteeing receipts, or a minimum level of usage (for example on toll roads) or consumption (for example with electricity supplies). The BOT construction is complete if all risks are transferred to the private sector. In some cases of a partial BOT construction, the export credits will be guaranteed by the party granting the concession. According to the logic of the BOT construction, interest and debt repayments are only covered by the cash flow, however, with the various lenders having equal status. As with project financing, with a BOT construction the credit insurers will have to create some coherence making the project amenable to financing in banking terms by covering specific risks

6.8.5 *Cofinancing*

Cofinancing with multilateral institutions – such as the International Finance Corporation (IFC), the European Bank for Reconstruction and Development (EBRD), the European Investment Bank (EIB), and the other regional banks (Asian Development Bank, African Development Bank, Inter-American Development Bank) – is a special form of project financing. Some of the multilateral institutions participate in the financing of private projects by means of long-term loans or a capital stake or both. Cofinancing occurs if multilateral institutions call upon commercial bankers to cofinance a project.

The reason why these institutions work towards cofinancing with private banks is two-fold:

1. The interventions by these institutions in the form of holdings or loans are limited to the amount of their own resources (i.e. the gearing ratio is 1:1). In view of the

enormous need for resources, cofinancing can be used to step up the flow of finance to developing countries in Central and Eastern Europe.
2. Cofinancing enables certain (country) risks to be reduced, enabling projects in difficult countries to acquire bank credits, albeit indirectly.

Box 6.8 elaborates on the use of cofinancing by the IFC.

Box 6.8: The use of cofinancing

The most successful cofinancing formula to date has been the IFC's Loan Participation Program, which also came to be used by the EBRD recently. Under this formula, commercial banks enjoy the benefits of the IFC's preferred creditor status. Hence it is that in certain countries (Belgium, France, the UK, the USA and others) bank supervisory authorities have exempted cofinancing loans from mandatory provisioning.

In the event of cofinancing, the IFC loan is provided in two tranches:

1. The 'A loan' is the IFC credit, provided on the basis of its own resources and subject to its own conditions.
2. The 'B loan' is provided (indirectly) by the commercial banks on the basis of agreed conditions (usually less favourable than those governing the 'A loan', i.e. with a shorter term and higher interest rate). In some cases the B loan is divided into two or more portions, each subject to its own conditions. The IFC acts as 'lender or record' and assumes responsibility for full credit administration. The participating banks are known to the lender. Finally, a participation agreement is signed between the IFC and the B-syndicate banks, including 'cross-default' and '*pari passu*' clauses, under which all participating banks have the same rights and commitments.

The IFC financing may also be accompanied by an export credit, insured by a public credit insurer and provided by commercial banks. In most cases, the latter will participate in the B loan of the parallel IFC credit, likewise on a pro-rata basis. The export credit does not, however, enjoy the IFC's preferred creditor status. An 'increditor agreement' is signed between the latter and the bank syndicate for the export credit, which includes only a 'cross-default' or '*pari passu*' clause for the commercial risks.

IFC loans were never restructured for political reasons, while the commercial banks' stakes were not eligible for the provision of what is termed 'new money'.

Further reading

Corluy, W. (1990) *Financiering en Risicobeheer in de Internationale Handel*, MIM.
Freshfields (1995) *International Project Finance Group*, Project Finance.
Generale Bank (1993) *De Nieuwe Technieken i.v.m. de Financiering op Halflange Termijn van de Belgische Uitvoer van Kapitaal Goederen en Diensten*, Bulletin Speciale Editie.
Guild, I. and **Harris, R.** (1985) *Forfaiting, An Alternative Approach to Export Trade Finance*, Woodhead-Faulkner and Euromoney Publications.
Madura, J. (1995) *International Financial Management*, West Publishing Company.
OECD (1990) *The Export Credit Financing Systems in OECD Member Countries*.
Stephens, M. (1995) *Emerging Markets: Projects 1995*. Text of a lecture given in Paris in January 1995 by the chairman of the Berne Union.

Appendix to Chapter 6: Modalities of cover offered by ECAs

1. As shown above, the risk is in principle never 100 per cent covered with credit insurance. The insured party's own risk or residual risk, namely its sharing in any losses, is deemed necessary in credit insurance in order to guarantee that party's cooperation in the management of the risk and in collecting its debts from other countries. In most countries the insured party has to bear in full the percentage not guaranteed by the ECA. Each additional insurance or any settlement that would contravene this regulation is prohibited on penalty of invalidating the insurance. Exceptions here include forfaiting and the distribution of the residual risk between the exporter and the bank in the event of a buyer's credit. The percentage of losses covered is normally:

   - 95 per cent when covering the risk of government debtors, and when covering the political risk associated with transactions with private debtors; or
   - 90 per cent when covering the commercial risk associated with transactions with private debtors. If the debtor or the guarantor is a bank, the figure is 95 per cent.

   The percentage covered may be reduced on account of the severity of the risks to be insured.

2. The reimbursement calculation differs according to whether it is a termination claim or a loss on the grounds of non-payment:

   - In the event of a termination claim, the basis taken for calculating the loss is the cost price (i.e. the total expenditure incurred by the insured party between ordering and the loss claim), from which are deducted the payments received and subsequent claims collected.
   - In the event of losses incurred on the grounds of non-payment, reimbursement is calculated on the basis of the amount of the unpaid claim or the unpaid part of the claim. This is therefore determined on the basis of the sale price (which may include transport and financing costs as well as profits).

3. The waiting period, that is, the time that must elapse before the ECA will pay against a claim, differs according to whether it is a termination claim or a case of

non-payment and according to the nature of the risks covered. In the case of the Belgian National Delcrederedienst (NDD), for example, this is as follows:

- In the event of termination losses: within 30 days after the amount of the losses has been finally established. If the amount cannot be established within six months of the breach of contract, the NDD makes a provisional payment, calculated on the basis of the probable damages.
- In the event of losses arising from non-payment: within 30 days of the last of the following dates: (a) the date on which the waiting period expires (six months in principle); or (b) the date on which the NDD has received the information and documents required to establish proof of the losses.

If the debtor's insolvency has been established before the waiting period has elapsed, the ECA makes payment immediately. The waiting period may also be extended on account of the severity of the risks to be insured.

4. No loss shall give entitlement to reimbursement if it is the insured party's own fault or the fault of any party for whom that party is liable. Fault may take one of the following forms:

   - technical or financial mistakes made within the context of the agreement and which would have caused losses even without any claim for damages;
   - failure to comply with the laws and regulations in force in the exporter's country or in another country, notably with regard to the authorisations and formalities required for imports, exports or transfer of payments;
   - lack of due care in dealing with the risks of non-transfer of payments in foreign currencies; for example, holding cash resources in the local currency of the debtor's country, which are not in proportion to the pace or volume of the work, or financing local expenditure by currency transfer, while financing could have been effected in the relevant currency;
   - accepting contractual clauses which are exceptional in relation to international customs, and which would abnormally restrict the rights of the insured party in the event of a loss claim.

   In such cases, fault may consist in penal clauses or clauses covering cancellation or *force majeure*, which encumber the event covered with abnormal consequences, or even in the acceptance of a legal competence of dubious status, regardless of whether this is judicial or by arbitration.

5. If the ECA is inclined to the view that there is an impending cause of a claim, it is entitled to impose any measure it considers suitable to prevent such losses occurring or to limit its impact.
   Among other things, it is entitled, if the cases of breaching are covered, to interrupt manufacturing or supplying or any implementation of the agreement or, conversely, to insist upon continuation regardless of the fact that one of the above events has occurred.

7 Concessional export financing

PART 1: EXPORT FINANCING

7.1 Introduction

There is usually strong pressure within donor countries for aid to generate commercial and political gains, which encourages concessional export financing. According to Morrissey (1993, p. 22), export competition among donors is one of the dominant driving forces behind aid, which is therefore provided either as an export subsidy – a mixed credit – or more generally as a support for exports, through aid tying.

It is clear that concessional export financing can supplant other means of export promotion such as tied official development assistance (ODA), and can equally serve to safeguard commercially viable export orders for domestic industry. This may explain why the gap due to the overall decline in the volume of export credits during the 1980s seems to have been filled by an increasing amount of ODA. In fact, according to the OECD, a large part of all export credits is now financed from aid budgets. Three considerations play a role in this respect:

1. The use of a mix of concessional aid and commercial funds results in softer credit terms than the market terms of commercial loans. Such financing therefore can lead to trade distortions, especially if used in export markets with already vigorous competition. If the concessionality level is low, a relatively small amount of aid can result in a substantial additional credit flow (while the whole amount is sometimes qualified as development aid).
2. It is feared that such concessional financing mitigates the developmental effects of aid, for example, because aid is diverted away from projects with low import content.
3. The willingness to coordinate aid will diminish if donors see each other as competitors.

It is argued that concessional export financing can make a positive contribution to development because it causes the total capital flow to recipients to increase, and the commercial credit terms to soften for countries with debt problems. It is also argued that as an instrument it is particularly suitable for countries which no longer need soft concessional financing, because of their level of development.

In this chapter, the concept of concessional export financing will first be reviewed. After establishing a definition of concessional export financing, some overall trends will be presented, followed by an examination of whether a theoretical case exists for its use. Actual experience with the instrument will be illustrated, by looking at policies carried out in France and Britain.

In the second part, the institutional background and rules regarding concessional export financing will be analysed. These rules have in common their aim to better reconcile the donors' developmental targets and the target of creating a level playing field in international competition.

7.2 Definitions

Export subsidies can take the form of export credits, export credit insurance (see Chapter 6) or ODA. An official export credit is a loan that is linked to an export transaction and which is provided by a governmental institution. It allows importing firms to spread payments over time, while immediately providing exporting firms with (part of) the revenues of the export transaction. Export credits are usually extended either to domestic exporters or commercial financial institutions (supplier credit), or to foreign importers (buyer credit) in the form of interest subsidies. Official export credit insurance is provided by national insurance agencies, and covers export transactions, which themselves may or may not be financed by export credits. The insurance represents an export subsidy if the premium rate lies below the going market rate. Finally, ODA consists of governmental loans at subsidised interest rates.

Concessional export financing will be defined here as a combination of ODA, in the form of aid credits or grants, with officially supported export credits or regular commercial credits. In this chapter, we will investigate concessional export financing by focusing on aid tying and mixed credits.

The subsidy which is implicit in a government export support programme can either be viewed as a benefit for the exporter or as the cost incurred by the government. These two approaches do not necessarily lead to the same estimates of the subsidy equivalents, because they involve different instruments. On the one hand subsidised supplier credits and subsidised export insurance lower the financing costs for exporting firms. On the other hand, subsidised buyer credits and ODA increase the importing firms' revenue, by providing favourable financing conditions for the importer instead of the exporting firm.

7.2.1 *Aid tying*

Aid can create a trade dependency between donor and recipient in many ways. If aid generates political goodwill, the recipient may feel obliged to purchase the donor's goods. This aid and trade link is made explicit when aid is tied, so that the recipient *must* import from the donor. It is useful to distinguish the effects of tying in two categories, formal and informal tying. In *formal tying* the granting of aid is contingent on purchasing goods from the donor. In practice, aid is rarely formally tied for an amount of over 70 per cent of aid. This category of formally tied aid generates the largest economic costs and inefficiencies. Tying is *informal* when it results from another donor policy, for example, where aid is given to countries which have strong trading ties with the donor or where the recipient is aware of the goodwill that would result if it purchased the donor's goods. Informal tying will commonly be closely related to donor trade interests but is difficult to identify.

Aid tying is an impediment to free trade by reducing competition, thereby increasing the price, and reducing the choice for developing countries. The volume of tied aid is substantial. In 1990, officially reported tied ODA commitments amounted to about 10 per cent of OECD – less developed country (LDC) trade. Within the OECD, this share varied from 6 per cent for the USA, 9 per cent for Japan and 12 per cent for the EC. Moreover, the average grant element in the Development Assistance Committee (DAC) tied aid commitments during the period 1989–91 was 44 per cent, ranging from 100 per cent for the USA, 29 per cent for the EC, down to 6 per cent for Japan. However, some figures, presenting the first results after the Helsinki package was concluded (see also Section 7.9), suggested a significant decline in tying percentages.

Depending on their international competitiveness, donor industries would win a share of global orders which, in the absence of tying, should at least in theory reflect their market share. Although tying is not a sufficient condition for donor benefits, it may help a donor to derive benefits from its increased trade, benefits which are more than proportional to its share of world export markets. Two issues are salient to the use of tied aid:

- It is necessary that tied aid is trade creating, that is, there is no net benefit if the export order would also have been won in the absence of aid;[29]
- donors offering a larger volume of tied aid are more likely to gain a net increase in market share than donors that only provide a small amount of tied aid.

Furthermore, even if tying is not net trade creating, there still is an incentive to use tying, because in its absence one may lose market share, because other producers do tie their aid. Once the process of tying has started it is therefore self-perpetuating. Donors justify tying, either by arguing that it creates trade or that they simply need to match the tying behaviour of other donors, who are competing for the same export markets.[30]

29. A survey related to the major donors concludes that some 30 to 50 per cent of tied aid is probably not creating net trade (Jepma, 1991, p. 37).

30. Note that if there is matching, tying is not creating net trade.

7.2.2 *Mixed credits and less concessional loans (LCLs)*

One particular form of export support that was increasingly used in the early 1980s is mixed credits. Mixed credits are tied aid credits in which a grant element (aid or soft loan) is offered to defray part of the cost of a commercial contract to the LDC government. Mixed credits are often compared with less concessional aid because of their relatively hard loan conditions.

Mixed credits are only granted to LDCs with export credit cover; requests for being able to provide a mixed credit are usually instigated by the company seeking the project rather than by the donor or by an aid agency. Their use is concentrated in a few industries only, but their relative impact is considerable. From a business perspective, they are often of greater benefit than other forms of aid, which explains why business lobbies are so vocally supportive of increased use of mixed credits. Indeed, they are far more overtly commercial and trade-supporting than ordinary aid.

The number of countries intensively using mixed credits is traditionally small. The country that uses this instrument most extensively is France, with some 50 per cent of its total use; Italy and the United Kingdom (UK) also significantly employ mixed credits. The issue of mixed credits has proved to be highly controversial: there have been many attempts to regulate their use in order to avoid 'beggar-thy-neighbour' policies which in the end will be to the disadvantage of all donor countries.

The common characteristic of less concessional loans (LCLs) and mixed credits – as apart from most other forms of aid – is the relative hardness of the loan conditions. While the average grant element of total ODA lies between 80 and 90 per cent, the concessionality level of mixed credits and LCLs is considerably lower. The minimum permissable concessionality level is 35 per cent for all countries, except for the least developed countries (LLDCs), where a minimum level of 50 per cent applies.

Mixed credits differ from LCLs in this respect, that the former offers two loan contracts: one for the concessional part and one for the commercial part; whereas in the case of LCLs, only one loan contract is offered, with a grant element of up to 50 per cent; there is usually mixing beforehand (which is called pre-blending or pre-mixing).

7.3 Trends

During the 1970s, the use of export credits expanded. Governments increasingly provided soft credits for export transactions, especially for the exports of capital goods,[31] because for various reasons, both at the supply and demand side, in the 1960s an excess capacity had arisen in this sector. Moreover, an increasing number of countries suffered from balance-of-payments problems. Therefore a growing importance was attached to the after-financing conditions for obtaining export orders. In other words,

31. The capital goods industry is considered by many governments to be of strategic importance to the economic development of their countries.

the focus gradually shifted from competitiveness of the product to competitiveness of the export financing.

Between 1960 and 1980, the volume of export credits expanded by a factor of five to about $70 billion. From the beginning of the 1980s onwards, however, the volume of export orders declined sharply, to a level of about $35 billion in 1987. This large decline was attributed to the economic world recession in general, and to the worsening debt situation of a number of LDCs in particular. Since 1988, the volume of export credits increased again. This recovery coincided with a revival of world trade and of capital goods exports.

While the volume of export credits to the LDCs in the 1980s declined drastically, the importance of aid funds as a source of financing of export transactions increased. The amount of aid loans that can be qualified as export support amounted in the early 1980s to about 20 per cent of the volume of export credits. At the end of the 1980s, however, the major part of export credits to LDCs was derived from the aid budget.

Changes did not only take place in financing conditions, but also in the form of finance. In the early 1980s, a substantial part of hard aid loans were mixed credits. At the end of the 1980s, however, the share of this form of finance had decreased. In 1981–82, the volume of mixed credits was over $4 billion, one-third of which consisted of ODA. In 1987, however, the volume of mixed credits dropped to 50 per cent, of which $1 billion consisted of ODA. An explanation for this decline is to be found in the reduced importance of the so-called stretching effect.[32] Whereas in the early 1980s a certain amount of aid money could attract about the same amount in terms of commercial credits, since 1987 the same amount of aid money would only attract one-third as many commercial credits.[33] A form of finance which has gained importance during recent years among others, because it is considerably simpler both procedurally and administratively, is the LCL.[34]

Recently, a gradually decreasing amount of low concessional aid loans went to the poorest countries, because aid loans were increasingly provided to the better-off LDCs and the spoiled markets in Asia.

7.4 Theory of export subsidies

Probably the dominant trade objective for which aid is used is to increase export competition. For the sake of simplicity, in the following analysis it is assumed that

32. By providing a concessional loan, additional commercial funds will be generated, so that a larger amount of credits can be extended.

33. The fact that problems are mounting in the export credit area is reflected by the trend in net cash flows of export credit agencies. The gap between claims and premiums has substantially widened since the mid-1980s. The net cash flow of export credit agencies went from zero in 1981 to a loss of SDR 6 billion in 1991. Although these cash flow data are not estimates of real losses, they do suggest an increase in direct budgetary costs.

34. Many countries adopted an LCL system in the 1980s, e.g. France, Japan, and The Netherlands. The Netherlands, however, abolished its system in 1991 to reduce the use of commercial funds within the Dutch Aid Budget.

concessional export financing can be considered as a sort of export subsidy. The theoretical analysis of the impact of concessional export financing can then be presented on the basis of a partial analysis of a supply and demand figure.

One of the insights from the theory of trade policy is that export support schemes may have a positive impact on individual business performance if targeted well and applied strategically. However, these schemes, except for some very specific market conditions, rarely increase a country's net welfare: from an overall welfare perspective the theoretical case for an export support scheme is therefore rather weak. This point is illustrated graphically in Figure 7.1.

In Figure 7.1, market equilibrium is established in F, where import demand and export supply are equal (d = s). This point corresponds with a price p and a volume of trade q. In the case of perfect competition, an export subsidy raises the export price of the home country, while lowering the corresponding price abroad, the difference between both prices in per cent being equal to the subsidy rate. So, if the domestic exporter receives a subsidy per unit of x, the price per unit received by the exporter will be x larger than the one paid by the importer. One can infer that such a price difference is only compatible with a market equilibrium at E (s′ = d). Now the prices for the importer and exporter are p^* and p^*+x respectively, while the volume traded has expanded to a level of q^*.

The impact of the export subsidy is twofold. First, the exporting sector has expanded and therefore increased its producer surplus. If the subsidy has no impact whatsoever on the non-exported part of the sales of the sector, the producer surplus is the difference between the total receipts related to the exports and total costs involved with these exports. Since after the export subsidy total receipts are equal to OCDH (as it was OBFI before the subsidy) and the related total costs equal to OJDH (instead of OJFI), the ensuing increased producer surplus amounts to BCDF (the shaded area). This amount represents the welfare gain for the exporting sector. Secondly, the

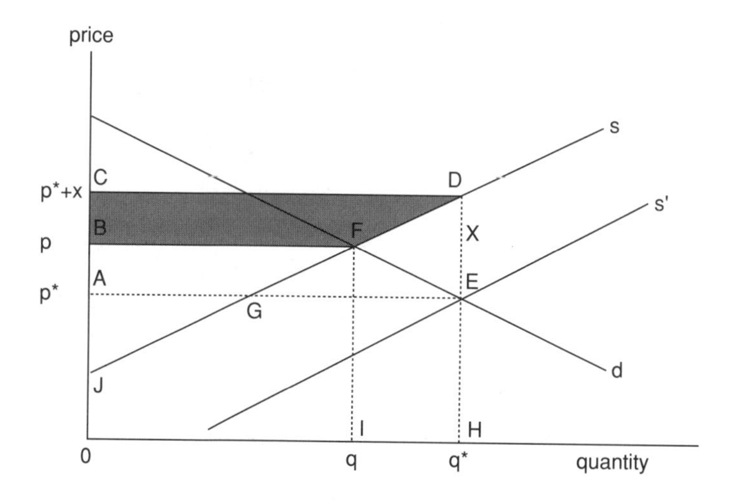

Figure 7.1 Effect of an export subsidy

government has to pay for the subsidy. This value obviously equals ACDE, that is, the volume traded times the subsidy, x per unit. This is the size of the subsidy the taxpayers in the exporting country have to pay.

The overall welfare effect for the exporting country is clearly negative. The triangle FDE in the figure can be interpreted as a deadweight loss. The overall national welfare loss equals the area ABFDE, which has two components. The upper half of the triangle FDE can be interpreted as a distortion loss; the lower half of FDE together with the area ABFE can be interpreted as a terms of trade loss. In other words, the taxpayers transfer an amount of resources to the exporter. They thereby increase the exporters' value added, but part of their sacrifice is leaking away to the importers by way of a terms of trade loss.

Export support schemes are thus a fairly expensive way of trying to improve the market position of, or employment in, a particular sector of the domestic export industry. Moreover, if the supply elasticity of exports is small, the expansion of the volume of exports due to the subsidy is also fairly small (from q to q^*). In the extreme case where export supply is totally inelastic – the supply curve will then be vertical – there will be no export expansion at all; the subsidy has then become a windfall gain that fully accrues to the domestic export supplier. So, according to the traditional static trade theory an export subsidy can never increase a donor's welfare, because the costs for the government are larger than the increased producer surplus for the domestic exporters.

Moreover, even if the benefits of export subsidies outweigh their costs, the resources for the export subsidy might well have been used more effectively. Further, if exports would have been lost in the absence of concessional financing, this does not imply that domestic resources would have remained unemployed. Finally, while some firms benefit, it may indirectly impose costs to other domestic firms.

The functioning of export support schemes in practice suggests a concentration in a few industries where the impact has been considerable. Moreover, the schemes tend to be focused on the better-off LDCs, less in need of ODA. The prime motive of these schemes seems to have been commercial rather than developmental. These contentions are corroborated by two case studies of the UK and France (Kock, 1993, pp. 66–79) which will be presented below.

7.4.1 *United Kingdom*

Initially the Aid and Trade Provision (ATP), Britain's mixed credit programme, was introduced to match assistance available to foreign firms and to help British firms acquire industrially and commercially viable orders with developmental potential in LDCs.

From its inception, however, ATP was a mercantile export subsidy; firms were not granted ATP on the basis of a coherent trade or aid policy, but in accordance with commercial arguments or political pressures. The commercial benefits were great and tended to be concentrated in engineering industries and, within those industries, in the large companies. In contrast to the more persuasive commercial arguments related to the employment potential, the ATP has not been a net benefit to the UK.

The obvious gain from ATP is that it supports exports. There is a direct commercial benefit to exporting companies and there may be direct benefits if ATP helps a firm penetrate new markets in which follow-on orders are subsequently obtained without aid support.[35] The fundamental issue is whether ATP is trade creating; if the export order could have been won without ATP, there is no net economic benefit to the economy, although the exporter benefits from the subsidy. Given the intensity of international competition and the aid support offered by other donors, it is probable that ATP helped UK firms to maintain their market share.

It is clear that ATP generates high commercial benefits per unit expenditure. If ATP were cut, for an average year between 1978 and 1986, some 14,000 jobs could conceivably have been lost. This would be at a cost of £180 million less in exports, a small fraction of total exports, but significant to some industries and firms. On average, each £1 million of ATP supported about 250 person-years of employment, made a net contribution to the trade surplus and repaid 50 to 75 per cent of its cost in increased tax revenue. Moreover, each £1 million of ATP supported some £3.2 million of exports and required total output worth up to £5.6 million.

As mentioned earlier, ATP is concentrated. Over the period 1978–85, 47.6 per cent of ATP went to electrical engineering, 22 per cent to mechanical engineering and 14.4 per cent to shipbuilding and other vehicles; 11 large companies accounted for 77 per cent of ATP (Toye and Clark, 1986). Relating this to the industries which receive the most aid support from other donors suggests that ATP has been focused in areas where foreign competition is strong.

Finally, ATP may be less likely to meet development objectives than normal aid, because it is initiated by companies so that commercial objectives have an explicitly higher weight than developmental objectives. This is especially significant given that ATP was expanded at a time when the real value of aid was falling.

7.4.2 *France*

The French export credit and insurance system is the most elaborate of the industrialised world. In the first half of 1990, the French authorities guaranteed outstanding credits to a total of $60 billion, one fourth of the OECD total (OECD, 1991, p. 23). For the sake of comparison, total outstanding credits guaranteed by the British authorities amounted to $37 billion in 1990, and those guaranteed by the German institutions to $25 billion.

By the end of the 1980s, export credit subsidies in France were of the order of 0.5 per cent of GNP. They were not only large but also concentrated. Two-thirds of export insurance subsidies, representing 0.15 per cent of French GNP, went to construction and associated business services. The more important interest rate subsidies, though less concentrated, were still heavily channelled into a few industries, with

35. Love and Dunlop (1990) argue that ATP support for one project allowed John Brown Engineering to win a number of commercial orders in China.

machinery and electronics receiving over 45 per cent of the total expenditure on subsidies, representing 0.25 per cent of the French GDP.

Consequently, almost half a percentage point of French GNP has been granted to a dozen firms. As a result, export subsidies calculated for a whole sector tend to underestimate the degree to which some firms or activities are subsidised. Estimates of average rates of export subsidisation in the early 1980s range from 8 to 20 per cent.

7.5 Concluding remarks

Concessional export financing, in the form of tied aid and mixed credits, was increasingly used in the 1980s as a device to promote domestic exports because of the decline in export credits. There seems to be no case for doing so based on traditional trade theory, because an export subsidy will always reduce global and national welfare. Moreover, the functioning of these schemes in practice, in particular in France and the UK, suggests their concentration on a few firms and industries and their large commercial orientation. Although there appear to be commercial benefits, these are not net economic benefits. In the next part, we will look at how the various international forums, and in particular the OECD, have responded to this increased use of concessional export financing.

PART 2: INTERNATIONAL ARRANGEMENTS – AN OVERVIEW

7.6 Introduction

In the post-Second World War period, the tariff barriers of the major developed countries were significantly reduced. However, at the same time, the slowdown in the growth of international trade in the early 1980s revived protectionist forces. Among other non-tariff barriers, export subsidies became an increasingly attractive instrument for defending and enhancing market share in a stagnating world market.

Governments were becoming more active in the export credit field because of the scarcity of capital on domestic markets and the non-convertibility of most currencies in the post-war period. Government-backed export credit agencies were established to provide exporters protection against risks in foreign markets and to assist in matching other countries' export credit terms. While the avoidance of losses is an objective, profit maximisation is not the aim of these agencies. Under these conditions, pressure towards soft terms for insurance and credit can be very strong.

International institutions were quick to recognise the dangers of an escalation in the absence of multilateral discipline. There was a risk of an officially supported export credit war by way of lowering interest rates, lengthening repayment periods and relaxing other credit conditions. The economic role of the effective cost of capital – to signal to borrowers and investors the opportunity cost of capital – is then frustrated. The pattern of resource use is distorted and moves away from its most efficient configuration, so that in the long run output and wealth are lowered.

The increasing use of concessional export financing thus led to prolonged discussions in international forums with the purpose of harmonising the conditions on which export financing was to be offered. A detailed review of the existing rules is essential since they profoundly affect the opportunities for subsidisation. It should be noted, however, that these arrangements still leave considerable room for export subsidisation.

In this part, the focus will be on international arrangements with respect to export credit subsidies in general and on concessional export financing in particular. This will be done by looking (briefly) at the frameworks of the EC (currently the EU) and the GATT (WTO). After that a lengthier review of the OECD, from the Consensus until the recently agreed Helsinki package, will be presented. The Helsinki package, which – at the time of its inception – represented a major breakthrough in limiting the abuse of ODA for trade objectives, will be reviewed in depth.

7.7 International forums

Cooperation in the field of export credits and export credit insurance goes back to 1934, when the Berne Union (now called the International Union of Credit and Investment Insurers) was established. In its early years it only dealt with insurance against commercial risks accompanying export contracts with private buyers. After the Second World War, insurance against political and economic risks began assuming much greater importance. The Berne Union agreed that the institutions of which it is composed should base their activities on the principle of being financially self-supporting. Moreover, it endeavours to ensure a degree of coordination with respect to the duration of the credit guarantees granted by its members, which is limited to a maximum of five years.

7.7.1 *General Agreement on Tariffs and Trade (GATT)*

Since 1955, Article XVI (4) of the GATT includes a prohibition of subsidies for all exports except those for primary products. More recent GATT rules for export credits are to be found in its Code on Subsidies and Countervailing Duties, which was negotiated in the Tokyo Round and went into effect in 1979. This Code provides that developed country signatories shall not extend export subsidies for industrial products, while developing country signatories are excused from this restriction, except that they 'should endeavour to reduce or to eliminate export subsidies'.

The GATT Subsidy Code condones export credits that are allowed by the OECD Consensus. Yet export insurance is not covered by the Consensus, but is prohibited by the GATT Subsidy Code. The GATT Subsidy Code considers as evidence of subsidisation the existence of long-term losses on official export insurance programmes, indicating that the insurance premiums charged are too low – the cost-to-the-government principle. This requires the difficult distinction between long-term and temporary losses. Are sustained losses over a decade to be considered as an export subsidy or as an unusual temporary accumulation of claims?

Economically speaking, GATT regulations on export insurance and credits permit significant subsidies to exporters because reference is not made to the ability of an exporter to secure funds at favourable rates, but to the cost to the government. Government agencies can provide export insurance at lower rates than the market if no long-term operating losses are incurred. Likewise, governments are allowed to grant export credits at their borrowing rate, which is very attractive to commercial borrowers.

7.7.2 *European Community (EC)*

When the EEC was established in 1958, the Treaty of Rome forbade any national export subsidies that (threaten to) distort competition between member states. This was followed by a consultation procedure in 1965, under which any proposed deviation from the Community's rules on export credits must be notified. Decisions are made according to the qualified majority voting system and are binding on the member countries concerned.

Restrictions on export credits are more comprehensive than those on export insurance. The EC Treaty rules out export credits to other EC member states. Export credits to third markets are allowed when they do not distort competition between EC states or when they match subsidies from non-EC suppliers and are approved by the Commission. It is difficult, however, to determine when export financing distorts competition between member states. The EC injury criteria are based on the concepts of competitive distortions and impact on trade. Increased import shares or differentiation on the importers' market are used as indicators.

In accordance with Article 92 of the Treaty, any aid granted by a member state or through state resources in any form whatsoever, which distorts competition by favouring certain undertakings or the production of certain goods, is incompatible with the common market. Article 92 thus forms part of the Community's internal rules on competition. All official export credits and export insurance, in so far as they distort competition among member states, are therefore ruled out.

In addition, the Commission requires that any capital provided by the state should earn a return, comparable to the return of a private investor under normal market conditions. The test is whether in similar circumstances a private shareholder, leaving aside all social, regional policy and sectoral considerations, would have provided the capital in question.

This requirement rules out any sustained losses of export credit agencies. It also indicates that a positive return on capital provided by the state does not suffice if the return is below normal market conditions. This requirement is closer to the benefit-to-the-firm principle than to the cost-to-the-government principle, in the sense that official premiums below comparable market rates are seen as a form of subsidisation.

It has the drawback that, quite often, no counterpart is available on the private market for the type of insurance provided by the official agency, so that subsidisation is very difficult to 'prove'.

In conclusion, both EC and GATT regulations refer to the use of public funds in defining inadmissible forms of export support. Article 92 of the EC Treaty rules out any involvement of government agencies or state resources in export insurance in so far as it would distort competition between Community members, and uses the benefit-to-the-firm principle. The GATT Code on Subsidies does not oppose involvement of official government agencies as long as the long-term operation of private and official export insurance systems are covered by insurance premiums, which is an application of the cost-to-the-government principle.

7.8 OECD arrangements

7.8.1 *The Consensus*

In 1955, the Organisation for European Economic Cooperation (OEEC) adopted rules governing measures designed to aid exports, which committed member states to abstain from artificial aid to exporters. When in 1960 the OEEC was transformed into the OECD, the obligations relating to export credits along with its other obligations on export subsidies were transferred to the GATT. Within the OECD concern over export credits continued, however.

This led to the Arrangement on Guidelines for Officially Supported Export Credits – the 'Consensus' – which became operative in April 1978. It is an arrangement between all OECD countries, except Turkey and Iceland, developed within the OECD framework. The Consensus is not an act of the OECD Council, however, and in a formal sense not a legal instrument, although it later became binding for EC countries. There are a number of exceptions to the Consensus, referred to as the 'Sector Understandings'. Separate arrangements were made with respect to defence and agriculture.

At the basis of the arrangement lies the matrix system. The matrix contains minimum interest rates for loans aimed at financing export transactions. A different minimum interest rate is specified depending on the export destination and on the time span of the export credit. Matrix rates are computed from the weighted average of government bond yields for the five currencies making up the special drawing right[36] of the IMF. Official export credit agencies are not allowed to grant financing below these minimum rates. Repayment terms of longer than six months are also not allowed. Nevertheless, exporters benefit from interest subsidies to the extent that market rates exceed Consensus matrix rates.

The Consensus's main purpose is to provide an institutional framework for an orderly export credit market. The Consensus does not restrict the export transaction

36. These currencies are: US dollar, German mark, Japanese yen, French franc and the UK pound.

itself, but imposes limits on the conditions and terms for officially supported export credits with a duration of two years or more. Moreover, it does not cover the conditions or terms of insurance or guarantees, but only the conditions or terms of the export credits that benefit from such insurance or guarantees. In this respect it differs from the earlier OEEC rules and the GATT Subsidy Code, since it does not refer to export credit insurance and guarantees whose premiums do not cover long-term costs.

Certain relaxations of these rules are possible, however. When commercial interest rates on comparable loans for a country's currency fall below matrix rates, the specified matrix rate no longer applies and any participant may lend in that currency at Commercial Interest Reference Rates (CIRR). CIRR is a monthly adjusted interest rate representative for commercial interest rates on loans in the domestic currency. Countries with high interest rates are allowed to subsidise the CIRR to the level of the matrix.

The Consensus uses the government-cost criterion to define export credit subsidies. The matrix system rules out granting loans at a rate lower than what it would cost the government to borrow on the capital market. Export credit financing should thus have no impact on government expenditures. Nevertheless, the adopted criterion is not perfect because it is a weighted average of financial conditions for different governments instead of reflecting each country's own government financing cost.

Economically speaking, firms derive a benefit from an official export credit when the interest rate on the official loan lies below the prevailing private commercial market rate for comparable loans. Because exporting firms are seldom able to obtain financing on the same conditions as governments do, financing at Consensus matrix rates is not available to most exporters. Official export credits at – or close to – matrix rates therefore represent a subsidy for the firm equal to the interest differential between the official and the private market rate. This subsidy is perfectly legal under the provisions of the OECD Consensus.

7.8.2 *The Wallen package*

When the debt crisis struck in 1982, a sharp deterioration in the international trading climate followed. In this contracting market, countries sought to maintain their exports by increasing their offers of tied aid credits. Tied aid credits, while still a relatively small part of total officially supported export credits, were becoming an important and distorting factor to competition among the OECD countries.

In the face of this growing competition in the use of tied aid, the OECD adopted a strategy of periodically increasing the minimum permissible grant element in both tied and partially untied aid financing, in order to strengthen the provisions of the Consensus. This culminated in 1987 in the acceptance of the Wallen package, which created a new formula (called the concessionality level) for calculating the grant element so as to make it reflect more closely market interest rates.[37] Moreover, the

37. The concessionality level is a ratio, which states what part of the financing package is granted out of developmental considerations. Since 1987, it is calculated on the basis of the CIRR.

package increased the minimum permissable concessionality level of aid credits to 35 per cent except for the LLDCs, where the level became 50 per cent.

The arrangements taken to counter trade distortions can be divided into measures for promoting a greater discipline and greater transparency. A greater discipline was sought through an increase in the costs of governmental export support, that is, by increasing the concessionality level, thereby discouraging tied aid credits. A greater transparency was to be achieved by establishing extensive notification and matching procedures.

By 1990, the OECD had come to the conclusion that the intentions of periodically increasing concessionality levels had not been realised. The purpose of increased concessionality levels was to mitigate the use of loans with a strongly export-oriented character, by making them more expensive and therefore less attractive for the donor. The opposite seems to have happened. Although interest rate subsidisation of export credits seems to have been reduced, the notifications of intent to offer hard aid credits actually rose after the package was implemented. Because of the higher concessionality levels, a larger part of the development budget was needed to finance the same export transaction. Moreover, data also indicate a movement in tied aid credits towards the better-off LDCs.

7.9 The Helsinki package

The OECD felt that further increases in minimum permissable concessionality levels were a dead end. As a result, the Trade Committee agreed that it needed a new basis for negotiation. The aim was to provide firm and clear rules that permit an export credit agency or a potential exporter to determine whether or not aid credits are allowed for a specific project. Even when exporters themselves are not seeking aid financing, they want to know if they can expect competition via other countries' aid credits or whether they can prepare their bids and financing proposals with the certainty that they will not be matched by competing softer offers.

In 1991 some new ideas were put forward which could be viewed as a fundamental breakthrough. The most innovative aspect of these was the rule that a project which is financially viable with commercial credits, or commercially viable, will not receive any aid credits. This meant a complete break with past efforts to separate trade credits from aid credits by periodically increasing concessionality levels. After a period of intensive consultation, with coordination especially onerous in the EC and between ministries with divergent interests, an agreement – the Helsinki package – was reached in December 1991.

Commercial viability is based on the principle that, if governmental aid funds are reserved for worthwhile aid projects which fail to secure commercial financing or officially supported export credits, then these funds are additional. In the absence of aid, worthwhile projects which are not commercially viable will not receive external financing. These are the projects towards which official aid should go, because otherwise they will either not take place or have to be financed out of the LDC's limited funds.

Once it has been decided to what extent a distinction should be made between commercially viable and non-viable projects, the question arises as to which of the commercially non-viable projects should be considered eligible for aid. Two key tests for evaluating aid eligibility were agreed upon:

- does the project lack capacity, in free market terms, to generate cash flow sufficient to cover the costs?
- is it reasonable to conclude that, after consulting other participants, it is unlikely that the project can be financed on market or Consensus terms?

7.9.1 *False starts*

Although the Helsinki package seems to have been developed relatively easily, the basis for the final agreement could only be reached after several false starts. A number of proposals were made to limit the number of projects eligible for aid. Moreover, it was suggested that ODA should not be provided unless special mutual donor consultations had taken place. In fact, suggestions along these lines were put forward based on the *a priori* argument that there is a fair chance that under these circumstances projects are either commercially viable or not very urgent from a developmental point of view. Some of the ideas that were considered – but ultimately not used in the Helsinki package – are the following:

- The aid quality of a project might be a better basis for a new rule than the concessionality level of its financing. The developmental potential of a project remains the same no matter what its financing terms are.
- The most effective way to reach the goals of the Wallen package is to *untie* aid credits and grants.
- It was considered whether to limit/forbid tied aid credits for projects in *spoiled markets*[38] and in *spoiled sectors*.[39] Exporters could then conduct business without having to contend with competition financed by concessional credits.
- Finally, a rule limiting or forbidding tied aid credits to large projects was considered. Very large projects would be subject to automatic consultations.

7.9.2 *Exceptions to the Helsinki rules*

The Helsinki rules' free trade philosophy received considerable support, although it met with resistance from aid protagonists. These new rules were based on the idea of aid only being available for commercially non-viable projects. This conflicted with the DAC guidelines on project appraisal, wherein the economic feasibility of projects is a key criterion. They also pointed to the potential incompatibility of interests if, for instance, a donor intends to allocate ODA to a project considered high priority from a developmental point of view which at the same time was commercially viable.

38. Developing countries, such as China and Indonesia, where it is virtually impossible to make a sale finance on normal commercial terms.

39. Sectors, such as mechanical engineering, where aid financing is widespread and expected.

In these cases, the above distinction could prevent the project from being financed at all.

The Helsinki package also incorporated a number of exceptions, however, which recognise the objectives mentioned above:

- Except for grants and very soft credits, tied aid financing should not be extended to those relatively well-off countries whose GNP makes them ineligible for long-term World Bank loans;[40]
- Aid credits to LLDCs should not be subject to the new rules, as LLDCs have great difficulty finding commercial financing, however attractive a project may be;
- Grants and very soft credits – with a concessionality level of over 80 per cent – are not subject to this rule;
- In order to limit the administrative burden, the new rule is limited to projects with a value of over $2 million;
- The new rules may be modified if there is a consensus that economic or political circumstances warrant it.

7.9.3 *The functioning of the Helsinki package*

The new rules do not yet cover all situations. For many projects it is not clear whether or not they are commercially viable. It will be hard to determine which projects come under the Helsinki rules, especially when relatively hard tied aid credits may be extended. If there is doubt as to whether or not a project meets the requirements for tied aid credits, or whether or not an aid offer is justified, any participant may request consultations[41] during which the others can express their views. If there is no support for the aid offer, the potential donor should reconsider going on, although it may proceed with a tied aid credit if it thinks it is necessary. It must then provide prior notification and explain the non-trade related national interests that forces such action.

Through these procedures a body of experience is expected to accumulate over time which will define *ex ante* guidance on the line between the two categories of projects. Export credit and aid agencies will tend to avoid projects where experience has shown that they lack support or tend to provoke disagreement. It will take several years before the new provisions are working well. It will require a similar period before a first estimate can be given of the functioning of the Helsinki rules in practice and of their effect on governments' aid and export credit policies and practices.

The first results on the functioning of the Helsinki package do suggest, however, that in its first ten months, from March until December 1992, the new rules seem to have had beneficial effects (see Table 7.1). The number of notifications of tied aid credit offers increased in 1992, from its already high 1991 level, to 824, totalling $15.4 billion. However, this increase was largely due to the notification of prior commitments in the first two months of 1992, before the Helsinki rules became operative.

40. In 1991 this was a GNP per capita of $2,555.

41. Prior consultations shall be automatic for all offers of large tied concessional or aid credits with a value of more than SDR 50 million.

Most of them were individual transactions under a prior committed credit line. Aid credits not covered by the Helsinki package remained at the same level.

The effect on credits covered by the Helsinki package has been profound. The rising trend of aid credits to better-off countries has stopped and the total value of 'Helsinki' type credits[42] has dropped precipitously. In sum, although the total value of aid notifications is more or less in line with that of previous years, there has been a shift away from 'Helsinki' type aid credits, possibly towards untied aid. Notification of all aid credits increased in 1992, largely because of the notable increase of hard aid credits concentrated in January and February. However, the volume of tied aid credits subject to the Helsinki package dropped sharply in the ten month period after the implementation of the Helsinki package, while the number of untied aid credits increased. If this trend is confirmed, this is an important effect of the Helsinki package.

These provisional figures seem to indicate a significant, albeit temporary, transition effect, during which participants anticipated the rule change. The participants seem to take the new guidelines very seriously. The figures also point to a significant increase in untied aid, which could have a permanent nature, and seems to be another important effect of the Helsinki package. Furthermore, it is not yet fully clear how the commercial viability concept will work in practice.

Birgitta Nygren, president of the OECD Consultation Group on Aid Credits, declared during a symposium organised by French employers (CNPF) held in Paris on 12 March 1993, with regard to the functioning of the Helsinki package:

> If participants think a notified transaction is not eligible, they can question the supplying country on its offer. Until now, some 300 transactions were notified of which 10 per cent was put before consultation. Less than one-third seemed to be commercially viable.... The first year of the Helsinki package has been one of learning and transition. The new qualitative Helsinki rules are very different from the earlier quantitative measures – increasing the concessionality level. Furthermore, the definition of commercial viability is still difficult to grasp.

The following data may serve to give a somewhat more concrete impression of the functioning of the new regime. Of the 824 notifications during 1992, 137 (totalling $3.8 billion) were potentially subject to the consultation process. For many of these, additional information was requested by one or more of the participants. Consequently, in four cases the offer was withdrawn; in 41 cases formal consultations were requested, 36 of which were completed as of 1 April 1993. In 13 of these cases the projects were deemed not commercially viable; in seven other cases the offering country received 'substantial support', while in the remaining 16 cases the project was deemed commercially viable. Of the latter, in seven cases the country went ahead with the offer, obliging it to explain in writing its 'overriding non-trade-related national interest'.

42. Relatively hard and large aid credits to intermediate developing countries.

Table 7.1 Notifications of aid credits (mln SDR)

Type of aid credit	1989	1990	1991[1]	1992[2]
a. Soft (concessionality level ≥ 80%)	3,846	2,463	4,575	767
b. Small (value < 2 million SDR)	41	71	126	39
c. Untied	1,239	1,554	946	5,194
d. for LLDCs	410	176	145	42
e. for ships	25	15	400	120
f. for better-off countries (GNP per Capita > $2,465)	196	609	636	0
g. for other countries	9,355	6,066	9,975	3,784
non-'Helsinki' type (a–e)	5,561	4,278	6,191	6,162
'Helsinki' type (f–g)	9,552	6,674	10,611	3,784
Prior commitments	326	240	128	2,336
TOTAL	15,438	11,192	16,929	12,282

Source: OECD, 1993, p. 9

1 Including notifications for the first two months of 1992 and adjusted by multiplying by 12/14.
2 Excluding notifications for the first two months of 1992 and adjusted by multiplying by 12/10.

7.10 Concluding remarks

While international arrangements impose important limits on concessional export financing, they leave room for export subsidisation. The basic idea underlying the main proposals was related to the risk of donor countries trying to outclass each other in export credit conditions. In those cases aid would basically serve as an export promotional device, distorting fair international competition and easily triggering an escalating process of competing export subsidies. The earlier adjustments with respect to the Consensus regime to prevent such an escalation – notably the increased grant component required to allow using aid for export support – have turned out to be insufficient.

To overcome the failures of the Consensus, and in the shadow of the Wallen package, the Helsinki package was concluded. The aim of this package was to provide firm, clear and easily workable rules. The first results show an increase in untied aid and a shift from Helsinki to non-Helsinki type credits. The Helsinki package may well have accomplished a turning point in the use of concessional export financing, although this contention is based on preliminary figures. It is still too early to conclude that the Helsinki package is working well.

Bibliography

References

Jepma, C.J. (1991) *The Tying of Aid*, OECD.

Kock, E.A.R.F. (1993) 'Concessional export financing: aid or trade?', *Development and Security*, no. 40, Centre for Development Studies/University of Groningen.

Love, J. and **Dunlop, S.** (1990) 'The domestic impact of overseas aid: a case study of the aid and trade provision', *National Westminster Bank Quarterly Review*, August, pp. 54–68.

Morrissey, W.O. (1993) The Mixing of Aid and Trade Policies, *The World Economy*, vol. 16, no. 1, pp. 69–84.

OECD (1991) *Economic outlook*, no. 49.

OECD (1993) *Experience with tied and partially untied aid finance under the new rules of the arrangement*, TD/Consensus(93)4.

Toye, J. and **Clark, G.** (1986) 'The Aid and Trade Provision: origins, dimensions and possible reforms', *Development Policy Review*, vol. 4, no. 4, pp. 291–313.

Further reading

Inspectie Ontwikkelingssamenwerking te Velde (IOV) (1990) *Hulp of handel?* Een evaluatie-onderzoek van het programma Ontwikkelingsrelevante Exporttransacties.

Jepma, C.J. (1993) *Towards Greater Untying of Aid*, DCD/DAC/FA(92)8/REV1.

Jepma, C.J. (1994) *Inter-nation Policy Coordination and Untying of Aid*, Avebury.

Ray, J.E. (1995) *Managing Official Export Credits: The Quest for a Global Regime*, Institute for International Economics/Longman Group.

8 The significance of political and cultural factors for international economic relations

8.1 Introduction

Political and cultural factors would not in general appear to play any major part in the theory of international economic relations. The fact is that economic theories that deal with international trade and direct investment confine themselves in many cases to the strictly economic domain and attempt to explain economic phenomena, such as consumption, production, prices and international trade, on the basis of exclusively economic variables. In analysing and explaining the direction and size of international trade flows, for example, the theories look in general at relative price differences, national incomes or comparative cost advantages of countries. Apart from these 'motors' of international trade, trade theories also look in many cases at economic factors placing a drag on trade flows. In general, a distinction is made between natural barriers to trade such as distance (transport costs and time involved) or physical accessibility or inaccessibility, and economic barriers to trade, such as import levies, quantity restrictions and a wide range of (customs) formalities and technical requirements that make it difficult to export a particular product, primarily because the relevant specifications often differ significantly from country to country. Economic factors, such as market size, differences in yields and the level of education in the population, usually figure most prominently in any analysis of foreign direct investments.

Economic analysis, however, overlooks important practical aspects of international economic relations. This chapter attempts to deal with this gap in theory to some extent. It starts by looking at diplomatic barriers to trade ('inhibitors') and political factors ('motors') (Section 8.2). Economic sanctions are always what come to mind first when thinking about trade barriers. A distinction is made here between negative sanctions and positive sanctions.

Apart from these explicit political factors, there are less tangible preferences among consumers and policy-makers. These factors, which are referred to in the following as political preferences, are discussed in Section 8.3. They are reflected in the flows of trade and the patterns of direct investment. They are particularly relevant to the deployment of the instruments of trade policy, such as anti-dumping measures and countervailing duties.

However, such preferences are by their nature not very tangible and therefore not easy to demonstrate. Apart from these political factors, finally, cultural factors play more of a structuring role (Section 8.4). These are such factors as the national character, language and traditions. Political and cultural factors together are found to influence trade patterns to a large degree and also play a major part in the assessment of countries' credit-worthiness (the transfer risk or country risk) by the international banking system and by multinationals (see Box 8.1).

Naturally, apart from the economic, political and cultural factors to be discussed in Sections 8.2 to 8.4, there are other factors that figure in explaining patterns of trade. The fact is that flows of trade are also affected by climatological factors, for example (consider harvest failures), or epidemics. In some cases chance or bad luck is a decisive factor: many export adventures have died an early death by a missed plane, slack service in a restaurant or lost luggage. This does not alter the fact that it is primarily the diplomatic climate and cultural factors that determine the scope for trade and the risks to international capital transactions. After all, the more serious conflicts at the political level or sharply diverging customs between countries are, the more real the risk of an exporter receiving adverse treatment: deliberate disadvantageous treatment by the government, consumer antipathy towards certain foreign products, hampering of access to foreign direct investment or of repatriation of profits. In short, diplomatic relations, political relations and cultural factors play an important role as determinants of international economic relations.

Box 8.1: Sources of information on international risks

Key information on country risks can most readily be found in the various international rankings as published several times a year in such publications as the *International Investor*, *The Economist* and *Euromoney*. There are some differences between these sources in terms of methodology and frequency. For example, the ranking published twice a year in the *Institutional Investor* is based on an anonymous survey conducted among a large group of leading international banks. They give the individual countries a score between 0 and 100, which is then reweighted according to the size of the bank. The ranking published quarterly in *The Economist* is based on a large number of objective criteria such as current-account position. Both the score given to a particular country and movements in it provide useful information about current or anticipated difficulties. The Dutch credit insurance company NCM also publishes information about export credit potential in a handy format. In addition, there are specialised publications on the analysis of internal and external political risks such as those from *Frost & Sullivan*. Then there are detailed country surveys by the Economist Intelligence Unit, for example, in which the various elements of the country risk are presented in an easy-to-understand format.

8.2 Economic sanctions

What characterises the economic instruments of modern diplomacy in the form of sanctions is their great variety. This section is confined to political sanctions, and does not look at trade wars or the forms of conditional protection propagated by the theory of strategic trade policy (van Bergeijk and Kabel, 1993). First of all, it is important to make a distinction between positive sanctions (rewards and promises) and negative sanctions (punitive measures or threats); see Box 8.2.

A second difference that matters from the analysis perspective is that between success and effectiveness. Effectiveness is concerned with the strictly economic question of the conditions that must be complied with for a sanction, in principle at least, to cause a certain level of economic damage (negative sanction), or to have some impact in increasing prosperity (positive sanction). If the sanction target, via the punitive economic measure for example, cannot be harmed to any significant degree, then the imposing of restrictions on economic trade cannot be deemed to have anything other than strictly symbolic significance. When it comes to the question of the success of economic sanctions, by contrast, what is at stake is the impact of the (potential) damage on the process of political change. It is only the combination of the two questions that can provide some answer to the problem of the possible effectiveness of a sanction as an instrument of foreign policy. The use of positive and negative sanctions does of course determine in part the trading climate and thus corporate decisions on servicing the market either via international trade, or via foreign direct investment in the particular country.

8.2.1 *Negative sanctions*

In principle, negative sanctions may be grouped into three main categories:

1. If the punitive measures are targeted at exports from a country, the term 'boycott' is used.
2. If the measures curb a country's own exports (and thus the import potential of the target country), the term 'embargo' is used.
3. Finally, there are sanctions aimed especially at curbing international capital flows. Such capital sanctions entail a freezing of bank assets in other countries, a hampering or blocking of international payments, a lowering or termination of development aid, the stopping of government guarantees for export credits or the prohibiting of international loans by the private banking system.

> **Box 8.2:** Economic sanctions
>
> - Negative sanctions are punitive measures or threats that entail some breaking or curbing of international economic relations.
> - Positive economic sanctions are rewards to friends and allies aimed at consolidating activities regarded as positive by the international community.

Recent examples of boycotts are the oil boycott of Iraq following the Iraqi invasion of Kuwait in 1990, the consumer boycott of Outspan oranges and the boycott of South African Krugerrands in the 1980s. Examples of recent embargoes are the oil embargo against South Africa and the arms embargo against Serbia. The first oil crisis, in 1973, was also in essence an embargo, as the Arab world was refusing on political grounds to supply oil to the United States and the Netherlands. Embargoes are targeted not only at goods, but in some cases also entail a ban on the use of certain international air routes as in the case of the UN air embargo against Libya in 1993. Capital sanctions are frequently implemented in conjunction with trade measures. In the case of sanctions against the Iraqi invasion of Kuwait, for example, Iraqi and Kuwaiti bank assets virtually throughout the world were frozen. The trade measures against the combatants in former Yugoslavia, to give another example, were accompanied by a freeze on international payments. This freeze extends to a wide variety of international transactions: commercial payments, benefits (pension and disability) and even transfer fees for professional footballers!

EFFECTIVENESS OF NEGATIVE SANCTIONS

In the standard neo-classical trade model the analysis of imposing a full, watertight sanction, which brings imports to and exports from the target country to a standstill, amounts to turning the traditional trade theory on its head. This model aims to illustrate the economic benefits of opening up a country to international trade on the basis of the terms of trade and associated effects. A sanction which relates to part of the import or export package or a sanction which is partially avoided can still be interpreted in these terms as a reduction in the terms of trade. The latter is of great importance as it indicates that it is a misinterpretation to assert that sanctions have failed if the goods affected by a sanction can still be purchased in the country against which the sanctions are targeted. The fact is that if the market mechanism is functioning, the fall in the supply of the goods will automatically be translated into a price rise, causing the total quantity to fall until a balance is achieved between supply and demand. In other words, the price mechanism ensures a distribution of the goods among consumers. An official rationing scheme will in principle only be required in so far as the price rise is deemed unacceptable or the commodity in question really is indispensable or the inevitable hoarding occurs on an unjustified scale.

It is also the case that sanction busting entails additional costs as, for example, the transport routes become longer, the origin of the goods has to be disguised by different packaging, more intermediaries have to be involved, and the risk of the sanction busters being prosecuted has to be borne by the sanction target. In consequence, net export revenues fall and the costs of imported goods rise. That means that far fewer import goods can be obtained from the same volume of export goods, and that the international purchasing power of the sanction target has fallen. According to the Shipping Research Bureau in Amsterdam, for example, South Africa paid between 10 and 20 per cent more for the oil it received during the oil embargo than it would have paid if buying on the free market (Hengeveld and Rodenburg, 1995). In brief, a boycott, an embargo or restrictions on capital transactions deprive the sanction target of (some of) the advantages of international trade, thus causing a fall in welfare.

The very threat of such a decline in welfare is a strong incentive to adjust, and the history of the sanction instrument also reveals cases therefore in which the threat of an economic sanction was in itself sufficient to bring about a change in political behaviour.

The possible damage or effectiveness of economic sanctions is determined according to the neoclassical trade model by a number of factors. The prospects for the success of a sanction will be enhanced in proportion to the following:

- the greater the importance of the import and export sector for the economy that is the target of a sanction, both quantitatively and qualitatively;
- the harder it is for goods that are affected by the sanction to be substituted by other products (low degree of substitution);
- the less scope there is for setting up import-replacing production;
- the shorter the duration of the sanction; and
- the shorter the time between taking the sanction decision and the time when the punitive measures are actually applied.

SUCCESS OF NEGATIVE SANCTIONS

Most economists believe that international economic sanctions are fairly blunt and ineffective instruments of foreign policy. Three reasons are advanced to support this pessimistic view.

Sanction busting and shifts in the pattern of trade. The pressure towards free trade is too great for a country to be effectively economically isolated. Economic players will always want to benefit from price differences on international markets that exceed transport costs. Consequently, punitive measures will ultimately be avoided by a shift in the flows of trade.

Politics and psychology. Economic damage is only one side of the coin. The psychological element is certainly just as important for the outcome of an economic sanction and in many cases can prove decisive. It is sometimes claimed that the probability of a change in behaviour that is intended as a result of economic damage is slight. A willingness to comply will erode the international prestige of the leaders of the country at which the sanctions are targeted and limit their support at home. Retaining respect and power will probably weigh more heavily than loss of economic potential.

A further important factor is that punitive action does not in all cases bring about the desired obligingness for other reasons. Take, for example, the case of sanctions designed to destabilise an unwanted government. Domestic criticism within the target country will only be targeted effectively against the government if the position of those in power is already weak. If the government has achieved a sufficiently stable power base, it can even use the external threats for its own purposes by channelling dissatisfaction against those imposing the sanctions. In this manner, the position of the government in the target country can actually be reinforced and the material capacity to resist the sanctions in both the short and long term can be increased. As a result, the conflict between those imposing the sanctions and the target may intensify and economic interaction between them may be permanently disrupted, while the economic sanctions will therefore not achieve the intended effect. One example is the commotion that occurred in 1992 following the Dutch threat to suspend development aid to Indonesia in connection with human-rights issues. The Indonesian government cleverly exploited the situation, seized the initiative, and actually *refused* any form of aid from the Netherlands and sent Dutch development workers home. These counter-sanctions proved extremely effective, both in generating support abroad for the Indonesian government, in marshalling feelings among the Indonesian population against Dutch policy and in realigning foreign policy in the Netherlands.

Low success rate. One major argument for not holding high expectations of sanctions is the numerical predominance of failed sanctions in the past and the low level of damage that the punitive measures have recorded. Of the 103 post-war sanctions – described by the American authors Gary Hufbauer, Jeffrey Schott and Kimberley Elliott (1990) – 69 cases (67 per cent) are deemed unsuccessful. That means that these sanctions had minimal or no impact on the sanction target's behaviour. Table 8.1 summarises the data on the number of sanctions, the number of successful sanctions and the success rates for five sub-periods calculated on this basis. A successful sanction is defined as one which led to the desired change in (political) behaviour. The table also reveals that the success rate has fallen continuously since the mid-1960s and at the start of the 1990s was below 20 per cent. Finally, it can be calculated on the basis of the data from Hufbauer, Schott and Elliott that the total damage from sanctions over the post-war period was less than half a per cent of world trade over the corresponding period. In 40 per cent of the cases the damage caused by a sanction was actually less than one tenth of a per cent of the sanction target's gross national

Table 8.1 The success of negative economic sanctions, 1946–89

Period	Number of sanctions	Number of successful sanctions	Success rate (as %)
	(1)	(2)	(2)/(1)
1946–55	13	3	23
1956–65	26	13	50
1966–75	17	6	35
1976–83	35	10	29
1983–89	12	2	17
1946–89	103	34	33

Source: Calculations by the author, based on Hufbauer, Schott and Elliott (1990)

product. Only in 30 per cent of the cases did the damage exceed the one per cent threshold.

A point to bear in mind when reviewing the results of Table 8.1 is that a very strict definition of success is used. By way of explanation, negative sanctions are usually deployed in the pursuit of several objectives. The UN sanctions against the Iraqi invasion of Kuwait, for example, had the further aim of closing down Iraq's nuclear and chemical military production facilities. In the study by Hufbauer, Schott and Elliott, the question of whether a sanction was successful or not was measured against the question whether the sub-objective that was most difficult to achieve by means of the sanction was in fact achieved. In popular terms, this definition therefore means that if someone sets out to become a millionaire, a leader of a political party, Prime Minister as well as President of the European Commission, that person will be deemed a failure according to this methodology if he or she fails to become President of the European Commission, totally overlooking the three successes out of four. The figures presented therefore underestimate the effectiveness of negative sanctions and the scope for applying them.

What is also intriguing is that a number of highly effective and efficient sanction threats are not officially included as sanctions, for example, if the threat of punitive economic measures has an immediate impact and the sanctions therefore do not need to be implemented. There are many examples of such highly efficient sanctions. One of the first sanctions in modern history was just such a sanction with immediate effect. The Yugoslavian invasion of Albania, in early November 1921, was grudgingly terminated by the aggressor within two weeks, when the Council of Ambassadors at the League of Nations (the precursor to the present United Nations) was requested to place only the possibility of economic sanctions on the agenda. Examples of sanctions with such a direct impact also occur in modern times. In 1975 the United States and Canada threatened to end supplies of civil reactors to South Korea. The threat in itself was sufficient to end South Korean attempts aimed at acquiring nuclear breeder facilities. Another example was the threat by the United States to reduce development aid to El Salvador (around 185 million dollars) by 10 per cent unless a number of specific provisions in El Salvador's amnesty legislation was modified. This relatively minor threat was of itself sufficient to bring about the desired change in political behaviour. In none of these cases can one speak of effective sanctions for the simple reason that there was no need to go any further than expressing a diplomatic threat. As a result, these sanction measures are generally excluded from discussions on the use of economic sanctions.

In short, the negative view of the usefulness of economic sanctions would appear to be caused partly by the unduly one-sided selection of cases examined, generally failing to pay sufficient heed to successful sanctions.

The numerical predominance of failed sanctions should not, moreover, be confused with the effectiveness of the sanction instrument in its own right. Failures that arise from the fact that the success criteria have not been complied with cannot be taken as scientific proof of the ineffectiveness of the sanction instrument in general. Figure 8.1 shows the success rates from Table 8.1 adjusted to take account of the obvious factor: the fact that international trade is tightly interwoven. This is defined on the

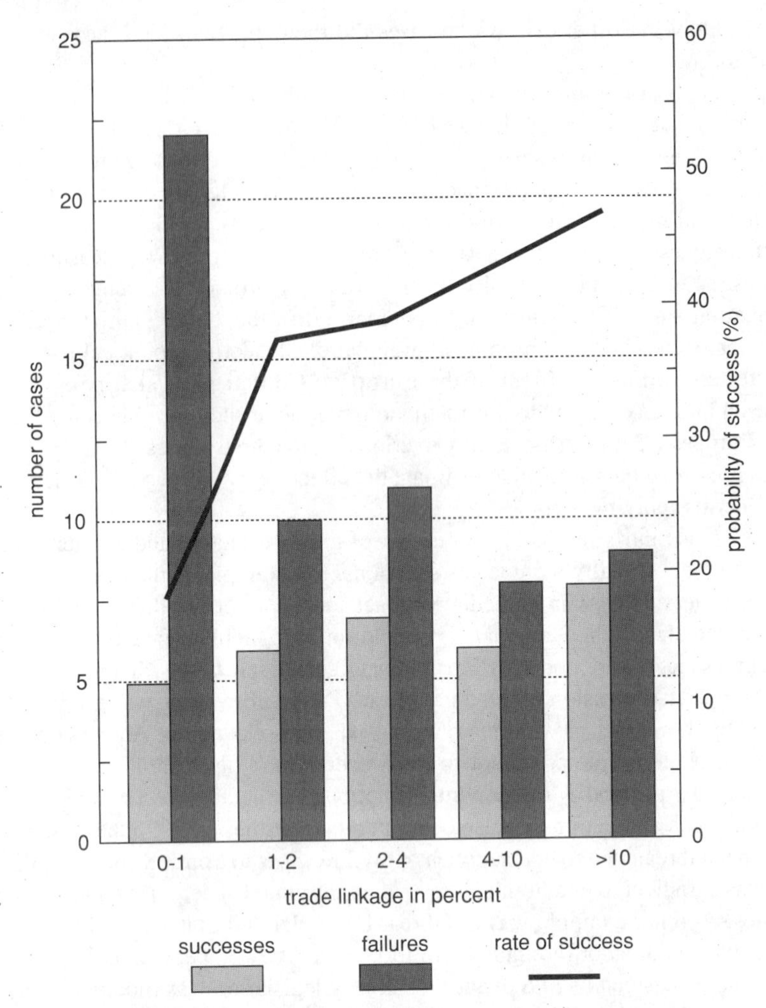

Figure 8.1 Trade linkage and sanction success: 80 sanctions (1945–89)

basis of trade flows (imports and exports) between the (group of) sanction taker(s) and the sanction target in the year preceding the sanction, and is expressed as a percentage of the gross national product of the sanction target. It is now clear that if the mutual trade flows are negligible, the success rate is below 30 per cent; as soon as the intertwining of trade links exceeds 5 per cent, however, the success rate rises towards 50 per cent. There may therefore be reasons why a particular sanction is almost doomed to failure, reasons which of themselves say nothing about the suitability of the sanction instrument in general. Conversely, there may also be cases where a sanction has been successful but which in themselves cannot be used as proof of the possible effectiveness of punitive economic measures in general. That would mean that the advocates of using economic sanctions were committing the same error as the opponents.

THE FUTURE FOR NEGATIVE SANCTIONS

International diplomacy can be expected to make increasing use of economic sanctions in the near future. First, the deployment of the military as part of UN missions, for example, has not proved very effective and in addition peaceful ways of resolving conflicts are increasingly being sought. The effort to counter the proliferation of nuclear and chemical weapons has an important part to play here. As part of what is termed strategic trade policy, an increase in barriers to trade – camouflaged by geo-political considerations or otherwise – is not inconceivable (Kaemfer and Lowenberg, 1992). Finally, there is a sharp rise in the use of trade barriers under international conventions designed to curb transnational environmental pollution and encroachment.

It is quite likely that an increasing use of negative economic sanctions will in due course blunt the effectiveness of this economic instrument. On the one hand, it would appear plausible that to implement a threat now will increase the credibility of a future threat being implemented. On the other, the potential impact of sanctions is diminished with regular use, since possible targets that are regularly hit will see this as grounds for arming themselves against possible punitive measures, for example by stockpiling or restricting or shifting international trade flows in advance. See Box 8.3 for negative sanctions used by the UN.

8.2.2 *Positive sanctions*

Negative sanctions are not the only economic instrument available to a government wishing to influence the behaviour of another country. The carrot has an important part to play alongside the stick in international politics. The significance of positive sanctions is often underestimated, because positive sanctions are frequently part and parcel of daily life and thus stand out less. Even with exceptional positive sanctions or those surrounded by a great deal of publicity, the significance for public opinion is of a different order than in the case of negative sanctions: a change in behaviour driven by a positive sanction, for example, does not lead to loss of face; in most cases, positive sanctions are actually interpreted as a consolidation of good relations.

IMPLICIT POSITIVE SANCTIONS

In many cases positive sanctions are implicit rewards or pay-offs for 'good behaviour', but no less important for that. The fact is that numerous economic activities can only be effected in a period of good international relations. A good understanding with one's neighbours means that waterways, air space and other transport links can be used. Other examples are certain forms of technology transfer and economic cooperation. When relations deteriorate, implicit positive sanctions will be reversed. When relations improve, positive sanctions will be stepped up again as a reward for good behaviour, a reward which will be withheld again as soon as undesirable political behaviour occurs. There are few, if any, costs associated with successful implicit positive sanctions: both parties only benefit as long as the desired behaviour occurs.

Box 8.3: The use of sanctions by the United Nations

One example of the increasing use of negative sanctions is the way in which the United Nations' Security Council is using the sanction instrument. During the Cold War, the United Nations resorted to economic sanctions on two occasions only. These sanctions against former Rhodesia and South Africa were designed to advance the process of decolonialisation in these countries. Since the ending of the conflict between the two superpowers (the US and the former Soviet Union), sanctions have been used by the United Nations to preserve the international status quo. Since the fall of the Berlin Wall in 1989, sanctions have developed into a major policy instrument used by the Security Council, and this economic weapon has been resorted to on seven occasions.

Table Security Council Sanctions (1946–94)

Rhodesia	1966–79
South Africa	1977–94
Iraq	1990–to date
Former Yugoslavia	1991–to date
Somalia	1992–to date
Libya	1992–to date
Liberia	1992–to date
Haiti	1993–to date
Angola	1993–to date

Source: Schrijver 1993

EXPLICIT POSITIVE SANCTIONS

In addition, positive sanctions entail international transfers of purchasing power or agreements in the field of technical and economic cooperation. Allies are often bought, the transnational negative consequences of certain international policy objectives may be offset, and misconduct can be bought off. Here are some telling examples of such transfers of purchasing power: the phased payments (reparations) held out by the Gulf states to Iran in the early 1980s, at the end of the Gulf War; Western aid in the 1990s to the reforming economies of Eastern Europe; the American aid package offered to those in power in Haiti in 1993–94 if the democratically elected president, Aristide, were to be allowed to return to the island. Apart from supporting capital flows, positive sanctions also play a part in goods transactions, as is often the case in military alliances. Even humanitarian aid (e.g. food) often proves to be political in nature, and the ending of punitive measures – something which became a real political option in response to the political changes in South Africa in the early 1990s, for example – may be regarded as a reward.

One important characteristic of explicit positive sanctions is that they only incur costs for those imposing them if a change in behaviour actually comes about. Positive sanctions are deemed particularly suitable in cases where the party imposing the sanctions does not rate very highly the prospects of the sanction target changing its behaviour or where the importance of a change in behaviour is very great to them or where there is negligible scope for causing economic damage. One could say that positive sanctions are the sole remaining non-military instrument, if the maximum achievable threat will not induce the sanction target to change its behaviour.

CONDITIONALITY

The applied 'donkey psychology', which lies at the heart of this analysis of positive and negative sanctions, teaches us that a donkey which already has the carrot stops walking. US President Reagan's 'constructive engagement policy', aimed at improving relations with South Africa, failed, for example, because no specific conditions were imposed upon South Africa in exchange for favours granted by the United States. This outcome was understandable, for rewards can in general only prove effective if the condition is attached that the undesirable behaviour is abandoned. Effective usage of positive economic sanctions in current international politics therefore requires the desired change in behaviour to be broken down into a number of achievable individual changes. Termination of some of the punitive economic measures may be promised if the individual change is achieved, for example.

There is a remarkable trend in the use of positive sanctions in economic diplomacy. This is the attaching to official economic transactions, conditions which clearly relate to national policy areas, for example the size of the defence machinery or the fabric of social life. The European Bank for Reconstruction and Development (EBRD, known as the Eastern European Bank), for example, is explicitly bound by its Articles of Agreement only to provide capital to countries that both opt for the capitalist market model and satisfy the condition that they have introduced a pluralist multi-party democracy. When granting loans, the World Bank is imposing – to give another example – green requirements for development projects, and is also attempting to influence strictly local environmental aspects pertaining to domestic policy. Even in the International Monetary Fund discussion has broken out about the imposing of the condition that a country's defence expenditure must be below a certain level, if it is to be eligible for balance of payments support programmes.

With these examples, what is relevant is not so much the fact that political circumstances are involved in economic decisions, for this was always done behind closed doors. Nor is it surprising that in the pursuit of domestic policy certain conditions have to be met in order to be eligible for international economic support, for requirements have always been laid down for *economic* policy. The real point at issue is that the international financial organisations no longer shrink back from making purely political demands explicit. This may indicate that in future increasing use will be made of political conditionality in countries' official economic relations.

8.3 Political trade preferences

Classical economists already recognised the impact of political and military-strategic preferences on world trade. For example, Adam Smith noted in his *Wealth of Nations* (1776) that a sound defence may be much more important than prosperity. That was why he supported the Navigation Acts, a form of protectionism with the aim of keeping sufficient vessels under sail to maintain England's maritime dominance. Nor is it uncommon when taking import decisions to take account of the wish to reward friendly nations, to punish others or to minimise (national security) risks. Such strategic policy preferences can be identified fairly readily in the arguments in the formulation or implementation of trade policy for deviating from (free) trade norms. Strategic policy preferences, it is found, can be measurably translated into trading patterns that differ from those that would be optimal on strictly economic grounds. There is more than just the economy at play in trade.

8.3.1 *Empirical findings*

Empirical studies of the impact of political factors on international trade flows revealed the major impact of political factors, such as colonial preferences and alliances, as long ago as the 1960s. The Dutch Nobel prize winner, Jan Tinbergen, had already developed a trade model which incorporated political factors. This model, econometric in design, was applied to 18 countries in 1959. Using the model, very large 'colonial or ex-colonial' trade multipliers of 10 to 20 were found; in other words colonial ties were the basis for a volume of trade between 10 and 20 times as large as one might expect on the basis of economic variables alone. Since the Tinbergen study, the impact of such invisible trade preferences has been demonstrated on several occasions (see van Bergeijk 1994). Table 8.2 summarises the results of a recent study of the impact of diplomatic cooperation and diplomatic conflicts. The study examines econometrically the impact of the diplomatic climate on the flows of trade between countries, using a fairly broad definition of diplomacy. Diplomacy is not confined to the activities of the Diplomatic Corps but includes behaviour exhibited by politicians and the public which may exercise a substantial impact on relations between countries. Under diplomatic cooperation it includes the impact of treaties, declarations of agreement and other activities pointing towards cooperation. These events have to be weighted by some means or other, for a diplomatic compliment or agreement with prevailing policy is of less weight, for example, than the actual exchange of ambassadors, the signing of a cultural treaty, or physically supporting a military ally.

Diplomatic conflicts – and we are talking here of unequal units such as a Soviet submarine turning up in Swedish territorial waters or disagreement on whether American government fiscal policy is correct – are examined in a comparable manner. The study spanned the 1,560 trade flows in 1986 based on a sample of 40 countries which together accounted for between 80 and 90 per cent of world production, population and trade.

In day-to-day practice of international trade, what is particularly interesting is the question of possible differences in reaction patterns of the various countries, and whether there are differences between the ways in which imports and exports are influenced. Table 8.2 shows the countries where the diplomatic climate really did have a significant impact on trade flows. The diplomatic climate was found to have a measurable impact on most of the other countries investigated, but it could not be claimed with sufficient statistical certainty that the impact really does exist. Actually, the established link between trade flows and the diplomatic climate could be based on chance in those cases.

A distinction is made in this study between the impact of diplomatic cooperation and diplomatic conflicts on trade; more conflict leads to less trade (imports and exports). In approximately three out of four cases, countries are found to react in the manner we could expect them to: cooperation leads to more trade, hostile behaviour to less trade. When it comes to export flows, there is a measurable counter-reaction from one in ten countries. A deterioration in the diplomatic climate is found to be accompanied by a rise in exports. (The countries involved are Venezuela, Pakistan and Finland; no such different reaction pattern was observed on the imports side).

No clear dividing line can be drawn between countries where the diplomatic climate does or does not have some impact, with the exception of the Scandinavian countries where no real relationship between trade and diplomacy was found. What is striking is that the empirical investigation fails to demonstrate that the diplomatic climate has any significant impact among the economic superpowers – Japan and West Germany. Equally surprising is the result for the United States and the United Kingdom. Even with these countries, which believe that they have little or no impact on private trade via their foreign policy, the diplomatic climate is found to have a significant impact on imports as well as exports and on the scale and direction of trade flows.

Table 8.2 Countries where an improvement or deterioration in the diplomatic climate led to a significant change in trade flows (1986)*

	Cooperation	Hostile behaviour
Export side	Sudan, East Germany, France, Czechoslovakia The Philippines, Spain, Canada, United Kingdom, Italy, Portugal, Finland	Portugal, Czechoslovakia Brazil, Switzerland, South Africa, Sudan
Import side	Czechoslovakia, France, United Kingdom, Poland, East Germany, Soviet Union, Gabon, Portugal, Canada, Spain, Sudan	Portugal, Poland, Canada, Pakistan, Brazil, Czechoslovakia

Source: Van Bergeijk 1994, Table 7.6, p. 161

* The countries in the table are shown by order of declining statistical certainty. In any event the links are so significant that with an unreliability interval of 10 per cent at most, a sound pronouncement can be made.

Although the diplomatic climate proves to be important for all types of country in their economic relations with the rest of the world, it would appear possible to make a distinction according to the way in which control of trade flows is shaped. Of the countries where the diplomatic climate is found to have a significant impact on exports, the majority (seven of the eleven) have a Western-style market economy. Economies that are centrally planned to a greater or lesser degree predominate when it comes to import flows. Evidently, a change in the diplomatic climate in a Western-style market economy leads to exports being modified, while political factors in a centrally planned economy influence imports from countries with a hostile attitude. The market economy selects its markets partly on the basis of political factors; the centrally managed economy on the basis of its suppliers. To some extent, the Western preference for export restrictions that has been identified reflects the commitments that have been entered into under the General Agreement on Tariffs and Trade (GATT; currently the World Trade Organisation, WTO). The GATT rules are of course aimed primarily at protecting home markets and therefore contain numerous provisions that hamper any changes to the geographical composition of imports. The relative predominance of centrally managed economies in the primacy of import-related trade policy may therefore also be caused in part by the fact that China, East Germany and the Soviet Union were not members of GATT in the period under review.

8.3.2 *Case study: Eastern Europe*

Political preferences are revealed not only in actual trade flows, but also in the deployment of the instruments of trade policy. Political considerations figure in the background in any decision on whether to use an instrument of trade policy. The greater the discretionary power of the trade authorities concerned, the more the instrument will be coloured by non-economic motives. Tariffs, for example, are in general applied uniformly, non-tariff barriers to trade such as quotas and technical requirements are often deployed on a different basis between countries. This is illustrated in Table 8.3 by the deployment of the anti-dumping instrument in the West, which was disproportionately targeted at the former Eastern bloc. Given an import share of around 10 per cent, the countries of Eastern Europe suffer disproportionately from the anti-dumping measures taken by the countries of the European Community.

Such political emphases in the range of trade instruments naturally have some impact on trade flows. In 1990, van Bergeijk and Oldersma calculated the possible long-term impact of the dismantling of the political barriers between East and West. The year 1985 was reviewed to see how the export potential might be affected in the medium term. The calculations showed a rise in the world export potential of 2 to 3 per cent of global production volume. In the case of Czechoslovakia, Hungary, Austria, Denmark and Finland the rise in the export potential actually exceeded 15 per cent of their gross national product. As illustrated in Table 8.4, the market players were able to adapt fairly rapidly to the new geopolitical constellation. This table shows the actual development of a number of international trade flows between East and West since the dismantling of the Iron Curtain for the fairly well-developed economies of Czechoslovakia, Hungary and Poland. Trade between these Central

Table 8.3 The deployment of the anti-dumping instrument by the EC (1980–90)

	Number of anti-dumping cases		Import share	Relative deployments
	No. (1)	Percentage (2)	(3)	(2)/(3)
OECD countries	445	49	60	0.8
Other countries	238	27	30	0.9
Eastern Bloc	220	24	10	2.4
Romania	36	4	0.7	5.7
Czechoslovakia	41	5	0.8	8.3
Yugoslavia	43	5	1	5.0

Source: Calculations by the author, based on Eymann and Schuknecht, 1991, p. 23, subject to the usual reservations.

Table 8.4 Trade with the OECD area of three economies in Central Europe since the reforms in 1990

	Exports 1990 in US$ mln.	Growth 1990–92 (%)	Imports 1990 in US$ mln.	Growth 1990–92 (%)
Czechoslovakia	4.865	110	4.867	195
Hungary	5.698	65	5.416	70
Poland	8.878	85	7.711	120

Source: Calculated on the basis of OECD, 1993, Table 25, p. 122, subject to the usual reservations.

European countries and the OECD area expanded by between 65 and 200 per cent within the span of three years.

What is striking in Table 8.4 is not only the high growth figures in the trade flows, but a further important factor is that East and West alike are reaping the benefits from the ending of the political conflicts in continental Europe. It should be noted that not all the countries of Central and Eastern Europe will achieve the same pace of growth, in the short term at least. In a number of cases, the short-term problems will predominate if companies in the relevant countries cannot cope with competition on the world market or are not yet in a position to do so.

8.4 Cultural factors

Political factors are subject to influence, even though political developments are frequently unpredictable. Consequently, the political background against which economic exchange takes place is fluid. Cultural factors, by contrast, are historically determined, and thus are more of a structural factor in the pattern of international specialisation and of less significance for short-term changes in international trade flows. Nevertheless, it is a good thing to include cultural differences and similarities in export decisions.

8.4.1 *Cultural barriers to trade*

Cultural factors influence trade relations by various routes. The most obvious example is language. First of all, there is a strictly economic aspect involved with language: having a common language reduces the costs of information transfer, such as advertisements and user instructions (lower print costs, no translation costs). The mirror image of this is costs associated with language differences, for example the various languages spoken in Europe create a situation where the internal market can never be perfect: the smaller linguistic communities in particular will continue to experience major barriers that segment the internal market. The impact of a common language is broader, however. Consumer preferences are in fact shaped partly by the media and therefore a common language used in a wide area is a major asset in the creation of international trade. Language is important not only on the demand side but also on the supply side, as products age if entrepreneurs fail to pick up new trends (or inadequately so) on account of linguistic barriers.

Some understanding of cultural backgrounds is also essential in negotiations on contracts. Many potential players wishing to enter the Japanese market saw their efforts founder due to a lack of understanding of who the decision-makers were and what the decision-making process was. Cultural factors such as the national character and traditional customs are also determinants of consumer preferences. One man's meat is another man's poison (for example, the sacred cow in India). Religion also figures in international trade patterns; any country producing pork will never be able to sell this into the Arab world, even at dumping prices.

8.4.2 *Impact on comparative advantages*

Under conditions of full, free international competition, a country will best be able to maintain its position in areas with which it has a strong cultural affinity. In this manner, cultural factors can measurably influence the comparative benefits of these countries. Hofstede (1980) studied IBM managers in 64 countries and established that countries can be classified on the basis of a typology with four dimensions. These are the essential elements that make up a national character or a culture:

- psychological aspects;
- individualism;
- avoidance of uncertainty;
- power distance.

The first dimension (feminine–masculine) measures the extent to which the culture of a country is feminine, that is, aimed at helping the 'weak' in society and maintaining personal relationships, or masculine in character, that is, aimed at performance and mutual competition. The second dimension (individualistic–collectivistic) measures the extent to which decision-making and behaviour is effected in an individualistic or collectivistic manner. One important element here is the relationship between individual opinion and group interest. The avoidance of uncertainty is more than risk aversion: it relates to a strong preference for professional solutions over the lay approach. Power distance is the extent to which a society considers inequality (for example in social position, wealth, income, etc.) to be normal.

A number of European clusters with strongly related cultures emerge from Hofstede's study. In economic terms, these are homogenous groups of consumers who together may constitute a common market. On the basis of Hofstede's method, there are three such homogenous clusters that can be identified in Europe:

- Belgium, France, Spain, Greece and Portugal;
- Great Britain, Ireland, Germany and Northern Italy;
- Norway, the Netherlands, Denmark, Sweden and Finland.

The background to the last cluster is the agricultural–seafaring tradition and the Hanseatic League (a protective and commercial association of free towns). Finally, as an example of this thinking being applied to the Netherlands' culture, Hofstede asserts that the feminine aspect predominates here. The Dutch are individualists and risk-avoiders. When it comes to the power distance factor, opinion is divided: on the one hand, the distribution of primary incomes in the Netherlands is extremely distorted, but on the other there is comprehensive redistribution and levelling. The Netherlands' comparative advantage can be explained on the basis of this cultural profile. If the Netherlands had been a 'macho' country with a high preference for risk, it would probably have focused its efforts on being good and effective in creating industrial products. However, the sociologically determined cultural advantage lies in services (trade, banking, insurance, accountancy etc.) and in creating living products (high-grade agriculture, biotechnology etc.).

Bibliography

Bergeijk, P.A.G., van (1994) *Economic Diplomacy, Trade and Commercial Policy: Positive and Negative Sanctions in a New World Order*, Edward Elgar.

Bergeijk, P.A.G., van and **Kabel, D.L.** (1993) 'Strategic trade theory and trade policy', *Journal of World Trade*, vol. 27 (6), pp. 175–86.

Bergeijk, P.A.G., van and **Oldersma, H.** (1990) 'Détente, market-oriented reform and German unification, potential consequences for the world trade system', *Kyklos*, vol. 42 (3), pp. 599–609.

Eymann, A. and **Schuknecht, L.** (1991) 'Anti-dumping enforcement in the European Community', *PRE Working Papers Series*, no. 743, World Bank.

Hengeveld, R. and **Rodenburg, J.** (eds) (1995) *Embargo: Apartheid's Oil Secrets Revealed*, Amsterdam University Press.

Hofstede, G. (1980) *Culture's Consequences, International Differences in Work-Related Values*, Sap.

Hufbauer, G.C., Schott, J.J. and **Elliot, K.A.** (1990) *Economic Sanctions Reconsidered: History and Current Policy*, 2nd edn, Institute for International Economics.

Kaempfer, W.H. and **Lowenberg, A.D.** (1992) *International Economic Sanctions: A Public Choice Perspective*, Westview.

Organisation for Economic Co-operation and Development (OECD) (1993) *Economic Outlook* 53.

Schrijver, N.J. (1993) 'The use of economic sanctions by the UN Security Council', University of Groningen, *Development & Security Series*, no. 39 (12).

Smith, A. (1976) *An Inquiry into the Nature and Causes of the Wealth of Nations*, Canna's edition, Clarendon Press (first published in 1776).

Tinbergen, J. (1962) *Shaping the World Economy – Suggestions for an International Economic Policy*, Twentieth Century Fund.

9 Anti-dumping and competitive advantage: gains and losses in international competition

9.1 Introduction: anti-dumping as a legal and economic phenomenon

Many people are familiar with dumping as a phenomenon that is subjected to analysis mainly in legal journals. That legal people should be interested in the phenomenon of dumping need not come as any surprise: anti-dumping procedures are a regularly recurring phenomenon; dumping is subject to regulations, and the application and interpretation of these regulations has become important for many companies. What does come as a surprise is that the phenomenon of dumping in general attracts so little attention in the economic press. One could get the impression that economists regard dumping primarily as an administrative and legal process, the details of which do not really merit closer scrutiny.

The central theme of this chapter is that economists (business and general economists alike) need to get more to grips with the practice of dumping, as this practice offers some interesting angles on economic analysis. Hence in what follows the emphasis will be on the practice of dumping and an analysis of the phenomenon from the perspective of business operations and economics.

Section 9.2 describes an actual case of dumping, based on sales of CDs by Japan and Korea on the EU market. Section 9.3 looks more closely at the definition of dumping and the various forms it takes, Section 9.4 establishes a link between the economic structure of a country – Japan – and dumping, while Section 9.5 looks at how this translates into economic theory. The concept of 'persistent dumping' is introduced at this juncture. Sections 9.6 and 9.7 build upon this by further developing the phenomenon from theory as well as practice.

9.2 A case study of dumping

In December 1986, three European manufacturers – Bang & Olufsen, Grundig and Philips[43] – submitted a complaint to the European Commission about the dumping

43. These three manufacturers have formed a temporary producers association called COMPACT (Committee of Mechoptronics Producers and Connected Technologies) and collectively account for more than 90 per cent of production in the EU.

of compact disc players by Japan and Korea on the European market. COMPACT, the temporary producers association of the European electronics companies, had first calculated the corresponding ex-works price in Japan on the basis of the actual shop price in Japan by adjusting for normal operating margins; this created an ex-works price of *f* 293.02 for an average CD player. This was then compared with the corresponding amount obtained by taking the price at which these CD players were sold in the EU, and again adjusting for the various relevant margins. An ex-works price of *f* 184.09 was then constructed in this manner on the basis of the European retail price. It was deduced from this that this was a case of dumping on the scale of *f* 108.93 per CD player, a dumping margin (dumping as a percentage of the CIF export value) of more than 58 per cent. The method of calculating the ex-works price in Japan and in the EU, along with the dumping margins, is shown in Table 9.1 on the basis of a concrete example.

The method of calculation illustrated in Table 9.1 is termed the constructed-value method. It is frequently employed by the party bringing the complaint in the belief it is being adversely affected by dumping; the fact is that the party bringing the complaint only needs to make a reasonable case for dumping. The method cannot be used, however, by the authorities that have to investigate the alleged dumping.[44] That means that they cannot proceed on the basis of consumer prices but must themselves perform an in-depth analysis of the prices of the exporting companies.

The above implies that knowledge of production costs in Japan is required in order to demonstrate dumping. In the case of CD players shown here, it was found that there had to be dumping on a scale of more than 30 per cent on the basis of the information collected for the purpose and the estimate of production costs derived from that. The result was therefore in line with the results of the constructed-value method, according to which in some cases there was selling on export markets at a price below production costs.

Market studies also showed that Japanese and Korean CD player models were being sold at prices far below the prices for similar models produced in the EU. The European producers also managed to demonstrate a major price drop as part of the dumping campaigns; the price drop could not be explained by technical improvements or learning-curve effects, one reason being that there was a major acceleration in the fall in prices for all Japanese and Korean exports.

Under threat of European action, the Japanese Ministry of International Trade and Industry (MITI) announced in early 1987 that an investigation into prices would be conducted and that Japanese producers would raise their prices, at the recommendation of the Japanese Government itself.[45] Evidently, it was recognised that a timely price increase, before the launching of the official investigation, really could have a

44. In the case of the EU the authority is the European Commission; it investigates both the dumping and the resultant damages. In the US it is the Department of Commerce that investigates dumping, and the International Trade Commission that determines whether any damage has ensued. The fact that both investigations in the EU are handled by the same body is explained by the fact that European anti-dumping levies are determined by the lower of the two, the scale of dumping or the damage (i.e. the amount of undercutting in relation to European-industry prices).

45. JiJi Press Ticker Service, 8 February 1988.

Table 9.1 Calculation of the dumping margin applied to a CD player imported from Japan and Korea

a. Normal value Japanese producer X, Model DX 50		
		Yen
Domestic price ex-retailer (actual price)		29,800
Margin of wholesale and retail trade	30%	6,877
Gross ex-works price		22,923
Commodity tax	15%	2,990
Normal value		19,933
Yen 1000 = Hfl. 14.70		293.02

b. Export price of firm X Model DX 110 (to compare with DX 50)		
		Hfl
Actual retail price		349.00
Value added tax	19%	55.72
Net retail price		293.28
Retailer's margin	25%	58.66
Price to retail trade		234.62
Wholesaler's margin	5%	11.17
Landed price		223.45
Import duty	19%	35.68
CIF export value		187.77
Shipment and Insurance	2%	3.68
Free-on-board price		184.09
Normal value		293.02
Export price		184.09
Dumping margin		108.93
as % of CIF export price		58.01%

beneficial impact on the investigation; a higher export-price level during the period of investigation will of course lead to a reduction in the dumping margin, if all other factors remain the same.

The European Commission's investigation into this anti-dumping case lasted more than three years and resulted in anti-dumping levies, ranging from 8 to 32 per cent per company in the country of origin of the dumped products. Companies that did not wish to cooperate in the investigation were subjected to a general 'residual duty'. A point to note is that the duties were only applied to CD players of Korean and Japanese origin: during the three years of the investigative procedure most producers were found to have moved final assembly of their CD players to other places in the Far East or to Europe. This changed the origin of the products, enabling the anti-dumping levies to be circumvented to a significant degree. Subsequently, it was also found that the announcement by the Japanese Government that it would enforce a price increase had had only limited effect.

It need not come as a surprise to learn that European consumer organisations were not very happy with the anti-dumping campaigns conducted by the European producers. The fact was that these campaigns drove up the price of CD players on the European market, which was not exactly welcome news to consumers as potential buyers of CD players. For example, the National Consumers Council (NCC) in the UK produced estimates of the losses to consumers caused by the anti-dumping campaigns. What subsequently emerged was that the method employed had overestimated the losses. The loss suffered by the British consumer when buying a CD player had been calculated by the NCC as the average price of a CD player multiplied by the average levy. This resulted in a significant overestimate of the losses as it failed to take account of the possibility of avoiding the levy by relocating production and changing the source. Besides, this method did not take any account of the effect that in due course these very campaigns would save European suppliers from possible decline, thus preventing foreign suppliers from being able to build up a monopoly on the European market.

The limited impact of the levies imposed led to follow-up complaints, which led to further investigation. Ultimately, the complainants decided against any further action, however. The scope for avoiding levies by setting up in new locations proved to be so ample that the costs to Japanese producers of covering themselves against anti-dumping campaigns from their existing location exceeded the costs involved in moving production to low-wage countries. As a result of all these developments a situation arose where the complaints on the European side were withdrawn and Japan and Korea requested that the levies be cancelled. A curious side effect of these relocations of production sites was that other Japanese companies, who had set up in the EU with the very aim of avoiding levies, suddenly experienced competition from countries from which other Japanese suppliers had dumped in the past.

All these developments helped to ensure that the prices of CD players on the European market fell substantially in the second half of the 1980s; this is illustrated in Figure 9.1.

9.3 Definition of dumping and the forms it takes

According to the 'Agreement on implementation of Article VI of the General Agreement on Tariffs and Trade 1994' dumping exists: 'if the *export price* of the product exported from one country to another is *less than* the comparable *price, in the ordinary course of trade,* for the like product when destined for consumption *in*

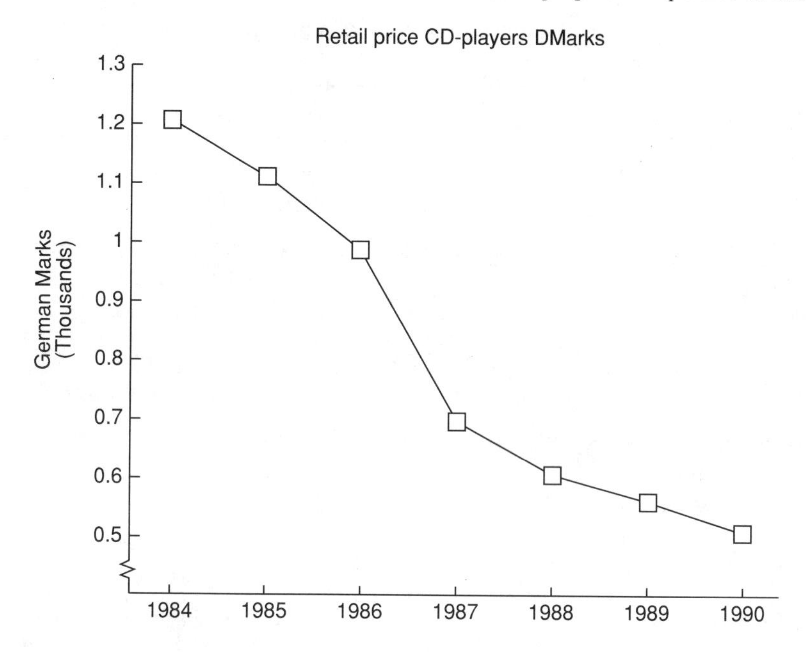

Figure 9.1 CD player prices since 1984 (German marks)

the exporting country.'[46] In exceptional cases where there is no *ordinary course of trade* or if the specific market conditions so require, the normal value for determining dumping can be established on the basis of the constructed value (structure) or even a price on third markets.[47] In normal cases, however, the dumping will have to be determined on the basis of the price structure and the comparison between the home market and the export market. An example illustrating this point is shown in Table 9.2. The numerical ratios in this table constitute a reasonably representative illustration of the case of mass consumer products.

The example shows that the consumer on the producer's home market pays 165, while 160 has to be paid for the same product on the export market. Nevertheless, the retail prices on both markets are not considered important for the formal determination of the dumping margin, nor are any underlying differences in wholesale and retail margin on the export and home market. The thinking here is that traders must be capable of eliminating price differences on various sub-markets, in so far as one is not dealing with the manufacturer's production costs plus uplift. In other words, in so far as the price on the home market differs from the corresponding price on the export

46. MTN/FA, 15–12–93 (MTN/FA A1A-8). This is the new code on the interpretation of GATT Article VI (on dumping and subsidies).

47. One example of a case where there is no *ordinary course of trade* is where a product is dumped during the introduction phase. A telling example of this occurred in the 1980s when a Japanese company wanted to sell cellular radios (portable telephone systems) on the American market below cost price, even before there had been any physical deliveries.

Table 9.2 An example of the price structure of a product on the home market and export market

Domestic market	165		160	Export market
Gross retail margin on domestic market	30	E	25	Gross retail margin on export market
Gross wholesale margin	5	D	5	Gross margin of import and wholesale trade or subsidiary of exporter
		C	10	Duties (6.67%) over A2 + B2 + 2 (transport and insurance)
Gross margin (selling, general and administrative costs plus profit) on domestic market	30	B	18	Gross margin (SG&A plus profit) on export products
Cost of manufacturing	100	A	100	Costs of manufacturing of export products

market on the basis of A to E in Table 9.2, it is up to the traders to eliminate such differences; dumping only exists in so far as a price difference is fully attributable to the manufacturer, with regard to the price structure A + B in Table 9.2, because traders are unable to eliminate this type of price differences by arbitrage.

According to this line of thinking, only the manufacturer's manufacturing and sales costs plus profit are considered for the purposes of calculating dumping. The dumping in Table 9.2, calculated on A + B is (100 + 30) – (100 + 18) = 12. Any anti-dumping levy will therefore be the tariff equivalent of 12 at most. If this is expressed as a percentage of the CIF value (118 + 2), this corresponds to 10 per cent. This percentage naturally comes on top of the import duties of 6.67 per cent in this case.

Calculating the dumping margin creates problems if the two columns in Table 9.2 are not comparable. If, for example, a proportion of the costs of sale and profit of a producer, who is a multinational, are incurred on the export market – as is often the case – the investigating authorities naturally have to make adjustments.

9.3.1 *Inter-company pricing*

It goes without saying that assessing the value of the internal supplies of multinationals across borders (termed inter-company pricing) can be a subject of dispute between customs authorities and multinational companies, particularly if the import levies are relatively high. Nevertheless, this theme has become less important over time. First of all, import duties in the Western world have been substantially lowered across the board with the passage of time. Secondly, the GATT code on customs valuation now accepts the invoice value as the customs value. Thirdly, there is an awareness that giving imports a low rating creates fewer import duties on the one hand, but on the other leads to more profit for the importing company and thus to a higher transfer through taxes on profits. The reverse occurs if imports are given a high valuation. In fact, what import levies and profit-tax levies have in common is that they are taxes with transfers that more or less correspond.

The importance of the theme of inter-company pricing from the point of view of anti-dumping remains as great as ever. What is at stake here are not the fiscal aspects but rather the competitive conditions. This means that in the event of anti-dumping there are quite frequently substantial additional levies on a customs value which in fiscal terms is deemed less important.

One topic of discussion in the past was whether the basis of assessment for establishing dumping ought to be item A in Table 9.2 or items A + B. This question is all the more important as the average margins on current trade may differ by country and distribution channel; unit profit is of course largely dependent upon the trading position. In some countries trade is powerful and may be able to enforce relatively high profit margins;[48] in other countries trade is in a relatively weak position.

Some countries with exporters that are regularly involved in anti-dumping campaigns proposed during the Uruguay Round of Multilateral GATT Negotiations that, when it comes to establishing dumping practices, the comparison between export and home-market prices should be restricted to level A in Table 9.2. This thinking was not accepted, however. The fact is that dumping does not occur at the level of manufacturing costs (A), but at the level at which a profit is made, that is, as a minimum on the basis of manufacturing plus sales (A + B). If one were to restrict the calculation to level A, this would fail to consider the effects of a commercial pricing policy.

9.4 Structural differences: Japanese vertical integration and dumping

One may well ask whether there are arguments for looking beyond levels A and B and including levels D and E in the analysis when it comes to proving dumping. This question is relevant if there are fundamental differences in market structure between countries, a point which is explained in further detail below. The comparison in Table 9.2 between the left-hand and right-hand columns becomes more complicated if the manufacturers have achieved strong vertical integration of sales on the home market, but have not done so with sales on the export market. In that case auditable costs and profit elements in the left-hand column are to be found not only in levels 2A and 2B,

48. Frequently, major chain stores are involved with own-brand products. Examples are Dixons and Rumbelows in the UK, Kaufhof in Germany, Grand Bazar in Belgium, Vendex in the Netherlands, and Carrefour in France. Products are bought by these chains from around the world; as a result of the strong position of their own brands in their store chains, they can squeeze relatively low prices from suppliers of better known brands.

but in 2D and 2E as well. The result is that the situations on the home and export market become difficult if not impossible to compare from the dumping perspective.

The point now is that the degree of vertical integration on the home market does vary substantially internationally, not so much between the US and the EU, but between the US and the EU on the one hand and Japan and, more recently and increasingly, Korea, for example, on the other. This means that this complication hardly gives rise to any problems at all in the event of dumping by the US on the European market or vice versa. The phenomenon of (abuse of) vertical integration is usually in contravention of anti-cartel legislation and policy. Vertical integration of producers and trade is common practice in Japan, however. A complex system of stake-holdings, bonuses and credits usually gives Japanese manufacturers a tight grip on their sales. Manufacturers' trading companies in Japan carry costs at the following stages of sales, which in the West are borne mainly by the manufacturer. The result is that as soon as dumping occurs in the relationship between Japan and the EU or Japan and the US, a comparison between the situation on the home and export markets is seriously compromised as a basis of calculation.

In practice, the above leads to serious complications when it comes to anti-dumping campaigns aimed at Japan. Although in theory in cases of strong vertical integration one could work backwards from the retail price to the ex-works price including selling, general and administrative costs (SG&A) and with due allowance for normal trading and cost margins, implementing such an approach runs up against major obstacles in practice. For example, one would have to check the books for all the interim stages from factory to sale to the consumer. According to the GATT rules, however, it is only the exporters' behaviour and thus only their book-keeping that is the decisive factor. If distribution networks are linked to the manufacturer, then the existing legislation in principle does not offer an adequate basis for establishing the level of dumping. In other words, since the anti-dumping procedures are legally confined to exporters, buyers connected to them legally or economically are not obliged to open their books for inspection.

As already observed, this objection relates primarily to Japanese companies. Furthermore, such companies usually refuse to allow the operations of their subsidiaries and other associated companies to be inspected. Extending the investigation to include buyers is not feasible in practice, as this would boil down to examining millions of transactions. Even if one were to succeed in this endeavour, it is not obvious that there would be any point: ultimately, it is not possible to make an effective comparison between domestic selling and export prices on account of structural differences in terms of trade and costs structure at home and abroad.

To illustrate this point, the Matsushita company – a producer with such brands as National, Panasonic, and Technics – not only has its own distribution company in Japan, but also more than 75 wholesale companies and 24,000 retail outlets linked to it. An analysis of all transactions along the route from factory to end consumer is therefore out of the question. What is more, the differences in systems render any comparison of costs and prices virtually impossible. To find a solution to this dilemma, investigators therefore have to construct a 'normal value', that is, a price on the home market under conditions such as would have obtained in the West. A similar problem also occurs with state-trade countries, where prices are often virtually devoid of economic significance.

This problem – that, in order to establish dumping, in practice A + B is relevant to European and American companies, while A to E is more relevant to Japanese companies – really lacks any effective solution. In the absence of any coherent method for determining the A + B level precisely for the Japanese situation, it remains possible for Japanese suppliers who are accused of dumping to make strategic switches between levels A + B and D + E. In fact, in order to determine the level of alleged dumping, one ought to be able to establish at which level in the column of Table 9.2 a buyer independent of the manufacturer appears. Some pundits take the view that sales from level A – because apparently trade is based on comparative cost advantages – should always be considered the first sales to independent third parties. This thinking is incorrect, however, as in Japan the first independent buyer is generally the consumer, while in Europe and the US it is usually the independent wholesaler or retail chain that brings together the wholesale and retail trade functions. In other words, it is usually A to E that is relevant in the case of Japan, while in the case of Europe A + B is generally more pertinent for the purposes of determining dumping. The pundits' suggestion fails to do justice to either.[49]

One important element incorporated into the GATT definition of dumping is that there must be a link between dumping and the injury it causes to industry in the importing country. A point to bear in mind with this addition is that the patterns of trade where dumping exists may be contrasted with the patterns one would expect if there were free trade with non-disrupted international prices; this then gives rise to a situation which is fundamentally at odds with the liberal GATT philosophy.[50] It is precisely in disrupting the opportunities for free international trade that the damage is caused to suppliers competing with the imports (at dumping prices). Hence it is that the scale of price undercutting, the rise in imports and the fall in their prices, the fall in profits and employment and the utilisation of capacity at producers in the country of import are major criteria in determining the injury caused by the dumping.

The EU, it should be noted, adopts the policy that if dumping can be proven, but the causal relation between dumping and the injury to the economy due to dumping cannot be proven, an anti-dumping levy may be introduced on the basis of the lower of the dumping margin and the margin of injury calculated; the latter is the undercutting of producer prices in the EU by the exporter who is dumping.[51]

In order to demonstrate a causal link between dumping and damage (and thus that the injury cannot be attributed to other factors) the complainant in the EU should supply a comprehensive list of information on the following: manufacturing costs, costs

49. During an interview in the BBC's 'Money Programme', Brian Hindley, one of the pundits, stated he had spent two years arriving at an understanding of the problem. In an article in the *Financial Times* of 6 January 1989 he presented a brief summary of his thinking, which is presented – with accompanying mathematical symbols – in Hindley (1989).

50. Agreement on Interpretation and Application of Articles VI, XI and XXIII of the General Agreement on Tariffs and Trade (Anti-Dumping Code) and Directive EEC 2324/88.

51. The calculation of the injury margin is the EU producers' price (weighted average), losses being eliminated and a target profit included, minus selling price of the exporter (weighted average).

of sale per type number, R&D costs and overheads, cost allocation, selling prices of models, sales distribution channels and the other elements listed above as injury criteria. The function of this list is that, if it leads to a generally negative picture, it can be included along with the price in determining the margin of injury.

9.5 Economic theory and dumping

As already indicated, dumping is totally at odds with the traditional free-trade philosophy. However, this philosophy was based on a world whose thinking was in terms of production and trade under conditions of perfect competition. In practice, however, this condition is by no means always satisfied. This means that the question that becomes relevant to entrepreneurs is the target price-volume combination for each individual's sales area and how they believe they can best cope with the competition (Brander and Krugman, 1983). For example, in a situation of imperfect competition a company may engage in price-fixing with an eye to its profits. If the various markets are separate from one another, the supplier will set prices that markets will bear. If elasticity of demand differs, pricing resulting from the equation of marginal revenue and marginal cost will vary according to differing demand elasticities. If, for example, the demand facing a company on the domestic market is fairly inelastic but fairly elastic on the international market, the endeavour to maximise profits will induce a company to charge a higher price at home than for exports of the same product. This is a typical example not just of price discrimination, but of dumping as well.

If one deviates from the atomistic free-trade model, in which the entrepreneur is assumed to be too small to influence the market price, modelling the behaviour of individual entrepreneurs *vis-à-vis* their competitors becomes important. In considering this type of entrepreneurial behaviour, various categories of dumping can be distinguished. For example, looking at the motives for underlying company behaviour, Kindleberger made a distinction between *sporadic, predatory* and *persistent* forms of dumping. The first category, *sporadic dumping,* consists of disposing of stocks in an irregular manner. The second category, *predatory dumping,* is the gaining of an export-market share at the expense of the competition by dumping and undercutting. The third category relates to the situation in which additional consignments are sold on third markets at slightly above variable costs with a view to increasing overall profits (Kindleberger, 1973, pp. 153–54).

A further distinction by type of dumping is that between *cyclical* and *currency dumping*; what the two categories have in common is that it was not necessarily the exporter's original intention to dump (European Parliament, 1983, p. 118). *Cyclical dumping* is caused by international economic waves giving rise at a particular moment to differences in the level of demand on various sub-markets. As discussed above, this creates a fertile breeding ground for price discrimination and dumping in the absence of perfect competition on separate sub-markets (Nicolaides, 1990). It is also conceivable that companies in certain countries will feel obliged at times of economic decline to maintain employment as far as possible and thus make feverish efforts to keep international sales up to the level before decline (see also below).

Currency dumping occurs when the value of the currency of the exporter's country rises, but the export price is consciously nudged downwards in relation to that of domestic suppliers on the export markets, to avoid undue erosion of the exporter's market share.

These two forms of dumping and their impact can be explained on the basis of Figure 9.2. A case of *cyclical dumping* could occur if demand on a particular market fell as a result of economic developments. This would also mean a fall in demand for the companies exporting to this market. Figure 9.2 shows this fall in demand by a shift from D_1 to D_2 in the demand curve which is relevant to the exporter. The consequence is, if we proceed from the export supply curve S_1, that the original equilibrium price P_E, and the original equilibrium volume, E_1, can no longer be sustained; the new market price now ends up between P_E and P_2; the volume of exports will also fall in the new situation, as the figure shows. In this situation it is conceivable that the exporter refuses simply to accept the fall in exports, and may, for example, endeavour to sustain the level of exports before economic decline. In that case the exporter will have to reduce the export price below the market price; the latter corresponds, we assume, with the price that domestic suppliers charge on this market. Two effects now occur as a result of this difference in price. First, consumers shift demand to the goods offered by the exporter to some degree and secondly, consumers' income rises indirectly as a result of this cheaper supply. One consequence of the latter is that the demand curve moves slightly to the right again, let us say to position D_3. The net effect is that the new point of equilibrium for the exporter happens to correspond with export volume E_2; this corresponds to the original sales volume, E_1.

In this situation, the exporter's market share does not drop, but there is a dumping margin of P_E–P_2. The exporter's market share will rise in comparison with that of the competing domestic producers. Therefore, this is a case of dumping causing injury.

The case of *currency dumping* can be illustrated more or less analogously. Imagine that the prices on the home and export markets were the same initially, that is, at level

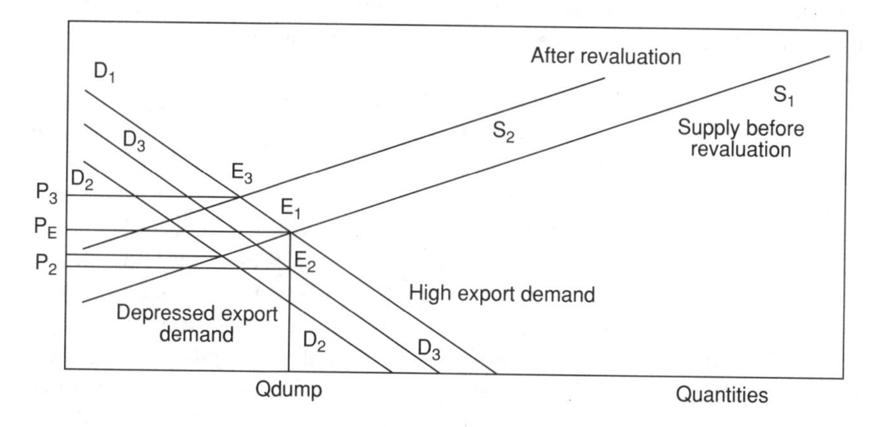

Figure 9.2 Cyclical and foreign exchange dumping

P_E. A revaluation of the exporter's currency in relation to the currency of the importing country would normally lead to a shift in the exporter's supply curve in the sense that the supply is now smaller for the same price (shift from S_1 to S_2). The fact is that the exporter receives a lower price for exports in the national currency as a result of the revaluation. Under normal circumstances the point of equilibrium for the exporter now moves to E_3 at a market price of P_3. The export volume falls, but the price has also risen for domestic suppliers.

Imagine, however, that the exporter does not consider the fall in the volume of exports to be acceptable and would like to continue selling at level E_1. This is only possible if, in contrast to the domestic suppliers, the exporter maintains the original export price P_E. In that event the exporter still comes out at an export volume of E_1. Here, too, there is price dumping on a scale of P_3–P_E formally speaking. If, furthermore, there is damage to local industry on any scale, this may lead to a complaint which ought to be honoured.

Currency and *cyclical dumping* may therefore only occur if exporters are able to influence the market and if their individual price-fixing behaviour is capable of leading to changes in their market share. This means that dumping can only occur when there is imperfect competition. In practice, therefore, anti-dumping is never found where conditions of perfect or virtually perfect competition exist. Furthermore, it is impossible to initiate proceedings with the associated investigations against, say, a hundred exporters. The following pronouncement in a recent report to the European Parliament confirms the assertion that dumping usually occurs only in markets with relatively few competitors: 'In over 40 per cent of cases there were five or fewer Community producers and in only 10 per cent of cases were there 21 or more Community producers. In terms of Community production at least, it appears that markets in which dumping investigations have been launched are relatively concentrated (European Parliament, 1993, p. 119). A further point to note is that in determining whether there is limited competition on the domestic market, one should also look at the number of exporters operating on it.

A special element in the discussion of dumping is what is termed the 'interface problem', that is, dumping as a result of structural differences between economies. In van Marion (1993) this problem is described by pointing out that international differences in market structure may lead to systematic differences between producers' price levels on their home market and that on their export market. He terms this 'systematic dumping'. In that case it depends upon the specific market conditions whether and to what extent the dumping causes damage. This case is discussed in further detail below.

The international differences in market structure – as already observed – occur, for instance, particularly in the comparison between the Western world and Japan. Competition in Japan, much more so than in the Western world, is focused on variation and innovation in the product offering, for example, in the form of a continuous process of change via differences in models and product designs, with a relatively rigid price level. This is in contrast with the Western model, where competition on price is much more of a factor. In contrast to the Western model, a fall in the price level on the home market is seen much more as a threat in Japan to the entire system of mutually dependent manufacturers, suppliers and distributors. As a result, price-maintenance behaviour predominates on the Japanese home market and volume behaviour on export markets (van Marion, 1993).

Dumping can occasionally be observed on the part of state-trade countries. This is usually a result of the great need for foreign currency, often at the central level, with a view to imports, and at the same time a lack of clarity in the price structure. Here too, dumping is *systematic* in nature, as it takes place regardless of the phase in the economic cycle, exchange rates or market conditions.

9.6 The theoretical basis of dumping with economies of scale

Figure 9.3 illustrates the case where a company has to contend with benefits of scale, and dumping is a rational option. With perfect competition and free access to home and export markets, the price would be at level P_a. This satisfies the condition that the price and the marginal costs are identical. If, however, a producer is able to protect its domestic market against foreign competitors by restrictions on imports or distribution, it will adopt a different strategy. On the domestic market the producer is operating under conditions of competition that are less perfect than abroad. It will, therefore, restrict its offering to the level at which marginal costs equate to marginal receipts (volume S_i; price P_1), at a higher price level than the perfect competitions level P_a and a smaller quantity than S_a. The producer will then endeavour to expand production via the export market until its marginal costs are equal to the average costs and foreign marginal revenues of exports (in Figure 9.3 equalled to price P_a). Sales therefore rise to level S_a; the producer exports $S_a - S_i$. As a result of these exports, unit costs of product supplied on the home market decrease from M, with exclusively domestic sales, to P_a with domestic sales plus exports. As a result of the addition of exports, profits rise from the area in dark grey in the figure to the dark grey area and the hatched area. The isolation of the home market and the export opportunity result in lower average cost and in increased domestic profit (this increase is the hatched area in Figure 9.3).

In fact, the supplier in Figure 9.3 is in a position of luxury, as long as the practice of dumping – which is really what is happening – can be continued. The supplier has a profit buffer on the basis of its protected market position on the domestic market, and export activities are the only way of increasing this profit. Consequently, the exporter is in a favourable starting position for strategic dumping. This occurs if the exporter consciously attempts to eliminate competitive suppliers on the various export markets. Precisely because of this profit buffer, the supplier will be able to sustain any battle quite easily and for a long time, and on those grounds alone discourage the other player.

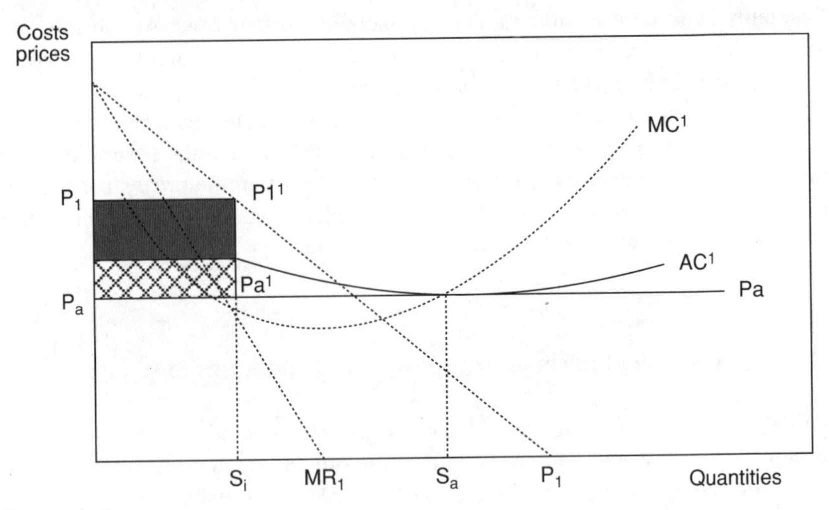

MC = marginal cost
AC = average cost
MR = marginal revenue
S_a = sales (volume) at perfect competition
S_i = sales (volume) when MC = MR
Pa = price at perfect competition
P1 = price when MC = MR

Figure 9.3 Imperfect competition and dumping

9.7 An example of predatory persistent dumping: practice and theory

The market for CD players is characterised by the following factors:

1. The market depends upon the introduction of CDs.
2. Market growth depends upon the number of hi-fi units in homes.
3. The product depends on after-sales service, which the trade must provide. Extending the dealer network for a single product pushes up the costs of sale dramatically on account of the need for training, financing and other support.
4. As a result of the previous factor, products are often offered by the 'specialist trade', who offer various consumer electronics products.
5. Average and marginal costs of manufacture fall. This means that the costs of sale are of great importance to behaviour. If methods can be found for increasing sales without increasing costs of sale at the same time, a significant cut in unit product costs can be achieved.
6. The product acts as a lead for other hi-fi equipment. Anyone buying a new hi-fi unit has an eye mainly on the CD quality.
7. Japanese companies jointly account for a market share of approximately 90 per cent. Japanese companies do not buy in from foreign companies.

One good way of selling outside the home market without increasing costs of sale is to supply to other companies on the basis of the buyer's brand or according to its specifications. This method of supplying finished products with the buyer's brand is called 'stencil-brand selling'. Supplies to manufacturers who have drawn up their own specifications are called OEM (original equipment manufacturers) supplies. One known method of making manufacturers fearful of in-house manufacture is to offer OEM products to them at a price which the buyers do not believe they can ever achieve, thus leaving them dependent upon OEM supplies from others. What is happening here is actually dumping, with the exporter frequently managing to squeeze unit product manufacturing costs without investing in distribution. Japanese suppliers that managed to overrun the television market in the US are using this method; the battle to decide VCR standards was also decided in this manner.

Box 9.1: A classification of cases of dumping

On the basis of the above discussion, a classification is presented here of the various cases of dumping according to the nature of the damage to the various competitors. The assumption is that dumping may lead to shifts in three cost positions: that of the dumping company X, that of the competing suppliers on X's domestic market, and that of competing suppliers on X's export market. Cost positions may change on account of economies of scale.

If dumping results in competing suppliers of X's export market assuming an unfavourable position on the cost curve while that of X improves, what we are witnessing is *predatory dumping*. X's profit now rises in due course while that of the disadvantaged parties falls. The salient point is that if there are economies of scale, X's competitive position improves in relation to domestic competitors who either do not or cannot export. If such dumping is neither persistent nor systematic, this is known as *non-persistent* dumping; otherwise one can speak of *persistent dumping*. A typical example of the latter is the previously mentioned 'systematic' dumping. As has been explained in further detail in the main text, this phenomenon is characteristic of the supply behaviour of some rather isolated economies or countries with a state-trade structure.

In the case of persistent dumping, there need not necessarily be predatory dumping at the same time. It is possible, for example, that relative competitive positions are not materially altered despite the dumping. The price level on the home market is then permanently higher than on the export market, but export prices do not necessarily have a permanent adverse effect on the competitive position.

Box 9.1 *Continued*

In cases of predatory persistent dumping, competitive relationships on both the home market and the export market may change. As a result of the dumping by X, sales rise and costs fall; the reverse applies among the competition on the home and export market alike. As a result, not only is competition on the international market slowly eliminated but on the domestic market as well. In the extreme case of great monopoly power, the *predatory persistent dumping* has done its work: X is now the market leader and the rationale for dumping has disappeared. Such situations are fortunately rare. One could assert that the cameras sector is somewhat close to this situation, because a limited number of Japanese producers have virtually succeeded in largely eliminating foreign competition and thus are able to push through the commercial practices of resale price maintenance on their export markets, practices which serve to restrict competition.

To summarise, dumping can be classified as follows:

	Persistent	Non-persistent
Predatory	Sustained dumping and sustained improvement in exporter's competitive position.	Dumping can have lasting influence on exporter's competitive position by dumping action.
Sporadic	Dumping consistently confronts producers in export markets with fluctuating demand.	Irregular export of oversupply.

Cases of *reciprocal dumping* come under *predatory non-persistent dumping* in the theory of strategic trade policy.

For some manufacturers, the CD player offered a good opportunity to increase their market share or even to establish a leading position in audio. Some Japanese manufacturers had already built up a reasonably strong brand position for their audio products on export markets, but for them the CD player was part of a strategic key technology: laser optics with digital applications in image and sound, data processing and display; these opportunities provided them with strong incentives to attempt to capture market share and to try to reduce production costs. Expansion of market share on their own Japanese and Korean markets was impossible: sales costs become prohibitively high if one transcends the limits of one's own captive trade channels. In other words, an attempt in this direction by undercutting in a market with individual brands and manufacturer-tied distribution would be suicidal; breaking into the distribution channels of another could only be achieved at exorbitant cost. As the demand for products from individual manufacturers by the 'trade keiretsu system' (i.e. a system by which distribution is firmly tied to manufacturers by means of all sorts of pressure in the financial and the commercial field) is inelastic, the only means left to Japanese suppliers for reducing production costs is via sales at low prices abroad. The same applies to Korean manufacturers. To them dumping is less dangerous than expanding domestic market share!

9.7.1 *Price and volume competition on various markets*

Section 9.2 outlined the dumping margins and levels of undercutting discovered in this case. It also showed the outcome: unfavourable for European producers. No theoretical underpinning was provided. It was shown above that it may be rational for certain suppliers to dump. If competitive relationships preclude volume competition on one's own market or make it unnecessary (Figure 9.2), exporting with dumping can increase profits. Such supply behaviour, as is sometimes encountered among exporters from Japan and Korea – aimed at maintaining the domestic price level and increasing sales via exports – can be described by means of the following simple comparisons, in terms of what is called Bertrand's model.

The profit achieved by a supplier, let us assume a Japanese market and price leader (π^1) is a function of its own price level (P) and that of the competitors (P^*):

$$\pi^1 = \pi^1(P;P^*)$$

The competitors' profit (π^* designated foreign here) is a function of their own price P^* and that of the Japanese market and price leader:

$$\pi^* = \pi^*(P^*;P)$$

Figure 9.4 shows the behaviour on the basis of reaction curves. The two straight lines are reaction curves; these are combinations of points forming the link between the minima of the iso profit curves, two of which are shown. The reason why reaction curves are the locus of the minima of the iso-profit curves is that in those points, at a given profit, the price (and thus the profit) of the competitor is kept as low as possible. The horizontal axis shows the price level P of the Japanese market leader/oligopolist. The vertical axis shows P^*, the price of foreign and other Japanese companies operating within a smaller trade keiretsu: (i.e. within a smaller network with closely tied distribution). The profit of the Japanese price leader, π^1, increases more via a rise in the company's own price than by a fall in the competitor's price.

Curve I–I is an iso-profit curve of the Japanese market leader; I^2–I^2 by analogy shows a higher iso-profit curve. Each company attempts to achieve the highest possible iso-profit curve. The problem is, however, that the other market player operates on an analogous approach; a movement to higher iso-profit curves for the other supplier (not drawn in the figure) means a movement to top right in the figure, as the reaction curve suggests. On the basis of the interaction, an equilibrium is established in point E. Both suppliers should see their profits increase if there is a shift in the equilibrium point towards top right in the figure, but this will not happen on account of the efforts made by each to achieve maximum profit, as can readily be seen in the figure. In fact, what is occurring here is a typical situation of price competition; the two suppliers do not attack each other with ever larger volumes so that prices fall.

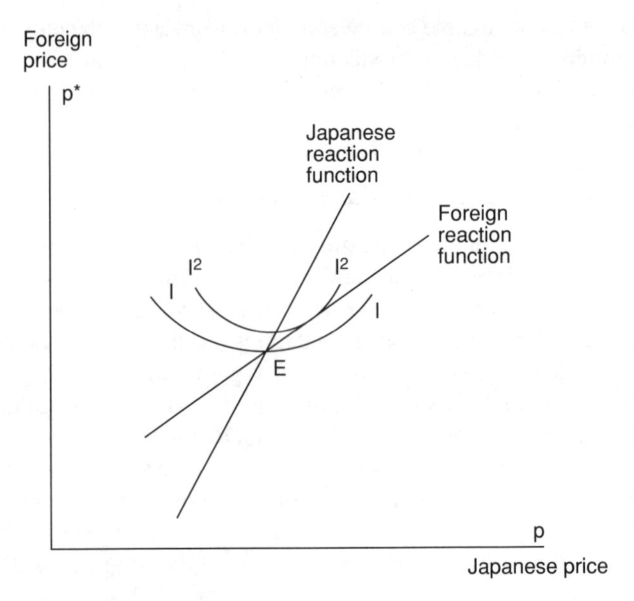

Figure 9.4 Bertrand behaviour

Source: Krugman, 1990, p. 251

In practice, the risk of price competition is greatest when there is ongoing product innovation, so that the price-fixing game can be played continuously without the players becoming prematurely lost in a typical situation of volume competition. In the case of CD players, Japanese companies for example sometimes will launch three new models each year in each price segment. In this sector one can therefore typically expect price maintenance.

The situation on the Japanese market, where such a supply situation occurs, can be illustrated more generally – and by corollary with the above – on the basis of the following model (Eaton and Grossman, 1986). The point here is to demonstrate that a protected market can still offer good profit opportunities for an exporter to such a market on account of the high price level. It is precisely because of this that the exporter will respect the price level on that market and thus restrict export sales, for the fact is that this situation represents the basis of the profit. This means that competition is not on volume but on quality and brand name. Often, there is also a reasonable degree of heterogeneity among the competing goods (Hideto, 1983). As a result, the price level is – generally speaking – relatively high.

The protection of the Japanese market by means of a distribution keiretsu serves to restrict the volume of imports. This is a further contributory factor to the isolation of the Japanese system from foreign competition. Since Japanese suppliers' total costs cannot fall by means of increasing sales on the domestic market on account of the market structure, but manufacturing costs can be squeezed by increasing sales via exports, there is a tendency among Japanese suppliers to export aggressively. This is then done at prices which either do not cover costs or which deliver sales where the profit on the home market at least offsets any losses on the export market. The keiretsu protection supports this: 'export promotion by import protection' (Krugman, 1984).

The net result is that profit in Japan is determined by price competition on the domestic market on the one hand and volume competition on the foreign market on the other. As far as exports are concerned, the market can again be described using reaction curves. Profit is now proposed as an increasing function of the volume of own sales, X, and a declining function of the sales of the other, X^*:

$$\pi^1 = \pi^1 (X;X^*)$$

$$\pi^* = \pi^* (X^*;X)$$

The reaction curves pertaining to this situation are shown in Figure 9.5. The exporter sets quantities (as in Figure 9.3, the quantity S_a-S_i) and waits for the prices and profits that result. This quantitative behaviour is called Cournot behaviour, after the first author on oligopolistic market behaviour. Profit is now determined for various volume combinations; once again, two iso-profit curves for the Japanese supplier are shown in the figure, a lower curve representing a higher profit level. J-J is the reaction curve for the Japanese supplier; F-F that for the foreign supplier. The volumes are shown on the axes.

The shift in a reaction curve from J–J to J'–J', as in the figure, could represent a theoretical shift from a situation of an accessible Japanese market to one where accessibility diminishes ever further. The fact is that as a result of this protection, the Japanese competitor could offer products with ever greater ease on the export market.

To summarise the above: a proportion (significant or otherwise) of dumping on the Japanese and Korean side can be explained on the basis of the international differences in economic systems. In itself, anti-dumping policy offers the possibility of

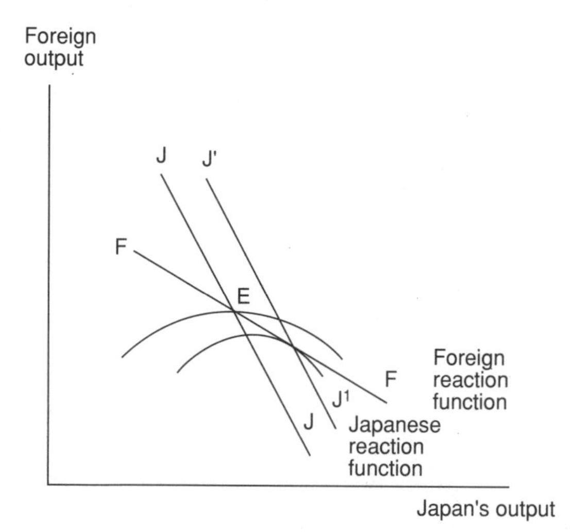

Figure 9.5 Cournot behaviour

countering dumping, albeit that in practical terms this is a fairly complicated and time-consuming method. Hence, reciprocal dumping is sometimes advocated as a counter-action, that is, dumping in the country which itself is dumping. In the case of Japan, this option is not available in sectors where there is captive distribution and intensive after-sales and support service: automotive, computing, office equipment, cosmetics, and so on. Apart from political pressure, defensive action will have to be taken on the European side by means of legal action in the anti-dumping arena.

Bibliography

Brander, J. and **Krugman, P.R.** (1983) 'A reciprocal dumping model of international trade', *Journal of International Economics*, 15, pp. 313–21.

Eaton, J. and **Grossman, G.M.** (1986) 'Optimal trade and industrial policy and oligopoly', *Quarterly Journal of Economics*, 101, pp. 383–406.

European Parliament (1993) The 'Ernst & Young' report: *The Economic Impact of Dumping and the Community's Anti-Dumping Policy*, Directorate General for Research, Internal Market Division.

Hideto, I. (1983) 'Anticompetitive practices in the distribution of goods and services in Japan: the problem of the distribution keiretsu', *Journal of Japanese Studies*, vol II, pp. 324–25.

Hindley, B. (1989) 'Dumping and the Far East trade of the European Community', *The World Economy*, vol. 11, issue 4, pp. 445–64.

Kindleberger, C.P. (1973) *International Economics,* Irwing Inc., 5th ed.

Krugman, P.R. (1984) 'Import protection as export promotion: international competition in the presence of oligopoly and economies of scale', in: H. Kierzowski (ed.) *Monopolistic Competition and International Trade,* Clarendon Press, pp. 180–93.

Krugman, P.R. (1990) *Rethinking International Trade,* MIT Press.

Marion, M.F., van (1993) *Liberal Trade and Japan; the Incompatibility Problem,* Physica Verlag.

Nicolaides, P. (1990) 'The competition effects of dumping', *Journal of World Trade*, vol. 24, no. 5, pp. 115–31.

Index